Praise for Joseph J. Ellis's

AMERICAN DIALOGUE

JOSEPH J. ELLIS

AMERICAN DIALOGUE

Joseph J. Ellis is the author of many works of American history, including *Founding Brothers: The Revolutionary Generation*, which was awarded the Pulitzer Prize, and *American Sphinx: The Character of Thomas Jefferson*, which won the National Book Award. He lives in Amherst, Massachusetts, with his wife and is the father of three sons.

www.josephellishistorian.com

AMERICAN DIALOGUE

AMERICAN DIALOGUE

The Founders and Us

JOSEPH J. ELLIS

VINTAGE BOOKS

A Division of Penguin Random House LLC

New York

FIRST VINTAGE BOOKS EDITION, NOVEMBER 2019

Copyright © 2018 by Joseph J. Ellis

All rights reserved. Published in the United States by Vintage Books, a division of Penguin Random House LLC, New York, and distributed in Canada by Penguin Random House Canada Limited, Toronto. Originally published in hardcover in the United States by Alfred A. Knopf, a division of Penguin Random House LLC, New York, in 2018.

Vintage and colophon are registered trademarks of Penguin Random House LLC.

The Library of Congress has cataloged the Knopf edition as follows:
Names: Ellis, Joseph J., author.
Title: American dialogue : the founders and us / Joseph J. Ellis.
Description: First edition. | New York : Knopf, 2018. | Includes index.
Identifiers: LCCN 2017050340 (print) | LCCN 2018009098 (ebook)
Subjects: LCSH: Political culture—United States—History. | Founding Fathers of the United States. | United States—Politics and government—1775–1783—Philosophy. | United States—Politics and government—2017– —Philosophy. | BISAC: HISTORY / United States / Revolutionary Period (1775–1800). | POLITICAL SCIENCE / History & Theory. | HISTORY / Revolutionary.
Classification: LCC E183 .E436 2018 (print) | LCC E183 (ebook) | DDC 973.3—dc23
LC record available at https://lccn.loc.gov/2017050340

Vintage Books Trade Paperback ISBN: 978-0-8041-7247-9
eBook ISBN: 978-0-385-35343-4

Author photograph © Dorothy Greco
Book design by Betty Lew

www.vintagebooks.com

Printed in the United States of America
10 9 8 7 6 5 4 3 2 1

In memory of Elting Morison, who trusted his questions and his students with a graceful patience I always admired but never achieved

This is probably all one can ask of history, and the history of ideas in particular: not to resolve issues, but to raise the level of the debate.

—Albert O. Hirschman, *The Passions and the Interests: Arguments for Capitalism Before Its Triumph* (1977)

So we beat on, boats against the current, borne back ceaselessly into the past.

—F. Scott Fitzgerald, *The Great Gatsby* (1925)

Contents

PREFACE

My Self-Evident Truth   3

CHAPTER 1: RACE

THEN

Thomas Jefferson   13

NOW

Abiding Backlash   49

CHAPTER 2: EQUALITY

THEN

John Adams   71

NOW

Our Gilded Age   103

CHAPTER 3: LAW

THEN

James Madison   119

NOW

Immaculate Misconceptions   151

CHAPTER 4: ABROAD

THEN

George Washington   *173*

NOW

At Peace with War   *207*

EPILOGUE

Leadership   *223*

ACKNOWLEDGMENTS   *241*

NOTES   *243*

INDEX   *267*

AMERICAN DIALOGUE

My Self-Evident Truth

> History is always unfinished in the sense that the future
> always uses its past in new ways.
>
> *Peter Gay,* Style in History *(1974)*

Self-evident truths are especially alluring because, by definition, no one needs to explain why they are true. The most famous example of this lovely paradox, which gave the term its name, is the second paragraph in the Declaration of Independence (i.e., "We hold these truths to be self-evident"), where Thomas Jefferson surreptitiously embedded the creedal statement of the American promise.

The ironies abound, since Jefferson almost certainly did not know he was drafting the American Creed, and subsequent generations worshipped his words for reasons different than he intended. Moreover, his initial draft described the truths as "sacred and undeniable," and it was probably Benjamin Franklin who suggested the change to "self-evident." But in the end, such nettlesome details have proven powerless against the sweeping influence of Jefferson's message, which defined the terms of the liberal tradition in American history.

My professional life as a writer and teacher of American history has been informed by another self-evident truth. As I try to put it into words, I worry that the very act of self-conscious articulation might drain away the unconscious magic of my working assumption and expose it as an illusion. But let me try. It goes like this: The study of history is an ongoing conversation between past and present from which we all have much to learn.

There, having said it, I can see that the formulation is helpfully vague. It does not dictate what we can learn and therefore casts a wide net that gathers in a messy variety of both personal and public lessons. Most of my experience comes from forty-plus years of teaching in a liberal arts college, where there is less distance between students and faculty. In such schools communication does not end with graduation but lives on in a feedback loop about the relevance and irrelevance of what had been learned years ago.

The dominant pattern was a random and wholly unpredictable kind of relevance. There was the Chinese student who had done a research paper for me on the Massachusetts Constitution, which was drafted single-handedly by John Adams. This served as the inspiration, so she claimed, for her work back in Shanghai, writing a putative constitution for post-communist China. At her twenty-fifth reunion, another student told me that her career as a corporate executive had been influenced by two lectures on the Civil War, one from the northern, the other from the southern perspective, which helped her to think ironically. Several former students, both women and men, reported that their efforts to negotiate the inescapable tension between career and family were informed by their reading of Abigail Adams's letters, citing most especially her indomitable resilience.

Such examples suggest that I was not completely fooling myself in believing that history has something to teach us all, even though it is impossible to know at the moment of learning just what that something might be. Self-conscious attempts to teach or preach relevance in history are therefore unnecessary, because the connection between then and now is embedded in the enterprise, fated to emerge in the future in unforeseeable ways. In that sense, reading history is like expanding your memory further back in time, and the more history you learn, the larger the memory bank you can draw on when life takes a turn for which you are otherwise unprepared.

Obviously, a few reassuring testimonials from former students do not a compelling case make. But since my belief in history's utility was an unquestioned article of faith, it did not require overwhelming evidence, only sufficient support to sustain its credibility. And on that score the historical record provided several dramatic illustrations of a usable past that caught my eye. My two favorite examples featured John Adams during the American Revolution and Abraham Lincoln on the issue of slavery.

In June 1776 Adams wrote to several friends in Boston, asking them to scour the Harvard library for books on military history, especially accounts of the Peloponnesian and Punic wars. He had just been appointed head of the Board of War and Ordnance, effectively making him secretary of war, a post for which he freely admitted he was wholly unprepared. He decided to give himself a crash course on how to manage an army.

Over the ensuing months he bombarded George Washington and the general officers of the Continental Army with advice gleaned from his reading. His most relevant strategic suggestion, which was based on his analysis of the battles between Thebes and Sparta as recorded by Thucydides, was to adopt a defensive strategy, what he called "a war of posts." Much like the Spartans, Adams argued, the British were virtually invincible on a conventional battlefield, so the Continental Army should engage only when it enjoyed tactical superiority in numbers or terrain. Such advice cut against all of Washington's aggressive instincts, but he eventually, if reluctantly, embraced it. The result was a protracted war that the British had to win, while the Americans had only not to lose. This proved a more attainable goal, eventually achieved when the British abandoned the conflict after the Battle of Yorktown in 1781.

In 1858 Abraham Lincoln also began a research project, in his case focused on the records of the Constitutional Convention and the early histories of that seminal event. Lincoln's research was prompted by the landmark Supreme Court decision *Dred Scott v. Sandford* (1857), in which Chief Justice Roger Taney, writing for the majority, ruled that the framers of the Constitution regarded slaves as property rather than persons, meaning that slave owners could not be deprived of their property without their consent, which led to the conclusion that any law prohibiting slavery in the western territories was unconstitutional.

Lincoln's reading of history led him to a dramatically different conclusion, namely that many of the founders sought to limit slavery's expansion, a view he presented in its fullest form in his Cooper Union Address (1860). He discovered that twenty-one of the thirty-nine signers of the Constitution were on record for banning or restricting slavery in the territories. Both Washington and Jefferson, as well as sixteen signers, endorsed the Northwest Ordinance, which prohibited slavery north of the Ohio River. Jefferson had even wanted to ban slavery in *all* the new territories.

As for the larger question of slavery itself, Lincoln argued that the founding generation regarded it as a moral embarrassment that clearly defied the principles announced in the Declaration of Independence, which was the major reason the delegates in Philadelphia refused to permit the toxic term to contaminate the language of the Constitution. As Lincoln described them, the founders thought of slavery as a cancer they could not surgically remove without killing the infant American republic in the cradle. Throughout the trials and tribulations of America's bloodiest war, Lincoln maintained he was acting as the agent of the founding generation, so that the Union cause spoke for the true meaning of the American Revolution.

It is worth noting that both Adams and Lincoln went back to the past with explicit political agendas, which is to say that they knew what they were looking for. So, for that matter, did Chief Justice Taney, who harbored a proslavery agenda. By definition, all efforts to harvest the accumulated wisdom of the past must begin from a location in the present, so the questions posed of the past are inevitably shaped either consciously or unconsciously by the historical context in which they are asked. Unlike my former students, who discovered relevant historical insights later in life, almost accidentally, the Adams and Lincoln examples were self-conscious attempts to generate historical evidence in support of preferred outcomes. When it comes to the writing of relevant history, there are no immaculate conceptions.

This is an inconvenient truth that most historians acknowledge under their breath, admitting that objectivity, in the sense that mathematicians or physicists use the term, is not a realistic goal for historians. The best they can strive for is some measure of detachment, which serves the useful purpose of stigmatizing the most flagrant forms of ideological prejudice (i.e., cherry-picking the evidence to claim that Thomas Jefferson was an evangelical Christian or Andrew Jackson a New Deal Democrat). But if you believe that the study of history is an ongoing conversation between past and present, detachment itself is delusional. In his *Style in History* (1974) Peter Gay put the point succinctly: "History is always unfinished in the sense that the future always uses the past in new ways." In fact, the past is not history, but a much vaster region of the dead, gone, unknowable, or forgotten. History is what we choose to remember, and we have no alternative but to do our choosing now.

My goal in the pages that follow is to provide a round-trip ticket to the late eighteenth century from our location in the second decade of the twenty-first. The founding era has been chosen as a destination for two reasons: First, of all of the terrain in American history, I know it best; second, it produced the Big Bang that created all the planets and orbits in our political universe, thereby establishing the institutional framework for what is still an ongoing argument about our destiny as a people and a nation. Thus my title.

The questions we will be carrying back to the founding from our sliver of time in the present are inescapably shaped by our location in a divided America that is currently incapable of sustained argument and unsure of its destiny. We inhabit a backlash moment in American history of uncertain duration. Our creedal convictions as Americans, all of which have their origin in the founding era, are bumping up against four unforeseen and unprecedented obstacles: the emergence of a truly multiracial society; the inherent inequalities of a globalized economy; the sclerotic blockages of an aging political architecture; and the impossible obligations facing any world power once the moral certainties provided by the Cold War vanished. These obstacles became more difficult to negotiate in 2016, when the most inexperienced, uninformed, and divisive presidential candidate in American history was elected to occupy the Oval Office.

The "Now" sections of the ensuing chapters represent my effort to place each of these topical areas—race, income inequality, jurisprudence, and foreign policy—in historical context by viewing them as recent entries in long-standing patterns. The "Then" sections focus on specific founders, chosen in part because of their prominence, but mostly because, based on my previous work in their papers, each founder speaks with special resonance to the subject under scrutiny. Much in the way the founders went back to the Greek and Roman classics for guidance during the political crisis of their time, we are going back to the founders, our classics, in ours.

Our goal, then, is to learn more about our origins in the fond hope that doing so will allow us to frame the salient questions of our time with greater wisdom than we are currently able to muster on our own. Moreover, the very act of posing such questions also enhances the prospects of viewing the founders themselves from new angles that cast their legacy in a different light. We can safely assume that the dialogue between now and then is an interactive process possessing the potential to change both sides of the chronological equation.

Although the founders are busy being dead, they still speak to us in the vast archive of letters and documents they left behind. The historical record is so rich because the revolutionary generation realized that they were "present at the creation," and they therefore preserved their thoughts in the belief that posterity would want to remember them. Over the years, a small army of editors has worked assiduously on that preservation project, producing the fullest account of any political elite in recorded history. My attempt to recover the American Dialogue is wholly dependent on that documentary record.

Of course, the suggestion that there is an ongoing conversation across the centuries is a literary conceit, but we pay homage to the dialogue every time we cite the seminal texts of the founding to fortify our current convictions. As a lovely song once put it, "The fundamental things apply / As time goes by."

In the pages that follow I will try to do justice to both sides of the dialogue. What did "all men are created equal" mean then and now? Did the "pursuit of happiness" imply the right to some semblance of economic equality? Does it now? Who was included in "We the people" then? Who is included now? Is it historically correct to describe the United States as an "exceptional" nation? If so, what are the current implications of this description? Did the founders leave a legacy of government as "us" or "them"? If the correct answer is both, which legacy best meets our needs now?

Given our current condition as a deeply divided people, my hope is that the founding era can become a safe place to gather together, not so much to find answers to those questions as to argue about them. Indeed, if I read the founders right, their greatest legacy is the recognition that argument itself is the answer.

CHAPTER 1

Race

Thomas Jefferson

Nothing is more certainly written in the book of fate than that these people are to be free. Nor is it less certain that the two races, equally free, cannot live in the same government. Nature, habit, opinion has drawn indelible lines of distinction between them.

Thomas Jefferson, Autobiography *(1821)*

More than any other prominent member of the revolutionary generation, Thomas Jefferson lived a life thoroughly embedded in the twin American dilemmas of slavery and racism. His earliest memory was of being carried on a pillow by a trusted if nameless slave. His last semi-conscious words as a dying man—a request to adjust his pillow—were mumbled to Burwell, his black manservant. When he made a formal census of "my family" at Monticello in 1800, he counted eleven "free whites" and ninety-three slaves, two of whom were his own children.[1]

If a painter were to pick the most paradoxical scene in the founding era, it could well be Jefferson's arrival in Philadelphia to serve in the Continental Congress in June 1775. The man soon to draft the most succinct statement about human equality in modern history dismounted from an ornate carriage accompanied by Jesse, Jupiter, and Richard, three formally attired slaves. If the central contradiction of American history is the coexistence of slavery and a creedal commitment to individual freedom, Jefferson lived both sides of that contradiction more conspicuously than any of America's founders.[2]

To put it differently, a racial fault line runs through the center of the American experience, and Jefferson straddles that divide with uncommon agility, making him our greatest saint and greatest sinner, the iconic embodiment of our triumphs and tragedies. Rather than side with his most ardent admirers or his most acerbic critics, we need to recognize not that the truth lies in between, but that Jefferson is a fusion of both sides in their most enigmatic shape, the Mona Lisa of American racial history.

The marble panels that ring the interior of the Jefferson Memorial contain his most lyrical tributes to human freedom and equality. A new panel now needs to be added containing his seminal statement on our racial identity: "Nothing is more certainly written in the book of fate than that these people are to be free. Nor is it less certain that the two races, equally free, cannot live in the same government. Nature, habit, opinion, has drawn indelible lines of distinction between them."[3]

This is the place to begin, not end, our investigation of the Jefferson legacy, namely with the realization that our most eloquent "apostle of freedom" is also our most dedicated racist, and that in his mind those two convictions were inseparable. We might also, at the start, notice the need to revise the classic formulation of James Parton, Jefferson's first biographer. "If Jefferson was wrong," wrote Parton in 1874, "America was wrong. If America is right, Jefferson was right." Our revised version might go like this: "If Jefferson was flawed, America is flawed. If America seeks to face its flaws, Jefferson is the man we most need to understand."[4]

＊ ✦ ＊

Recovering Jefferson's early years is an exercise in inspired guesswork, largely because of what his biographers have called "the problem of the Shadwell fire," which destroyed most of Jefferson's papers in 1770. We know that his father, Peter Jefferson, was a moderately successful planter and surveyor who died in 1757, leaving his widow,

Jane Randolph Jefferson, an inheritance of two hundred hogs, seventy cows, twenty-five horses, and sixty slaves. That list accurately expressed the unspoken assumption of the Virginia planter class into which Jefferson was born, a world in which slaves were a form of property akin to livestock. His early notebooks, which somehow survived the blaze, are silent on the slavery question, revealing instead a young man whose penmanship shifted dramatically, as if written by different people, searching for his own voice and style. When he went off to the College of William and Mary in 1759, he was accompanied by Jupiter, a young slave who had been a favorite playmate during Jefferson's childhood, and who remained his personal servant for the next thirty-three years. During that time, the record of their relationship is virtually nonexistent.[5]

Slavery enters the story most conspicuously in 1768, when Jefferson decided to build his own home atop an 867-foot-high mountain in the foothills of the Blue Ridge range on land he inherited from his father. First named the Hermitage, it was soon christened Monticello, or "little mountain." It would become his lifetime architectural project and permanent retreat from what he called "the woes of this world." A French visitor nicely caught the psychological significance of Monticello: "It seems indeed as though, ever since his youth, he had placed his mind, like his house, on a lofty height, whence he might contemplate the universe." Unmentioned, though impossible for a visitor not to notice, were the fifty-two slaves Jefferson brought with him to Monticello and who played a major role in building it.[6]

Four years later, on New Year's Day 1772, Jefferson brought his new wife to Monticello, where legend has it that the household slaves gathered around to celebrate her arrival, creating an apparent scene of domestic harmony. Martha Wayles Skelton was an attractive and delicate young widow whose dowry included 135 slaves, thereby increasing the slave population at Monticello to about 200 souls, making Jefferson the second-largest slaveholder in Albemarle County. The very place that Jefferson was constructing and dreaming about as his elevated refuge from earthly problems in fact embodied in its most palpable form the central problem of his age. At least at first glance, then, Jefferson seems to be a typical Virginia planter, whose most distinguishing feature is his almost eerie ability to float above the unmentionable problem in some rarified region of his mind that Monticello was designed to duplicate.

But appearances, it turns out, are not reliable measures of his slave-owning mentality. The earliest glimpse of a distinctively different attitude toward slavery occurred during his first term in the Virginia House of Burgesses in 1769. Jefferson was poised to propose a bill permitting owners to free their slaves without acquiring permission from the governor or council, as Virginia law then required. But because of his junior status, he deferred to Richard Bland, a senior colleague, and only seconded the motion for his own bill. He then watched as Bland was buried under an avalanche of invective from which, at least according to Jefferson, his political career never recovered. While the cautionary lesson Jefferson drew from this episode proved enduring, it is noteworthy that his first act on the political stage in Virginia was a futile effort to make the emancipation of slaves easier. This was not the behavior of a typical Virginia slave owner.[7]

Another sighting of a distinctive presence among the planter class occurred the following year, when Jefferson, in his other identity as an aspiring lawyer, agreed to take the case of a young man, the grandson of a mulatto slave, who was suing for his freedom. Virginia law clearly specified that slave status was inherited from the maternal side of the gene pool, and it made no exception for the children or grandchildren of a mulatto. Jefferson challenged the law, not just in technical terms (i.e., how to define *mulatto*), but in language that undermined the radical assumptions on which slavery itself rested. "We assert that under the law of nature," Jefferson contended, "all men are born free, and every one comes into the world with a right to his own person." The judge, of course, dismissed Jefferson's argument as a sentimental irrelevancy, though hindsight permits us to recognize it as the preview of some highly significant coming attractions in the Jefferson story.[8]

And then, in 1774, a quite remarkable statement appeared in a pamphlet published in Williamsburg entitled *A Summary View of the Rights of British America*. Jefferson had not intended its publication, believing instead that he was drafting instructions for Virginia's delegates to the Continental Congress. But buried in a paragraph criticizing George III's treatment of his loyal subjects in the American colonies were the following words: "The abolition of domestic slavery is the great object of desire in these colonies where it was unhappily introduced in their infant state. But previous to the enfranchisement of the slaves we already have, it is necessary to exclude all further importations from Africa. Yet our repeated attempts to effect this by prohibition . . . have been hitherto defeated by his majesty's negative." Exactly where this out-of-the-blue statement about abolishing both the slave trade and slavery itself came from was not explained.[9]

Summary View, it turned out, became Jefferson's first appearance on a national stage because it was reprinted in Philadelphia, New York, and Boston. As John Adams later recalled, no one had ever heard of this young Virginian before, but he suddenly acquired "the reputation of a masterly pen . . . in consequences of a very handsome public paper which he had written for the House of Burgesses, which had given him the character of a fine writer." Apart from his way with words, what Adams and everyone else noticed about *Summary View* was its novel argument that Parliament not only lacked the authority to tax the colonies, but also could not legislate for them at all, a significant shift in the American position on British policy that was just then becoming viable.[10]

There were two other items that no one seemed to notice, or at least did not mention at the time. First, Jefferson had expanded the critique of British imperialism beyond Parliament to include George III, who until now had been regarded as off-limits. Second, and for our purposes most significantly, he had included both the slave trade and slavery itself in the list of transgressions by the British monarch, insisting, without any evidence, that there was an unspoken agreement within the American colonies that slavery was a vestige of British policy that must be ended.

No other Virginia slave owner had ever made such a claim. There *was* a significant segment of the planter class in Virginia that favored an end of the slave trade, not primarily for moral reasons but rather because their plantations were already overstocked, and they stood to gain by selling their excess slaves to South Carolina and Georgia if the flow of imports from Africa stopped. But the claim that American colonists south of the Potomac were poised to end the institution of slavery was a total fabrication. Perhaps it drew no comments because no one took it seriously.

—— ❧ ——

The next chapter in this story played out in the early summer of 1776 and culminated with the debate in the Continental Congress over the language of the Declaration of Independence. For obvious reasons this much-traveled ground is also enveloped in semi-sacred shadows, making any succinct account of the historical context seem almost sacrilegious. Given our focus on the slavery question, however, a selective summary becomes almost mandatory.

On June 7 Richard Henry Lee of Virginia moved the resolution "that these United Colonies are, and of right ought to be, independent States." The Continental Congress decided to delay a vote on Lee's resolution until July 1 in deference to delegations requiring guidance from their respective state legislators. In the meantime a five-member committee was appointed to draft a document announcing American independence to the world if and when Lee's resolution won approval.

On June 11 Jefferson met with John Adams, Benjamin Franklin, Roger Sherman, and Robert Livingston in Franklin's quarters. After Franklin declined the assignment, the committee chose Jefferson to prepare a draft, which he proceeded to write in his Market Street apartment during the second week of June. He then shared his draft with Adams and Franklin, later recalling that "they were the two members of whose judgments and amendments I wished most to have the benefit." They suggested one minor revision, replacing "sacred and undeniable truths" with "self-evident truths." The committee then placed the document before the Continental Congress on June 28, the scene depicted in the iconic painting by John Trumbull.[11]

After voting unanimously on July 2 in favor of Lee's resolution (New York abstained) and thereby making independence official, the delegates put themselves into committee-of-the-whole format to debate Jefferson's draft of the Declaration. No record of the debates exists because none was kept. They made multiple changes, revising or deleting over 20 percent of the text, then forwarded the edited version to the printer on July 4. They dropped completely the following paragraph that Jefferson had included in his list of grievances against George III:

> He has waged cruel war against human nature itself, violating its most sacred rights of life and liberty in the persons of a distant people who never offended him, captivating and carrying them into slavery in another hemisphere, or to incur miserable death in their transportation hither. This piratical warfare, the opprobrium of INFIDEL powers, is the warfare of the CHRISTIAN king of Great Britain. Determined to keep open a market where MEN should be bought and sold, he has prostituted his negative for suppressing every legislative attempt to prohibit or to restrain this execrable commerce. And that this assemblage of horrors might want no fact of distinguished die, he is now exciting those very people to rise in arms against us and to purchase that liberty of which he has deprived them by murdering the people on whom he has obtruded them, thus paying off former crimes committed against the liberties of one people, with crimes which he urges them to commit against the LIVES of another.[12]

For both stylistic and substantive reasons, this lengthy paragraph is arguably the most dazzlingly incoherent piece of prose that Jefferson ever wrote. The convoluted syntax, strained vocabulary, and operative tone were, by themselves, sufficient reasons for his fellow delegates to the Continental Congress to remove the paragraph from a document purportedly designed to sound a stately note. Substantively, the claim that George III was responsible for imposing the slave trade, and by implication slavery itself, on innocent and unwilling American colonists was a blatant fiction. Moreover, the very mention of slavery violated the unspoken code of silence on a subject possessing the explosive potential to blow up the fragile political consensus essential if the movement for American independence was to succeed.

What was Jefferson thinking? Well, we know that he sat in sullen silence throughout the debate, leaving to Adams the task of defending his every word. (His bumpy but lifelong friendship with Adams dates from this moment.) We also know that he was thin-skinned about the entire editorial process, subsequently telling his friends that he regarded every deletion as a defacement.[13]

One way of reading the offensive paragraph is to view it as a message aimed specifically at a Virginia audience. The claim that George III was "exciting those very people to rise in arms against us" referred to a proclamation by the governor of Virginia, Lord Dunmore, that offered freedom to all Virginia slaves who rallied to the British cause. As noted earlier, the Virginia legislature was on record for ending the slave trade, so Jefferson's condemnation of it as a moral travesty was politically popular within the Old Dominion. But ending slavery itself was not only unpopular, it was unthinkable. By stigmatizing Dunmore's offer of emancipation, Jefferson actually exposed the moral contradiction at the core of Virginia's position and inadvertently mentioned the unmentionable subject of slavery itself, which he had previously, in *Summary View*, described as being on the road to extinction. Little of this made rational sense.

It did, however, make a kind of revolutionary sense to fold slavery into the list of grievances against George III, using the political crisis to create a patriotic story line in which an evil king imposes a diabolical institution on innocent and unwilling colonists. This was a preposterous piece of propaganda, but in the superheated moment, when blaming George III for "a long train of abuses" had become rhetorically possible and even politically mandatory, adding slavery to the bill of indictment was a tactically shrewd maneuver that laid the political foundation for emancipation in a document declaring America's own independence. The tortured character of Jefferson's prose in the deleted paragraph suggests he was struggling with some version of this patriotic fiction but in the end chose to limit the indictment to the slave trade because that was less controversial.

His other antislavery references in the Declaration were implicit rather than explicit, and both occurred in the second paragraph of the text, which his editors in the Congress passed over without comment, presumably regarding this early section of the draft as a mere rhetorical overture. This is richly ironic, since subsequent generations, including our own, have focused almost exclusively on this section of Jefferson's text and discovered there the seminal statement of what Gunnar Myrdal first called the American Creed. Neither his editors nor Jefferson himself realized at the time the latent implications of his verbal felicities.[14]

The claim that "all men are created equal" has assumed many mystical meanings, but all of them are incompatible with slavery, and there is no reason to believe that Jefferson was oblivious to that fact. Two months earlier, when George Mason deployed analogous language in his draft of the Virginia Constitution, several delegates worried out loud that such language could be construed as a rejection of slavery. They therefore insisted upon adding "when they enter into society" to qualify the equality statement. Jefferson was well aware of these exchanges in Williamsburg, which were reported in the Philadelphia newspapers.

He smuggled another covert antislavery argument into the same paragraph when he revised the trinity of rights most famously proposed by John Locke in his *Second Treatise on Government* (1690). Instead of "life, liberty, and property," Jefferson wrote "life, liberty, and the pursuit of happiness." Jefferson borrowed the new phrase from Mason, who had used it in his draft of the Virginia Constitution as a supplement to Locke's "property." By dropping "property" altogether, Jefferson deftly deprived slave owners of being able to claim that owning slaves was a natural right protected by law. On this score there can be little doubt that he knew what he was doing.[15]

———— ✦ ————

Jefferson's public role as a rather rarified critic of slavery continued through the war years. His opposition to slavery operated at an elevated region of his mind, which never descended to the ground that he walked and that his slaves at Monticello worked. There is no evidence he gave any consideration to emancipating his own slaves, or ever declaring his intention to do so at some point in the future, in part because such an action would have been politically suicidal in Virginia, in part because he was temperamentally averse to all forms of controversy. Nevertheless, when asked to join a five-man committee to revise Virginia's code of laws, his antislavery agenda surged to the surface again, in a way that provides a window into his distinctive mode of thinking about slavery.

The task, which occupied the bulk of his intellectual energies from 1777 to 1780, involved purging Virginia's laws of anachronistic English precedents, then replacing them with the legal architecture of a state-size republic. The obvious candidates for elimination were the vestiges of primogeniture and entail, the barbaric criminal code that included torture, and an established Anglican church. Jefferson's singular contribution was to add slavery to the list.[16]

Jefferson had always assumed that the American Revolution was more than a political movement to withdraw from the British Empire. It was also a political transition from a monarchical to a republican framework in which each former colony became a state-based laboratory for the establishment of republican principles. Moreover, that political transition was part of a larger shift in the global templates from a medieval to a modern society. The term *Enlightenment* had not yet been coined, but Jefferson was living its meaning with all its visionary implications as a decisive break with over a thousand years of entrenched feudal traditions, which he dismissively described as "the dead hand of the past." And within this quasi-utopian scheme, slavery was an institutional embodiment of a barbaric bygone era, much like the belief in miracles, divine right monarchies, and religious relics, which now needed to be consigned to the oblivion they so richly deserved.

Jefferson's vision operated at a very high altitude. His antislavery convictions did not derive from some sudden realization that he was living a lie at Monticello. He opposed slavery not because it was a sin, but because it was an anachronism. His clairvoyant certainty was bloodless but beguiling. He knew where history had been and where it was now headed. In his mind's eye he saw that the end of slavery was already baked into Virginia's future.

This distinctive way of thinking explains the specific proposal he drafted, probably in 1782, for implementing a policy of gradual emancipation in Virginia. As he saw it, his task was to provide a path forward toward a foreordained future. In his scheme, all slaves born after an unspecified date would be freed at birth. They would continue to live with their enslaved parents through childhood as they acquired the skills essential for subsequent careers as farmers and artisans. They would then be transported outside Virginia, presumably to the unsettled western territories. In order to replace the labor lost by their departure, an equal number of European peasants would be imported and dispersed throughout the state. Jefferson calculated that this plan would end slavery in the Dominion by the middle of the next century and would liberate 300,000 souls. The Virginia legislature simply ignored the proposal.[17]

One final surge of inspired futility occurred two years later, in 1784. While serving as a Virginia delegate to the newly created Confederation Congress, Jefferson was appointed to chair the committee charged with establishing rules for the creation of territories and then states in the vast regions between the Alleghenies and the Mississippi acquired in the Treaty of Paris (1783). The result was the Ordinance of 1784, a thoroughly Jeffersonian document that set three conditions for the admission of territories as states: complete equality with the other states in the union; the prohibition of hereditary titles and aristocratic privileges; and an end to all forms of slavery by no later than 1800. This last provision was seriously considered but lost by one vote. As Jefferson lamented shortly afterward, "the fate of millions yet unborn [was] hanging on the tongue of one man, and Heaven was silent in that awful moment."[18]

As it turned out, he was not exaggerating. For if Jefferson's proposal to ban slavery in all incoming states had been enacted, it would have settled at the start the very question that later generations could not solve short of civil war. In retrospect, he had offered his own generation an opportunity that, once missed, would never come again. As it also turned out, Jefferson's effort to block slavery's expansion was also his last act as a public advocate for emancipation. Perhaps the most charitable way to put it is that he had done his best, but the American Revolution, as he had imagined it, failed to live up to his expectations.

＋－－ ═◆═ －－＋

During his five-year sojourn in Paris as America's minister to France, a discernible shift occurred in Jefferson's posture toward slavery. The agent of change was publication of his *Notes on the State of Virginia* in 1785, which contained remarks on both slavery and the enslaved population that propelled Jefferson to center stage in the ongoing debate, a position he found intolerable. He had written *Notes* during the summer of 1781 and made several revisions over the next three years but never intended it for publication. It was, in fact, the only book Jefferson ever published, since he preferred to target different audiences with different voices; a published book, unlike letters, did not permit multiple Jeffersons. He confessed as much to James Madison, his emerging protégé back in Virginia: "But these are sentiments on some subjects [in *Notes*] which I apprehend might be displeasing to the country [i.e., Virginia] and perhaps to the assembly or some who lead it. I do not wish to be exposed to their censure." Madison wrote back, in code, to confirm that "the *freedom of your strictures on some particular measures and opinions will displease their respective abettors.*"[19]

Madison's deliberately elliptical language, designed to confound snoopers at the post office, was referring to Jefferson's plan for gradual emancipation in Virginia, now made public for the first time. Almost certainly, Madison was also referring to Jefferson's vivid characterization of slavery as "a perpetual exercise of the most boisterous passions, the most unremitting despotism on the one part, and degrading submissions on the other." And then there was his nearly apocalyptic conclusion. "Indeed I tremble for my country when I reflect that God is just; that his justice cannot sleep forever. . . . The Almighty has no attribute which can take sides with us." In between these uncompromising denunciations, Jefferson had inserted a lengthy diatribe against the effects of slavery on the white population, claiming that the greatest crime was not the suffering of black slaves, but the moral corruption of white masters. Not only had Jefferson previously envisioned emancipation as inevitable to a planter class wholly unprepared for the prediction, he now unleashed his verbal prowess against slavery as an all-consuming culture of depravity that, unless ended, would sink Virginia into an economic abyss from which it would never recover.[20]

Madison made no explicit reference to Jefferson's lengthy discussion in *Notes* of the reasons why all freed slaves must be settled elsewhere: "Why not retain and incorporate the blacks into the state . . . ? Deep rooted precipices entertained by the whites; ten thousand recollections by the blacks of injuries they have sustained; new provocations; the real distinctions that nature had made." There then followed a catalog of those distinctions, all of which lay behind what Jefferson called "that immovable veil of black": they secrete more by the glands than the kidneys, giving them a permanently vile odor; they were capable of sensation but not reflection; their capacity for love was confined to physical expression; they were inherently lazy and worked only when watched; compared to Native Americans, their efforts at art were primitive and at oratory never rose above plain narration.

Jefferson's conclusion was qualified but clear. "The opinion that they are inferior in the faculties of reason and imagination must be hazarded with diffidence," but he was prepared to offer the opinion, "as a suspicion only," that blacks were inherently inferior because they were black rather than because they were enslaved. The historical and biological sources of the differences were currently beyond the reach of science, he acknowledged. Yet whatever their origins, Jefferson regarded it as self-evident that "blacks are inferior to whites in the endowments of both mind and body." Since any mixing of the two races would therefore generate an inferior American race, "when freed they must be removed beyond the reach of mixture."[21]

David Ramsay, who was composing a history of the American Revolution in South Carolina, wrote to congratulate Jefferson for his critique of slavery in *Notes*, but disagreed with his conclusion about black inferiority: "I think you have depressed the negroes too low. I believe all mankind to be originally the same and diversified by accidental circumstances. I flatter myself that in a few centuries the negroes will lose their black color. I think they are already less black in Jersey than Carolina, their lips less thick, their noses less flat."[22]

Most northern commentators agreed with Ramsay, arguing that Jefferson's rigid racial categories were vestiges of an outdated, indeed medieval view of human nature, which was not what one should expect from a self-proclaimed champion of modernity. Enlightened thinkers emphasized the environmental causes of racial differences, thereby connecting the inferior condition of enslaved blacks to slavery rather than their African origins. As Benjamin Rush, the Philadelphia physician and revolutionary gadfly, put it, "the unhappy sons of Africa, in spite of the degrading influence of slavery, are in no wise inferior to the more fortunate inhabitants of Europe and America." This was also the view of Samuel Stanhope Smith, a Pennsylvania minister and lecturer at Princeton who was the most learned student of racial science in America. Like Ramsay and Rush, Smith insisted that all human beings were the product of climate, diet, and the circumstances in which they lived. This explained their sincere conviction that, once removed from the intense heat of equatorial Africa, blacks in the United States would gradually become white. No one at the time, not Jefferson or his critics, enjoyed access to the insights of Charles Darwin on evolution or Gregor Mendel on genes.[23]

And so while Virginia planters found the sections of *Notes* on slavery the most difficult to digest, progressive thinkers of an antislavery persuasion were confused by Jefferson's anachronistic view of race, most especially his emphasis on the *inherent* inferiority of anyone with African blood. This claim seemed incongruous when contrasted with his insistence, also argued in *Notes*, that Native Americans were *not* racially inferior to whites and ought, one day, to be assimilated into the mainstream of the American population without any worry about biological degradation.[24]

Jefferson preferred not to engage his critics. His previous denunciations of slavery were all elevated arguments about its incompatibility with the principles of the American Revolution and its misguided defiance of the direction that history required. Such arguments floated above the more nettlesome questions about the political and economic conditions in which slavery was embedded south of the Potomac, and the even more palpable racial context of the ideal world he was creating at Monticello. The publication of *Notes* (new editions soon appeared in England and America) forced Jefferson down from his accustomed height above the fray and into a conspicuous position of leadership on the most controversial issue of the day. He was temperamentally incapable of playing that role.

Starting in 1785, a discernible shift toward reticence appeared throughout his correspondence, initially taking the form of a plea to slow history down on the emancipation question, lest a faster pace only energize the opposition and thereby delay the outcome. "In a few years there will be no slaves Northward of Maryland," he predicted; this would happen naturally, without any need for encouragement. Meanwhile, the rising generations of Virginia, "suckled in the principles of liberty as it were with their mother's milk," would eventually rise to the task, "and it is to them that I look with anxiety to turn the

fate of the questions." References to "the work of the next generation" became a familiar refrain.[25]

The public controversy generated by *Notes* also forced Jefferson to
face more squarely the problem of what to do with the slaves once they
were freed. His previous prescriptions—provide them with essential
skills and then dispatch them at adulthood to some unspecified location in the western territories—now seemed inadequate, vulnerable
to such practical questions as how and where. "As far as I can judge
from the experiments which have been made," he now explained, "to
give liberty to, or rather to abandon persons whose habits have been
formed in slavery is like abandoning children."

His new appreciation of the postemancipation problem also served
to reinforce his reticence on the larger question of slavery itself. For it
made no sense to accelerate the emancipation schedule until a work-
able plan for managing the transition was in place. Here we can detect
the origins of what was to become his enduring posture as master of
Monticello. His highest duty was not to stake out a leadership role in
Virginia by freeing his slaves, but rather to keep families intact under
his patriarchal gaze while the stars aligned as he believed they would.
Leadership meant waiting.[26]

⸻ ⸱⸱⸱ ⸻

During his last years in Paris a new ingredient entered the Jeffersonian
equation that further altered the chemistry of his thinking about slavery. A fourteen-year-old mulatto slave named Sally Hemings arrived
in Paris, sent from Monticello to accompany Jefferson's younger
daughter, Polly. Descriptions of Hemings emphasize her attractive-
ness according to white criteria for beauty, that she was "very handsome, [had] long straight hair down her back," also that she was
"mighty near white." Her white father, John Wayles, was Jefferson's
father-in-law, making Hemings the half sister of Jefferson's deceased
e.[27]

t some point between 1787 and 1789 Jefferson and Hemings
he sexual partners, and Hemings became pregnant with his child.

Under French law, Hemings could have remained in Paris and automatically been freed, but she chose to return with Jefferson on the condition that he promise to free all their children upon adulthood, a promise Jefferson subsequently kept by freeing all four of her six offspring who reached maturity. Hemings remained Jefferson's mistress at Monticello for thirty-six years, until his death in 1826.[28]

We can dispense with all the lurid speculations about "Tom and Sally" that began with the exposure of their liaison in 1802 and were then revived when DNA evidence confirmed Jefferson's highly probable paternity of Eston Hemings, the youngest child, in 1997. The intimate relationship in fact made eminent sense for both sides. For Jefferson, who had vowed on his wife's deathbed never to marry again, the arrangement gave him a lifelong sexual partner he could trust because she was under his complete control. For Hemings, the arrangement ensured freedom for her children and favored treatment within the household at Monticello; she was in effect pursuing the same path as her mother before her and thereby sustaining the genetic link between the Hemings and Jefferson family lines. The admittedly fragmentary evidence suggests that both sides regarded the mutual understanding as a solemn vow of fidelity they both kept.[29]

Jefferson's relationship with Hemings occurred almost a decade after he had sounded the warning against racial mixing in *Notes*. But it gave a new kind of coloration to his public rationale for separating blacks from whites after emancipation. He was living a lie, and he knew it, which was also one reason he needed to conceal it.

His private secretary in Paris, William Short, whose presence in Jefferson's quarters made him privy to the liaison with Hemings, had the temerity to suggest in a letter that the relationship might cause Jefferson to rethink his wholly negative view of racial amalgamation. What difference would it make, Short asked rhetorically, "if whites should advance to the middle ground between their present color and black?" There were already, Short observed, "in our own country some people darker than the gradual mixture of blacks can ever make us, and yet I do not know that they suffer from thence." Perhaps a mixed-race America, Short was suggesting, would not constitute the degradation that Jefferson feared. Jefferson never answered Short's letter; nor did he revise his rationale for making emancipation contingent upon deporting all freed blacks; nor did he abandon his sexual partnership with Sally Hemings.[30]

The Jefferson who departed Paris in 1789, then, was not the same clear-eyed critic of slavery who had arrived four years earlier. In the upper reaches of his mind, where the most visionary Jeffersonian ideas always flourished, he maintained moral certainty that slavery was a doomed institution, and that the energies released by the American Revolution would eventually overwhelm it for all the right reasons. But below the moral high ground, in his day-to-day life, all the abiding truths seemed to collide in crisscrossing patterns, none of which seemed to lead anywhere. A few years later, a French visitor to Monticello, the Duc de La Rochefoucauld-Liancourt, captured the contradictions of the new Jeffersonian posture on slavery:

> The generous and enlightened Mr. Jefferson cannot but demonstrate a desire to see these negroes emancipated. But he sees so many difficulties in their emancipation, even postponed, he adds so many conditions to render it practicable, that it is thus reduced to the impossible. He keeps, for example, the opinion he advanced in his notes that the negroes of Virginia can only be emancipated all at once, and by exporting to a distance the whole black race. He bases his opinion on the certain danger, if there were nothing else, of seeing blood mixed without means of preventing it.[31]

At the time of the good duke's visit, Sally Hemings was nursing Jefferson's second child.

→—=◆=—→

Except for a three-year interlude at Monticello (1793–96), Jefferson spent the next eighteen years in public office at the national level as secretary of state (1790–93), vice president (1796–1800), and president (1800–1808). At no point during that time was he required to address the slavery question directly, primarily because Congress had seen fit to take the most threatening topic off the national agenda. In response to two Quaker petitions demanding the end of the slave trade and slavery itself, the House passed a resolution in the spring of 1790, declaring that "Congress has no authority to interfere in the emancipation of slaves, or the treatment of them within any of the states; it remaining with the several states alone to provide any regulation therein." This became the seminal statement of the slavocracy's constitutional position for the next seventy years, that is, until the Civil War, when it became the political rationale for the Confederate States of America.[32]

During the 1790s, working behind the scenes with Madison to create an opposition party that denounced the economic program of Alexander Hamilton, most especially the federal assumption of state debts and the establishment of a National Bank, Jefferson developed a more expansive version of states' rights doctrine. In what one historian has called the "Jeffersonian Persuasion," not just slavery but all domestic policy was off-limits to the federal government, which Jefferson described as a "foreign power" that had no more authority to legislate for the states than Parliament had had to legislate for the colonies. The political agenda of the Republican Party,* eventually formalized in the Kentucky and Virginia Resolutions (1798), claimed to represent a restoration of "the ancient Whig principles" and "the

---

*Although several American history textbooks use the term *Democratic-Republican* to describe the political party that Jefferson and Madison founded in the 1790s, the term they used was *Republican*. Because the Jeffersonian Republicans morphed into the Jacksonian Democrats in the 1820s, the label *Democratic-Republican* seems sensible, since it anticipates the verbal evolution of the Jeffersonian persuasion, but it is historically incorrect. *Democratic-Republican* does not enter the mainstream political lexicon until 1816 with the presidency of James Monroe. To further confuse readers, modern-day Republicans trace their origins to what became Abraham Lincoln's party in 1854. And to make it even more complicated, the party of Lincoln can trace its origins to the Whigs of the 1830s and, before them, the Federalists of the 1790s.

spirit of '76," which had been betrayed by the Federalists, who themselves claimed to speak for the constitutional settlement and "the spirit of '87."[33]

It is tempting to regard the elaborate ideological lacework Jefferson and Madison created in the 1790s as a highly partisan subterfuge designed to protect what they called "the agrarian interest," which was a euphemism for slavery. This makes political sense because the Republicans were predominantly a southern party with headquarters in Virginia; and it makes historical sense because we know that more explicit defenders of slavery in the antebellum era like John C. Calhoun deployed the same states' rights argument to stigmatize federal authority over "that species of property."

But a close reading of the Jefferson-Madison correspondence throughout the decade, much of which was conducted in code, reveals not a single occasion when either of them blurted out the otherwise unspoken truth, namely that their doctrinal hostility toward federal power was merely a mask to conceal their implicit defense of slavery. Quite the opposite, Jefferson devoutly believed that his denial of federal authority over domestic policy was a principled position with roots in the same arguments he had hurled at Parliament and George III in *Summary View*. (It apparently never crossed his mind that the colonists had not been represented in Parliament as they now were in Congress, or that the Constitution had given the federal government enumerated powers over the states.) He was not being disingenuous when he reiterated his personal hatred of slavery, and his deep regret that the most potent weapon for ending it was simply unavailable for principled reasons he could not compromise. In the end, of course, it made no practical difference. But in terms of understanding Jefferson's mentality, it does make a difference to acknowledge that his political paralysis on slavery at the national level was not a contrived pose but rather a product of his heartfelt conviction that any energetic projection of federal power was a repudiation of revolutionary principles. But then, as he himself acknowledged, so was slavery.[34]

By the time he reached the presidency, his self-imposed paralysis had evolved into an official policy of silence. "I have most carefully avoided every public act or manifestation on that subject," he wrote to one antislavery advocate. "Should an occasion ever occur in which I can interpose with decisive effect, I shall certainly know and do my duty with promptitude and zeal." But in the meantime "it would only be disarming myself of influence to be taking small means." In fact, when he wrote these words in 1805, the occasion Jefferson referred to had just occurred.[35]

The occasion was the Louisiana Purchase (1803). For $15 million, the rough equivalent of $270 million today, the United States doubled its size, adding all the land from the Mississippi River to the Rocky Mountains and from the Canadian border to the Gulf of Mexico. The diplomacy surrounding the purchase had as many twists and turns as the Mississippi itself, but the central player in the story was Jefferson, who violated his creedal conviction about the inherent limitations on executive power by making one of the most consequential executive decisions in American history. He was fully aware of the quasi-monarchical character of the precedent he was setting, but he defended it on the grounds that such a providential opportunity to expand American borders across the continent could not be missed. And the Congress, sharing the same sense that dithering about constitutional scruples would be sheer madness when continental destiny was on the march, quickly passed what was termed "enabling legislation" that granted Jefferson unlimited authority to set federal policy for the entire Louisiana Territory.[36]

Suddenly, in one dramatic and wholly unpredictable set of circumstances, the conditions for resolving the slavery dilemma had converged, creating the providential opportunity to take decisive action that Jefferson, with utter sincerity, claimed he was waiting for. And he possessed nearly dictatorial power to seize that opportunity with an executive action that could change the direction of American history in accord with his own words in the Declaration of Independence.

All the necessary decisions followed naturally from policies he had previously advocated. First, slavery would be prohibited in all the

Louisiana Territory, the same policy he had proposed for all western territories in 1784. Second, a portion of the revenue from the sale of the unsettled land would be set aside as an endowed fund to compensate owners for freeing their slaves, thereby ending slavery gradually in the southern states east of the Mississippi. Third, a section of the enormous new tract would be designated as a homeland for resettling the freed slaves and their descendants, which would constitute a national version of the plan Jefferson had previously proposed for Virginia's slaves after emancipation.

This course of action did not require extraordinary imagination or vision. All the elements of the plan had, at one time or another, occurred to a younger Jefferson. To be sure, implementing such a plan required a display of executive authority that Jefferson claimed to abhor, but he had already chosen to act imperiously in making the Louisiana Purchase itself. And if putting slavery on the road to extinction was a moral and political priority, as he so often insisted, if he truly was poised to act decisively when the opportunity arose, then it strains credibility to conclude that the opportunity came and went because of sheer obliviousness.

His blind spot was race. He made one change in the language of the treaty approving the purchase, which described the range of rights enjoyed by "the inhabitants of the ceded territory," inserting "white" before "inhabitants." In an earlier letter about America's continental destiny to James Monroe, he had waxed eloquent about the extraordinary prospects of an American "empire of liberty," concluding with a caveat: "It is impossible not to look forward to distant times, when our rapid multiplication will cover the whole northern, if not the southern continent, with a people speaking the same language, governed in similar forms and by similar laws; nor can we contemplate with satisfaction either blot or mixture on that surface."[37]

Blot meant blacks. Jefferson was fully prepared to envision the Louisiana Territory as the appropriate destination for the Native American population currently residing east of the Mississippi. But the freed slaves would need to be transported back to Africa or—this was his new preference—somewhere in the West Indies, perhaps Santo Domingo. "Nature seems to have formed these islands," he predicted, "to become the receptacle of the blacks transplanted into the hemisphere." As a result, the Louisiana Purchase did not offer a solution to the postemancipation problem as Jefferson now envisioned it, because he could not imagine a biracial American society of whites and blacks. The word he used to describe the relocation of freed slaves was *expatriation*, which accurately conveyed his sense that they must be carried outside the borders of the United States. And once the vast interior of the American West was removed from the emancipation equation, what was already a difficult logistical problem became virtually intractable.[38]

The Louisiana Purchase afforded the last realistic opportunity to implement a policy of gradual emancipation, in part because the number of slaves was growing exponentially, in part because cotton production in the Deep South and the emergence of the Cotton Kingdom soon revitalized the slave economy in ways that Jefferson could not foresee. He had inadvertently contributed to the creation of the Cotton Kingdom as secretary of state. One of his duties was to approve patents for new inventions, and in 1793 he endorsed the application of a recent Yale graduate named Eli Whitney for a machine called the cotton gin, asking only "does it work?"[39]

For the rest of his life, the impossibility of it all became the centerpiece of Jefferson's position on the slavery question. He made multiple efforts to calculate the cost of deporting all freed slaves, the last attempt in 1824, only two years before his death. On that occasion he estimated that the price tag for removing 1.5 million ex-slaves over a twenty-five-year period at $900 million. As he put it, once you looked at that number, "it is impossible to look at this question a second time." Emancipation was inherently impractical because expatriation was logistically and economically incomprehensible. Once you grasped that intractable fact, procrastination became the only credible course, indeed the only sensible stance atop the high moral ground, all the while waiting for history to align itself with one's fondest hopes.[40]

Jefferson's fullest explanation of his rationale for silence came in response to a request from Edward Coles, a young Virginian slave owner who was contemplating the emancipation of his slaves and looked to the Sage of Monticello for advice. Jefferson reviewed his earlier efforts to limit or end slavery, then his subsequent disappointment at the failure of the younger generation to carry his youthful project to fruition. But he was adamant that no plan for emancipation could proceed until a postemancipation plan for the removal of all ex-slaves was in place:

> For men probably of any color, but of his color we know, brought from their infancy without necessity for thought or forecast, are by their habits rendered as incapable as children of taking care of themselves. . . . In the meantime they are pests in society by their idleness, and the degradation to which this leads them. Their amalgamation with the other color produces a degradation to which no lover of his country, no lover of excellence in the human character, can innocently consent.

Given his relationship with Sally Hemings, these words defy credibility as an expression of monumental hypocrisy that Coles most probably recognized—the Sally story was well known within Virginia's planter class—but chose to ignore according to unspoken white Virginia etiquette. At the end, Jefferson advised Coles to resist his otherwise admirable urge to free his slaves and instead focus his energies on caring for them as a benevolent patriarch. Coles rejected the advice, eventually choosing to take his emancipated slaves with him to Illinois.[41]

Jefferson's most dramatic and memorable version of the same message came in response to the Missouri Crisis (1820). Even though he had created the constitutional precedent for federal authority over the Louisiana Territory, now he argued that the federal government could not prohibit slavery in Missouri, the first of the new territories to apply for statehood. He described the very act of raising the slavery question as a "Federalist plot" to foment slave insurrections in the southern states, an ominous manipulation of the slavery dilemma that struck him "like a firebell in the night." No man on earth, he claimed, would be more disposed to end slavery than he was, "if it could be done in a practical way. The cession of that kind of property, for so it is misnamed, is a bagatelle which would not cost me a second thought, if a general emancipation and expatriation could be effected. . . . But as it is, we have the wolf by the ears, and we can neither hold him, nor safely let him go. Justice is on one scale, and self-preservation in the other." By "self-preservation" he meant the preservation of the white race.[42]

Visitors to Monticello reported that Jefferson was obsessed with the Missouri question, which prompted apocalyptic predictions of a race war that are littered throughout his correspondence at the time. He warned that once Congress was granted the authority to prohibit slavery in the territories—an authority he had once championed— "its majority may, and probably will, next declare that the condition of all men within the United States shall be that of freedom; in which case all the whites south of the Potomac and Ohio must evacuate their states, and most fortunate are those who can do it first." The most ardent and alarmist members of the emerging slavocracy could not have put it better.[43]

The same man who had once argued that ending slavery was the great piece of unfinished business for the revolutionary generation now claimed that prohibiting the expansion of slavery into the western territories was a repudiation of the revolutionary legacy. "I regret that I am now to die in the belief," he lamented, "that the useless sacrifice of themselves by the generation of 1776 is to be thrown away by the unwise and unworthy passions of their sons, and that my only consolation is to be, that I live not to weep over it."[44]

Perhaps out of desperation, he embraced an idea called "diffusion," which was simultaneously visionary and delusional. As he somewhat clumsily put it, "their diffusion over a greater surface would make them [i.e., slaves] individually happier, and proportionately facilitate the accomplishment of their emancipation by dividing the burden on a greater number of coadjutors." He seemed to be suggesting that allowing slavery to spread into the vast regions of the West would dilute, then dissolve, the toxic properties of the slavery dilemma by permitting it to evaporate in a western version of outer space. When John Adams learned that Jefferson had embraced the doctrine of diffusion, he worried that his old friend had apparently lost his mind, since no sane person could believe that a cancer could be killed by letting it spread throughout the body. From Jefferson's perspective, the diffusion theory had the splendid advantage of resolving the intractable problem of what to do with the freed slaves. As the term suggested, in some mystical manner they simply disappeared beyond the western vistas.[45]

Jefferson turned out to be right about the Missouri Crisis. It was "a firebell in the night" that foreshadowed the unresolvable political problem of slavery in the western territories that, just as he predicted, would become the issue that split the union when President Abraham Lincoln insisted on prohibiting slavery's expansion, and the slave states responded to his election by seceding. For our purposes, however, the Missouri Crisis was also an "airburst in the night" that exposed the devolution of Jefferson's previously principled opposition to slavery into empty rhetoric. From 1820 onward, Jefferson became indistinguishable from most ardent proslavery advocates in using his states' rights philosophy to construct a firewall designed to block any and all restrictions on slavery.

In 1823 he drafted and sent to Madison a proposal entitled "The Solemn Declaration and Protest of the Commonwealth of Virginia" in which he described all federal laws promoting internal improvements (i.e., roads, canals) as a diabolical conspiracy designed to establish federal control over Virginia's sovereign right to manage its own response to slavery. He compared this federal initiative to Parliament's imperial agenda against the American colonies in the 1760s, and he suggested that Virginia should feel justified in seceding from the union for the same reasons she had seceded from the British Empire. The ever prudent Madison persuaded him to keep the proposal to himself.

A younger Jefferson had insisted that the central principles of the American Revolution were inherently incompatible with slavery. The aging patriarch now argued that "the spirit of '76" precluded any attempt by the federal government to end slavery. It was a sad and pathetic spectacle, for he was linking his revolutionary legacy to the most reactionary segment of southern political culture and, in the end, to the destruction of the republic he had helped to create.[46]

The graphic contrast between the younger and the older Jefferson materialized in late autumn of 1824 during the ten-day visit of the Marquis de Lafayette, who made Monticello a mandatory destination in his ceremonial tour of all twenty-four states. Lafayette was at pains to remind Jefferson of their common presumption as young revolutionaries that slavery would die an early death in the emerging American republic. And yet almost a half century later, they were walking around a plantation populated by nearly a hundred slaves, and slavery remained a glaring anomaly that Lafayette could not explain. "I would like, before I die," Lafayette implored, "to be assured that progressive and earnest measures have been adopted to attain in due time so desirable, so necessary an object. Prudence as well as honor seems to me to require it."[47]

Jefferson fell back on what had become a familiar refrain. Like Lafayette, he too was surprised that slavery had resisted the liberating energies of their revolutionary project. But somehow it had, and now he could only deplore the misguided efforts of northern politicians to impose a tyrannical solution, which only made matters worse by agitating sectional differences that risked civil war. As for his own slaves, he was prepared to act decisively and with great relief once a feasible plan for the deportation of all Virginia slaves, either to Santo Domingo or to Liberia, could be enacted by state legislation. In the meantime his highest calling was to care for the slaves under his custody as he would for members of his own family.[48]

This was an updated version of the same multilayered defense of his self-imposed paralysis that Jefferson had been offering to curious visitors and correspondents throughout his retirement years at Monticello. It was a blatantly self-serving story, since it cast him, as much as his slaves, in the role of helpless victim, trapped in an awkward historical moment not of his making and beyond his control. But he had told the story so many times that he had come to believe it himself. The key ingredient in the Jeffersonian narrative was the insistence that any emancipation scheme must include a viable plan for expatriation, a condition that defied resolution but for that very reason conveniently provided Jefferson with a foolproof rationale for inaction.

His last word on the subject, sent to William Short, his former secretary in Paris, seemed to leave little doubt that he was reconciled to failure as an emancipator. He could not endorse any plan ending slavery, he explained, that betrayed American destiny by blackening the Anglo-Saxon population, thereby producing a mongrel race of enduring inferiority:

> On the subject of emancipation I have ceased to think because it is not to be the work of my day. The plan of converting the blacks into Serfs would certainly be better than keeping them in their present condition, but I consider that of expatriation to the governments of the West Indies of their own colour as entirely practicable, and greatly preferable to the mixture of colour here. To this I have great aversion, but I repeat my abandonment of the subject.[49]

There is a clear answer to the perennial question: How could the author of the Declaration of Independence fail to free his slaves or lead the movement for emancipation? His fear of racial amalgamation after slavery ended, it turned out, proved stronger than his conviction that "all men are created equal." The chief problem with this conclusion was that Monticello, where he lived out the last seventeen years of his life, was a veritable laboratory for precisely the kind of racial mixing he purportedly dreaded.

⊷ ⋙✦⋘ ⊷

The slave population at Monticello was divided by color into two distinctive communities. There were the black field hands, who lived in log cabins on four farms spread up and down the mountain. The flood of visitors who came to see the Sage of Monticello after his retirement in 1809 seldom saw these slaves, and Jefferson himself encountered them only at harvesttime, or when he left the mansion to supervise his overseers or laborers on construction projects. (Despite his famous celebration of farmers as "the chosen people of God," Jefferson never walked behind a plow and found farming deeply dull.) Then there were the light-skinned slaves, some of whom appeared almost completely white, who staffed the house and the adjoining dependencies on Mulberry Row. Almost all were members of the extended Hemings family. A French visitor described the scene: "In Virginia mongrel negroes are found in greater number than in Carolina and Georgia; and I have seen, especially at Mr. Jefferson's, slaves, who neither in point of colour or features, showed the least trace of their original descent [from Africa]; but their mothers being slaves, they retain, of consequence, the same condition."[50]

The biological source of this racial mosaic was Elizabeth (Betty) Hemings, the mulatto matriarch of the Hemings family who arrived at Monticello in 1772 as part of the dowry Martha Wayles Skelton brought to the marriage. Betty Hemings brought ten children with her, six probably fathered by John Wayles, Jefferson's father-in-law. Sally Hemings was her youngest child, born in 1773. Sally and her six sisters were all described as physically attractive according to white standards of beauty, and most, perhaps all of them, followed in their mother's footsteps by forming sexual partnerships with white men. For obvious reasons, the liaison between Jefferson and Sally Hemings has attracted the lion's share of historical attention, but it was only one part of a larger pattern of racial mixing at Monticello that gave slavery its distinctive biracial coloration. Tobacco had failed as a cash crop, and the interest on Jefferson's debt to bankers in England and Scotland hovered like a dark cloud over all his idyllic dreams of pastoral splendor, but miscegenation at Monticello was a flourishing enterprise.

The pattern of sexual interaction at Monticello was simultaneously typical and distinctive. On the former score, the most recent studies of plantation records in antebellum Virginia suggest that previous scholarship underestimated the frequency of interracial sex between masters and slaves, which had concluded that less than 10 percent of the children born on southern plantations were fathered by whites. But these numbers were based on manumission records in which white owners acknowledged paternity. Because sexual relations between the races on most plantations remained covert and secretive affairs, unlikely to leave a trail in the written record, more recent assessments have tended to double the earlier estimates. The level of racial mixing at Monticello falls within that higher range. On the other hand, Monticello was distinctive because sexual interaction was primarily concentrated within one extended slave family, the Hemingses, and because that family became the public face of slavery at the most visited plantation in Virginia.[51]

When historians talk about the architecture of Monticello, they are almost always referring to the Palladian style that Jefferson had come to love during his travels in southern France. But the architecture of Monticello as a plantation is of a different genre altogether, and the design was distinctively Jeffersonian, meaning structured to make the black workforce almost invisible and to feature the light-skinned household laborers, who looked and acted less like slaves than like members of the family because, in fact, they were. This physical arrangement disguised the full meaning of the slave experience at Monticello for visitors, while providing Jefferson himself with the role he preferred, as paternalistic employer or guardian rather than slave master. And like a commander ensconced at headquarters, he conveyed a clear signal to his overseers in the fields that unpleasant incidents should not filter their way back up the mountain.

The ironies abound, since the core appeal of this Jeffersonian biracial façade was the lighter color of the up-front slaves, all Hemingses, whose privileged status and domestic demeanor seemed to defy the coercive conditions customarily associated with the institution of slavery. And yet the Hemings family also embodied the conspicuous consequences of racial mixing that Jefferson was on record as abhorring. In effect, the reason slavery looked more benign and palatable in its Jeffersonian version was also the reason Jefferson used to justify his resistance to ending slavery. This is the kind of profound paradox that almost invites psychiatric speculation.

It also raises some questions that must, by their very nature, remain forever unanswerable: Did Jefferson regard his own children as biologically inferior mongrels? What was he thinking when he watched his own enslaved children performing household duties? Were his moments of physical intimacy with Sally Hemings totally bereft of emotional content? Did his extended exposure to the fidelity and composure of his biracial slave "family" cause him to question his convictions about racial degradation? There is, in fact, the glimmering of an answer to the last question.

Jefferson was predisposed to free those biracial slaves who could pass as white. When asked by a fellow slaveholder how he interpreted the Virginia law defining the different gradations of "mulatto," he explained that inferior African blood remained dominant in the first and second crossings with white partners, but with the third crossing "the blood cleared," making anyone who was seven-eighths white legally so and almost always physically indistinguishable from white Americans or Europeans.

All of his children by Sally Hemings fit that description. He allowed his two oldest children, Harriet and Beverly, to walk away from Monticello in 1822—the entry in the Farm Book read "ran away"—and he freed his two youngest children, Madison and Eston, in his will in

1826, though not until they reached maturity. He never freed Sally Hemings, who was three-quarters white. In freeing his own children, Jefferson honored the promise made to Sally Hemings in Paris, but he also acted in accord with his racial convictions, which apparently remained intact. Blacks could be assimilated into American society only when they ceased appearing to be black.[52]

In Jefferson's case, the denial syndrome had become a widespread habit of mind so prevalent that it justifies using *Jeffersonian* as a distinctive mental or psychological label. Consider the following examples of what might be called Jefferson's flair for functional delusions. He sincerely declared his hatred of political parties as poisonous snakes in the republican garden at the same time as he and Madison were creating the Republican Party. As secretary of state in the Washington administration, he spread rumors that Washington was senile, then seemed genuinely surprised when his slanders were exposed, and he wrote Washington in several letters brimming over with personal assurance that he was totally innocent of such indiscretions. He did the same thing with John Adams in the election of 1800, this time paying a scandalmonger, James Callender, to libel Adams, again expressing complete confusion when Callender published their clandestine correspondence, and later assuring Abigail Adams that the whole episode would forever remain a mystery to him.[53]

At Monticello this Jeffersonian syndrome operated primarily as a shield to protect the bucolic and domestic paradise that Jefferson had created in his imagination from the inevitable intrusions of the real world. Modern-day tourists, for example, see an authentic replica of Monticello that never existed in such a completed condition during Jefferson's lifetime, when the Palladian vision was still a construction site replete with roofless rooms, broken bricks, and teams of black and white laborers digging and hammering away.

Jefferson's domestic dream also had to filter out other nettlesome contradictions. There was the awkward presence of Thomas Mann Randolph, his daughter Martha's husband, who became a deranged alcoholic banished to live alone in one of the outlying dependencies.

Then there was the shadow cast over the Monticellan dream by Jefferson's staggering debt of several hundred thousand dollars, the modern equivalent of millions, owed to English and Scottish bankers and growing every year. (In a strictly legal sense, Jefferson could not free his slaves because he no longer owned them, his creditors did, though the Atlantic Ocean made enforcement unlikely.) All these topics were taboo on the mountaintop, where the Jeffersonian editorial process removed them from the conversation.[54]

Debt proved a downfall that could not be edited out. Jefferson managed to deny the hopelessness of his economic predicament until the very end, when he was rescued from total despair only by the inimitable Jefferson style. "A call on me to the amount of my endorsements," he wrote Madison, "would indeed close my course by a catastrophe I had never calculated." Madison would also die bankrupt, as would James Monroe and most of Virginia's planter class, all victims of an inherently unprofitable slave economy.

Buoyed by the false hope that a public lottery might allow him to salvage at least some portion of his estate to pass on to his heirs, he mustered up one final surge of eloquence in response to a request for his thoughts on the fiftieth anniversary of the Declaration of Independence. "All eyes are opened or opening to the rights of man," he wrote. "The general spread of the light of science has already laid open to every view the palpable truth, that the mass of mankind has not been born with saddles on their backs, nor a favored few, booted and spurred, ready to ride them legitimately, by the grace of God."

If these inspiring words were still floating in the air at Monticello during the public auction six months later, no one heard them, least of all the "130 valuable Negros" who were sold to the highest bidder, a fate that Jefferson had promised would never happen. It was a tragedy for all concerned. Slave families were broken up and dispersed throughout Virginia and "down the river" to the brutal cotton fields of Mississippi, Arkansas, and Louisiana. Jefferson's surviving daughter and eleven grandchildren were made wards of the state, dependent on charitable contributions from several city and state governments.

(Virginia offered no financial assistance, in large part because its economy, much like Monticello's, was bankrupted by slavery, and its only cash crop—here again the fate of Monticello was emblematic—was its surplus slaves.) Jefferson himself had the good fortune to be safely under the ground, shielded once again, this time forever, from the inevitable implications of his fondest illusions.[55]

From our perspective nearly two centuries later, Jefferson's personal tragedy pales in comparison with the fate of the enslaved population at Monticello. More broadly, even before his story ended so sadly, all our expectations for a visionary Jefferson, defending the principles he so lyrically declared in 1776 against the most obvious exception to his own founding creed, have been shattered beyond recognition. The arc of his career as a critic of slavery is all downward after 1785; the dominant direction is retreat; the final destination is a Virginia-writ-large version of America already auditioning for its role as a keystone in the Confederate States of America.

Jefferson seems destined to disappoint all but his most ardent disciples. He was in a unique position as president to seize the most fortuitous opportunity history ever offered to implement a gradual emancipation policy that would put slavery on the road to extinction, but he failed to do so. And by lending his enormous prestige to the most reactionary elements in Virginia politics during his retirement, he ushered the Old Dominion from the epicenter to the periphery of American history. To borrow a phrase Jefferson used to describe his theory of black inferiority, his self-imposed paralysis on the most consequential and controversial question of his time invites "a suspicion only" that his political ambitions and personal comforts outweighed his antislavery convictions. One of the many ironies raised to relief by his sad ending is that both Virginia and Monticello became victims of an inherently unprofitable slave labor force. Emancipation was economically as well as morally the historically correct choice, rendered impossible in Jefferson's mind for racial reasons that were themselves incompatible with his own personal and sexual conduct. At some point, faithful Jeffersonians must be forgiven for throwing up their hands in frustration.[56]

His racial views are more difficult to assess with historical detachment because they are simultaneously offensive to modern sensibilities and more racist than the norm in postrevolutionary and antebellum America. As noted, Jefferson's insistence on the *inherent* inferiority of blacks was an extreme position within the spectrum of racial thinking at the time, but his inability to imagine a biracial society after emancipation was broadly shared by the most prominent founders, and almost all the plans for gradual emancipation at the national level included schemes for sending the freed slaves elsewhere. As a recent scholar of the subject has put it, "for much of the nineteenth century, the most respectable way to express one's loathing for slavery was to endorse the logic of colonization."[57]

In all the northern states that ended slavery after the American Revolution, the racial problem could be solved by segregation, because the number of freed slaves was negotiable, though one could anticipate the timing of state emancipation laws with complete confidence by knowing the size of the slave population (i.e., Vermont with the smallest population came first, New York with the largest came last). On the national level, however, the sheer numbers south of the Potomac rendered segregation an unacceptable solution. With few exceptions, even the most staunch abolitionists assumed that emancipation would be followed by deportation. In her appendix to *Uncle Tom's Cabin* (1852), for example, Harriet Beecher Stowe described Liberia as the preferred location for ex-slaves. Although Jefferson's racial views were distinctive, his belief in exportation was a central premise shared by even the most progressive opponents of slavery.[58]

A few ardent advocates of racial equality in America, mindful of Jefferson's dark side on the racial question, have recently called for removing the Jefferson Memorial from the Tidal Basin. (No one to my knowledge has yet proposed taking sledgehammers to his profile on Mount Rushmore.) Adding a panel that provides his views on race as well as slavery strikes me as the wiser course, in part because the troublesome connection between our most noble and ignoble values is a point worth confronting, and Jefferson embodies that fusion more fully than any other figure in American history. Attempting to erase Jefferson from our memory will do nothing to change the long and deep history of racism in the United States. Forgetting that history will only deprive us of understanding what we are up against in the ongoing struggle for racial equality, a struggle embedded in over three centuries of racial prejudice.

Since its dedication in 1943, the Jefferson Memorial has been a shrine that celebrates the twin goals of human freedom and equality, most eloquently expressed in those magic words he wrote in Philadelphia in June 1776. They usefully served as an inspirational rallying cry for the war against German and Japanese totalitarianism, then against Soviet-style communism. A modified Jefferson Memorial would make his darker legacy relevant in much the same haunting ways that the Vietnam War Memorial and the Holocaust Museum force us to remember a tragic war and genocide. The thoughts and conversations prompted by this flawed Jefferson would add a historical dimension to our ongoing debate about racial justice that frames the issue at stake in both a broader and a deeper fashion than our present perspective permits. We should begin with the realization that our battle against racism, like the war against cancer, is an ongoing struggle that must be conducted without having an end in sight.[59]

Abiding Backlash

In the context of the Negro problem neither whites nor blacks, for excellent reasons of their own, have the faintest desire to look back; but I think the past is all that makes the present coherent, and further that the past will remain horrible for exactly so long as we refuse to assess it honestly. . . . Appearances to the contrary, no one in America escapes its effects and everyone in America bears some responsibility for it.

James Baldwin, Notes of a Native Son *(1955)*

Martin Luther King, Jr., liked to buoy the spirits of his supporters by observing that "the arc of the moral universe bends upward toward justice," a thought he borrowed from Theodore Parker, the nineteenth-century antislavery theologian. But nearly a century and a half after slavery was ended, the dark side of the Jeffersonian legacy continues to cast a shadow over King's hopeful words, reminding us that Jefferson never intended his lyrical version of the American promise to include blacks, and the very belief that it should was a recent, mid-twentieth-century idea. Each lurch forward along the arc of racial equality, in fact, has generated a backward surge that exposes residual prejudices called to the surface of American life from some deep pool of racial resentment that was always there and, if Jefferson was right, always will be. Instead of an upward arc, then, the dominant racial pattern since the end of slavery has been a cycle in which progress actually generates resistance to its continuation.

We can glimpse that pattern in our current context. The first black president completed two successful terms, though a near majority of Republican voters, in the face of all evidence, continue to believe he is not an American citizen and was therefore never a legitimate president. The African American Museum of History and Culture now occupies space on the National Mall, but the dominant protest movement is Black Lives Matter, a response to the routinized killing of black men and boys by police in our urban war zones. For the first time in American history, the majority of students in our public schools are racial minorities, but the most celebrated black memoir is *Between the World and Me* by Ta-Nehisi Coates, which is an open letter to his son, declaring his sense of hopelessness about the racial prejudice his son will be forced to face in a white world.

We need to gain perspective on this backlash pattern. For while all problems in American society have a history, none of them is as incomprehensible, when viewed myopically or ahistorically, as our racial dilemma. James Baldwin put it most succinctly when he wrote that "the past is all that makes the present coherent." In his *Notes of a Native Son* (1955) he went on to offer the most profoundly relevant observation on the racial challenge that American history has forced upon present and future generations: "The establishment of democracy on the American continent was scarcely as radical a break with the [European] past as was the necessity, which Americans faced, of broadening the concept to include black men."

⊷ ▰◆▰ ⊷

According to the most recent census, there are 45 million African Americans in the United States, 13 percent of the total population. Two overlapping questions, both misleadingly simple, become obvious: How did they get here, and what does *here* mean? The answer is three massive immigrations, two that happened and one that did not.

The first and largest migration occurred between 1500 and 1860, the notorious Middle Passage from Africa to the Americas, which crested in the middle years of the eighteenth century. Approximately 10 million Africans were forcibly transported to the New World as slaves, the vast majority going to South America and the Caribbean. Only 400,000 were carried to the English colonies in North America, where slave traders imported a roughly equal number of women and men in order to generate a self-sufficient population that replaced itself rather than depend primarily on future imports from Africa. By 1776, out of a total population of 2.5 million, 20 percent, or 500,000, were African Americans, 90 percent of whom were enslaved and living south of the Chesapeake. (As a percentage of the total population, the African American population reached its zenith in the year the United States declared its independence.) Between the American Revolution and the Civil War, the black and white populations grew at the same explosive rate, doubling every quarter century, generating a black population of slightly over 4 million in 1860. In part because the great influx of European migrants occurred in the nineteenth century, modern-day blacks can collectively trace their origins further back in American history than whites.

The second migration, which never happened, was a standard feature in all plans for gradual emancipation in the early republic and antebellum eras; it envisioned the involuntary deportation of all ex-slaves to locations in Africa and the West Indies. This migration never materialized, in part because logistical and economic problems proved insoluble in the absence of a national consensus on emancipation itself, and in part because emancipation happened suddenly rather than gradually in a wholly improvisational context during and after the Civil War.

Recall that Lincoln initially insisted the Civil War was about saving the Union, not ending slavery. And the Emancipation Proclamation (1863) was a military decision designed to deprive the South of its captive labor force, not yet a statement of national policy. We know that Lincoln was considering a deportation scheme, since he apprised a visiting delegation of free blacks to prepare their people for a mass exodus once the war was won, and he dispatched a presidential commission to Panama in order to explore the viability of a black homeland there. But we can never know what Lincoln would have done, since he died a martyr to the cause just as the war ended. Three days before his assassination, in his final speech, he condemned a vindictive peace, urging a conciliatory policy toward Confederate leaders, but said nothing about the fate of the freed slaves.

Neither his successor, Andrew Johnson, who was an unapologetic racist, nor the Radical Republicans in Congress, who sought to provide social and economic equality for ex-slaves at the expense of the white planter class, made any proposal to colonize the black population elsewhere. The net result was an outcome that few opponents of slavery before the war had anticipated, and for which even fewer white Americans in the South were prepared: the permanent presence of nearly 5 million third- or fourth-generation Americans of African descent in the United States, the vast majority located in a region dedicated to their enduring subordination.

The third migration was an exodus of 6 million blacks from that region to cities in the Northeast and the Midwest. Starting as a trickle in the 1890s, what came to be called the Great Migration surged during World War I, when the reduction in European migration created job openings in the urban North, declined during the Great Depression, then surged again during and after World War II. Usually traveling in family units, black migrants deserted their long-standing homeland for what Richard Wright called "the warmth of other suns" in Baltimore, Chicago, Cleveland, Detroit, New York, Philadelphia, St. Louis, and Washington, D.C. The result was a shift in the racial landscape of the United States. By 1970 nearly half the black population lived outside the South, and there were more blacks in Chicago than in all of Mississippi.

The migrants were fleeing for much the same reasons that European Jews fled the pogroms for the open-ended possibilities of the New World, though the New World for the black migrants was the Promised Land to the north, and they were deserting what the preeminent historian of the South, C. Vann Woodward, called "the strange career of Jim Crow." In truth, there was nothing strange about the creation of a race-based class system in the states of the former Confederacy after Reconstruction ended in 1877. Quite predictably, southern states repudiated the racial agenda imposed on them against their will in the Fourteenth and Fifteenth Amendments, rejected as unimaginable the idea of black social and political equality, and reestablished a racially segregated society based on the same level of white domination that had existed under slavery. In some ways the Jim Crow era was more virulently racist than slavery, because under slavery control could be assumed but after emancipation needed to be more conspicuously confirmed by Black Codes, lynching campaigns, and terrorist organizations like the Ku Klux Klan.

Much like European immigrants, it was the children and grandchildren of former slaves who created successful lives and careers in their new northern surroundings. Here are just a few highly selective examples of second- or third-generation beneficiaries of the Great Migration who might well have languished in obscurity in the Jim Crow South: in literature, James Baldwin, Ralph Ellison, Toni Morrison, Richard Wright; in sports, Joe Louis, Jesse Owens, Jackie Robinson; in music, Aretha Franklin, Michael Jackson, Diana Ross.

But there was also a dark side to the Great Migration that became increasingly visible in the middle decades of the twentieth century. The inner cities of urban America became black ghettos after middle-class blacks and whites escaped to the suburbs, leaving a black underclass trapped within racially segregated spaces whose borders were defined by restrictive white covenants and redlining realtors. The result was Jim Crow with a northern accent, a new kind of structural racism immune to conventional civil rights legislation, and a de facto brand of segregation that produced a class division within America's black population. By the late twentieth century, the black ghettos had become the new face of America's racial dilemma.

→ ⊶⊷ →

If the migrations that shaped our current racial framework happened in long-term waves, the efforts at racial reform, what we have come to call civil rights movements, happened in briefer bursts. The first occurred during the twelve years after the Civil War (1865–77), a crowded moment of intensive debate over the fate of the freed blacks dubbed Reconstruction. The second, often called Second Reconstruction, occurred during the twenty years after World War II (1948–68). The most intriguing irony within this historical pattern is that the central achievements of Second Reconstruction—full citizenship for blacks, to include voting rights—were merely reaffirmations of legal rights already guaranteed by the Fourteenth and Fifteenth Amendments.

Reconstruction was, as the black activist and intellectual W. E. B. Du Bois described it, "a splendid failure," splendid because it enshrined legal and political equality for ex-slaves in amendments to the Constitution, a failure because it did not provide the economic foundation those new rights required in order to become more than paper promises. Nothing less than a second American Revolution was necessary to achieve that goal, which in practice would have meant that the planter class of the Confederacy be regarded and treated like Loyalists after the war for independence, their estates confiscated and the land distributed among their former slaves. A few Radical Republicans endorsed such a policy, and a gesture in that direction was made with the creation of the Freedmen's Bureau and its "forty acres and a mule" agenda. But the will to implement such a policy could never extend beyond a radical fringe in Congress and never enjoyed support from the white population in the North, where blacks were still regarded as second-class citizens who lived in segregated communities.

Without land of their own, the freedmen were effectively marooned in the postwar South, fated to assume quasi-slave status as tenants of their former masters, poised to become victims of Jim Crow policies once federal troops were withdrawn in 1877. In retrospect, what was economically essential to implement a racial revolution was politically impossible, because the vast majority of white citizens, North and South, found the wholesale transfer of property from whites to blacks unimaginable. As Du Bois was the first to recognize, once the opportunity to redistribute the wealth of the white planter class was missed during Reconstruction, economic inequality became a permanently embedded feature in America's racial equation that reinforced and verified long-standing presumptions of racial inferiority.

❧

If we move our lens forward to Second Reconstruction, one prominent feature of the terrain has fallen out of memory and needs to be restored, because it defined the intellectual framework within which the civil rights movement developed. In 1938 the Carnegie Foundation recruited a prominent Swedish economist, Gunnar Myrdal, to replicate the success achieved by Alexis de Tocqueville a century earlier in his classic *Democracy in America* (1835), believing that a European might bring a more detached perspective to America's distinctive racial problem. Myrdal and his team of researchers fanned out across the American South, gathering evidence that filled two fat volumes with graphs, charts, and analysis. Taken together, these comprised the most comprehensive documentation of racial discrimination in America ever assembled. It was published as *An American Dilemma: The Negro Problem and Modern Democracy* in 1944, the year after the Jefferson Memorial was dedicated.

The connection to Jefferson, it turned out, was not a mere coincidence. For Myrdal identified the natural rights section of the Declaration of Independence as the seminal source for what he called the American Creed and thereby injected a new ingredient into the modern conversation about civil rights. Lincoln, of course, had previously cited Jefferson's lyrical language (i.e., "all men are created equal") to justify ending slavery. Now Myrdal extended the reach of the same words to stigmatize all forms of racial discrimination. As we know, Jefferson had explicitly disavowed such an expansive meaning, and Lincoln had also distinguished between a Jeffersonian rationale for ending slavery, which he embraced, and one for justifying racial equality, which, like Jefferson, he rejected. Myrdal now claimed that the latent meaning of the Jeffersonian promise had always been broad and inclusive, and that by the middle of the twentieth century the truths that Jefferson had declared self-evident in the eighteenth century, and that Lincoln had reaffirmed in the nineteenth, were blooming again with a new biracial flowering.

Myrdal also presented his revision of the American Creed in a distinctive Jeffersonian format, as a set of eternal principles levitating above the laws and mores of American society that created a gravitational field pulling history forward in an egalitarian direction. Within this framework the Jim Crow policies of the South, like slavery before them, were doomed vestiges of an older order. It helped that *An American Dilemma* appeared in the same year that American and allied troops landed at Normandy and began advancing across Europe in defense of values eerily similar to Myrdal's creedal principles, though black troops were still serving in segregated units.

That anomaly was corrected in 1948, when President Harry Truman signed the executive order desegregating America's armed forces, which launched the modern civil rights movement. A second surge came six years later in the landmark case of the twentieth century, *Brown v. Board of Education*, when the Supreme Court ruled that segregated public schools were inherently unequal and therefore violated the equal rights provision of the Fourteenth Amendment. It merits attention that both of these rulings came from branches of the federal government furthest removed from popular opinion, and both met with stiff resistance within states of the old Confederacy. But both reforms also followed the script for racial equality that Myrdal had described as foreordained.

Second Reconstruction reached a crescendo in the mid-1960s, with Martin Luther King's "I Have a Dream" speech in 1963, then passage of the Civil Rights Act of 1964 and the Voting Rights Act of 1965. Though he spoke from the steps of the Lincoln Memorial, King declared that he had come to collect on a "promissory note" issued by Thomas Jefferson, thereby linking the goals of the civil rights movement back to the original formulation of the American Creed, which King also described as an expanding mandate that now included the descendants of Jefferson's slaves. What Lincoln had called "a new birth of freedom" at Gettysburg in 1863, King claimed was being born again exactly a century later, this time enveloping all black Americans under its egalitarian canopy. The dedication of the Martin Luther King, Jr. Memorial in 2014 gave iconic status on the Mall to the liberal narrative of American history as an ongoing conversation within the trinity of Jefferson, Lincoln, and King about what "all men are created equal" meant then and means now.

In King's version, it meant that all explicit forms of racial discrimination as practiced in the segregationist South since the end of First Reconstruction were both illegal and anachronistic. The civil rights legislation of 1964 and 1965 essentially declared that the federal government was now prepared to enforce these laws in the states of the former Confederacy. Even that modest goal came at considerable cost, however, since the vast majority of southern whites did not believe King's version of Jefferson's words, just as their ancestors had not believed Lincoln's version. Their reading of the American Creed remained true to the historical Jefferson's core convictions about black inferiority and the right of states to defy federal laws imposed on them without their consent. Richard Russell, the segregationist senator from Georgia, warned President Lyndon Johnson that if he signed the Voting Rights Act, the Democratic Party would lose the South for the next thirty years, which turned out to be a conservative estimate. Johnson declared that the moral principle at stake was worth the political sacrifice, arguably an act of presidential leadership without parallel in the twentieth century. Most of the southern states soon made the transition from Democrat to Republican and from overt to covert forms of racial discrimination.

Within the long sweep of what Myrdal called the American Dilemma, Second Reconstruction marked a milestone. After two hundred years of slavery and another hundred years of what King called "the dream deferred," the United States made the decision to assimilate its most long-standing immigrants as full-fledged citizens. And that decision was rooted in equivalently long-standing American values embodied most lyrically in Jefferson's famous words about human equality. King understood the civil rights movement as a chapter in an ongoing national story in which the latent energies of the American Revolution kept radiating out their full implications until they enveloped all people regardless of creed, color, or gender. Within this narrative, all explicit expressions of racial prejudice were placed on the permanent defensive, outspoken advocates of white supremacy were now relegated to the political fringes, and America's racial conversation for the first time spoke with a discernibly liberal accent. The new narrative featured the upside of the Jeffersonian legacy while dismissing the downside as a premodern vestige of values that were now, at last, gone with the proverbial wind.

This last assumption has proven woefully naïve, most especially the belief that ending segregation was synonymous with ending racism. Moreover, two ominous features of the racial terrain, clearly visible in retrospect, were either not noticed at the time or beyond the range of the available political telescopes. First, as in First Reconstruction, there was no economic component to the reform agenda of the 1960s. Over half the black population at the time lived below the poverty line, and the median black household possessed less than 10 percent of the wealth of the median white household. The optimistic title of Booker T. Washington's classic memoir, *Up from Slavery* (1901), remained a fond hope a full century after slavery ended, and once the opportunity to redistribute the estates of the planter class was missed during First Reconstruction, the prospects for economic reparations disappeared forever. It was one thing to acknowledge the rights to vote and to sit together on a bus, quite another to share resources; and lacking that radical commitment, the legal and political rights bestowed during Second Reconstruction rested atop an apparently permanent black underclass whose very existence, much like slavery before it, fed unspoken white assumptions of black inferiority.

Second, this overlap between race and class was most pronounced in those northern cities where nearly 40 percent of the black population now resided. Myrdal's *American Dilemma* had focused almost exclusively on the Jim Crow policies of the rural South, as had King's nonviolent protest campaign in the early 1960s, leaving unaddressed the de facto segregation in the urban North and the more covert kinds of racism that flowed from epicenters of concentrated poverty and unemployment. Indeed, by the last decade of the twentieth century, it was misleading to speak of black Americans as a homogeneous whole. There were middle-class and working-class blacks who stood to benefit from the opportunities created during Second Reconstruction; then there was the black underclass, trapped in urban ghettos of forced confinement where gangs, guns, and drugs defined a social agenda in a nightmare version of the American Dream.

—⊷≡⊶—

The underside of the Jeffersonian legacy remained alive and well in the late twentieth century, but concealment became an essential strategy for any and all opponents of racial equality. The climate of opinion created by Second Reconstruction did not permit explicitly racist language in mainstream American politics, so the race card needed to be facedown in the new game, and the players could only wink and nod in silent recognition when coded terms like *law and order* and *voter fraud* entered the conversation. Social scientists coined the term *structural racism* to describe the new stealth strategy, which put a premium on duplicity, deniability, even self-deception, all modernized versions of the more ignoble Jeffersonian values.

Racism had always been an elusive term to define, much less measure. But earlier incarnations, especially in the Jim Crow South, were conspicuous. The distinguishing feature of post–civil rights racism is its covert character, indeed its ability to pose as something else. The efforts of social scientists to provide a new language for modern-day racism, while laudable, is elusively abstract. Instead, let me offer a palpable example of what we might call color-blind racism in action.

Consider the war on drugs, first declared by Ronald Reagan in

1982. The decision to make the prosecution of drug dealers and users a national priority had two unfortunate consequences: first, an exponential expansion of the prison population in the United States from 300,000 in 1980 to over 2 million in 2010, an incarceration rate nearly ten times higher than that of any industrialized nation in the world; second, the impact of the new drug war fell disproportionately on the black population, chiefly black males in America's inner cities, where imprisonment became the presumed fate for a statistical majority of ghetto youth, the equivalent of going to college for white suburban males. And the establishment of mandatory minimum sentences, even for first-time offenders, meant that a generation of black men could expect to spend five or ten years of their early adulthood behind bars and the rest of their lives burdened with criminal records. In response to the often-asked question "Where are the missing black fathers in ghetto families?" the answer became "Most of them are in jail."

Here is a case where the rarified term *structural racism* comes to life. For while the war on drugs unquestionably had racial consequences, whether those consequences had explicit racist causes is an arguable question. In *The New Jim Crow* (2010) Michelle Alexander announced her affirmative answer in her title, concluding that the criminal justice system "is engaged in a stunningly effective and well disguised system of racialized control," which, she claimed, was consciously designed "to take black males off the street" and fill the prisons with a hugely disproportionate number of blacks. In addition to the sheer size of the black casualty rate in the war on drugs, Alexander made two arguments to support her case that a self-conscious racial strategy is at work: first, penalties and sentences for using or distributing crack cocaine, the drug of choice for blacks in the inner cities, are much more severe than for powder cocaine, the drug of choice for suburban whites; and conviction rates for black defendants in drug cases are several times higher than the rates for whites.

Those disposed to deny that any racist strategy exists can argue that racial minorities are convicted of drug offenses more frequently than whites because they commit more drug crimes. The burden of proof, they argue, rests on those making charges of racism, and the targeting of inner-city blacks cannot be characterized as racist for the simple reason that epidemic levels of drug-related crimes are concentrated in the black ghettos, so the higher incarceration levels of blacks is only collateral damage in the drug war.

A predominantly white jury drawn from the northern suburbs of Chicago is likely to find such an argument persuasive. A predominantly black jury drawn from the neighborhoods of Chicago's South Side is likely to reach a different verdict, concurring with Michelle Alexander that "New Jim Crow" is an accurate description of their experience with police raids, especially by SWAT teams in military gear with automatic weapons, which are reminiscent of the Klan attacks in the night their grandparents told them about.

The two juries are obviously living in parallel universes. Both sides are capable of agreeing that most black residents of Chicago's South Side are not criminals and that most police officers are not predisposed to random acts of violence. But once the pathological conditions of the South Side become the zone of racial interaction, violent conflict and mutual misunderstanding become inevitable. And the recent availability of cell phone cameras that document blatant acts of police brutality ignites the racial tinderbox, which then explodes into riots featured on the nightly news that white and black audiences view through fundamentally different racial prisms. Many whites regard the term *structural racism* as a euphemism for welfare programs they are supposed to fund. Many blacks regard the term *law and order* as a euphemism for state-sponsored terrorism. As long as the urban ghetto remains the toxic environment in which a significant portion of America's black population is effectively trapped, this predictable pattern will persist, continue to feed stereotypes on both sides of the racial divide, and render a truly biracial conversation virtually impossible.

--- ◦≡◦≡◦ ---

This is a dispiriting conclusion, made more depressing by listening to shrill voices on each side of the racial chasm. Within this cacophony, the voice of William Julius Wilson sounds a distinctive note. His body of work as a sociologist of the black underclass merits extended attention as another way of thinking about our current racial predicament.

Wilson first attracted national attention as a young scholar at the University of Chicago with a book whose very title, *The Declining Significance of Race,* provoked criticism from the black community. His point, it turned out, was that there was no such thing as a "black community," because a class division separated middle- and working-class blacks from inner-city blacks. The former were beneficiaries of the civil rights movement and affirmative action programs. The latter were a category unto themselves, mired in zones of concentrated poverty beyond the reach of liberal legislation, a permanent black proletariat. In effect, there were two black narratives: one group, a slight majority of the black population, was advancing, albeit slowly and incrementally, into the mainstream of American society; the other group, a sizable minority, remained outside the pale without any prospects for social or economic salvation. Depending on where you stood along this bimodal spectrum, things were better or worse than ever before.

Wilson recognized that race played a significant role in creating and then sustaining segregated neighborhoods, which other scholars have characterized as "American apartheid." "Racism put African Americans in their economic place," Wilson observed, "then stepped aside to watch changes in the modern economy make the place in which they found themselves even more precarious." When St. Clair Drake and Horace Cayton wrote their pioneering study of Chicago, *Black Metropolis* (1945), a sprinkling of working-class whites and a sizable black middle class coexisted alongside more impoverished black residents. But in the wake of the civil rights movement, these upwardly mobile segments of the urban population escaped to the suburbs, leaving a black underclass marooned in what became the black holes of America's urban universe. By the late twentieth century, these insulated inner-city spaces had become raw material for racial stereotyping, best symbolized by predatory black males on the prowl, insolent and armed, the criminal heroes of gangsta rap. Much in the way the degenerate condition of enslaved blacks fed racist convictions in the nineteenth century, the black ghettos have become urban jungles dominated by tribal gangs in hooded sweatshirts that seem almost designed to populate the most horrific racial nightmares of suburban whites.

Although he recognized that the black ghetto generates racist reactions, Wilson insisted that economic and demographic conditions are the root causes of the racial problem. And he therefore proposed that race-neutral economic reforms are the only viable solution to the most recent and virulent version of the American Dilemma. His thinking was driven by a self-consciously pragmatic appreciation of the ingrained hostility that any race-specific solution will generate on what is still a predominantly white society. As a result, only a biracial approach that addresses economic equality as a class rather than a racial problem has any hope of succeeding; therefore he advocated a robust jobs program, a kind of Marshall Plan for American cities, designed to target poor blacks and whites alike.

This is a stealth strategy (he first entitled one of his books *Hidden Agenda*) designed to make inner-city blacks the chief beneficiaries of economic reforms with no explicitly racial goal. Predictably, many of his black colleagues in the academic world have accused him of being a traitor to his race, a price Wilson seems fully prepared to pay. Scanning the scholarly horizon, no social scientist has thought as deeply about the most intractable racial challenge of our time, or brooded as realistically about how best to navigate the pitfalls and prejudices along the way.

A final voice offering a different kind of clarity for all of us struggling amid the current racial cacophony comes from James Baldwin. It is a surprising source, given that Baldwin has been gone for over a generation, and even in his own day he enjoyed alienating all parties and partisans in the racial debate. "On one side of town I was an Uncle Tom," Baldwin defiantly declared, "and on the other the Angry Young Man." The "town" where he was actually living when he made that remark was Paris, his permanent residence as an expatriate, which would also seem to disqualify him as an American visionary.

Yet somehow, almost because of rather than in spite of his unwillingness to inhabit the militant or moderate racial categories of his own time, Baldwin has become more relevant in our own. Perhaps his multiple identities as a black, gay, patriotic expatriate equipped him with uncommon mental and emotional dexterity, speaking to blacks and whites, women and men, in ways that were both biracial and bisexual. Moreover, no American fiction writer, with the singular exception of William Faulkner, more fully grasped the pull of the past on our racial dilemma. As Baldwin succinctly put it, "The people are trapped in history and history is trapped in them."

If history for Jefferson was a burden, what he called "a dead hand," for Baldwin it was more like a river whose currents could not be successfully ignored or resisted. For blacks this meant recognizing that America was their proper homeland, occupied by their ancestors the year before English Puritans landed at Plymouth Rock, and therefore all separatist visions along the lines of those espoused by Marcus Garvey or the Nation of Islam were delusions: "Negroes are Americans and their destiny is the country's destiny," Baldwin declared. "They have no other experience besides their experience on this continent and it is an experience which cannot be rejected." For good measure, he added that "the black man" was "as American as the Americans who despise him, the Americans who fear him, the Americans who love him."

For whites, this meant accommodating themselves to the painful but ultimately liberating realization that America always was and always will be a biracial society, so the only question became: What kind of biracial society? The answer to that question, Baldwin insisted, placed a burden on every white citizen "to find a way of living with the Negro in order to be able to live with himself." In Baldwin's view, the belief in white supremacy was just as delusional as the belief in black separatism. "It is only now beginning to be borne in on us," he wrote in *Notes of a Native Son*, "that this vision of the world [i.e., white supremacy] is dangerously inaccurate, and perfectly useless." What Myrdal called the American Dilemma was really the White Man's Burden, which was to face the fact that "this world is white no longer, and it never will be again." On this score, Americans' biracial history prepared them to lead all modern nations into the future because "it is precisely this black-white experience which may prove of indispensable value to us in the world we face today." Ironically, Baldwin's experience as an expatriate in France led him to the conclusion that America's distinctive history of routinized racial interactions prepared the United States, more than Europe, for the emerging global mosaic.

Racism was the obvious cloud that hovered over that hopeful fate, and Baldwin tended to describe it as America's long-standing addiction to self-deception. "Color is not a human or personal reality," he wrote, "it is a political reality," meaning a white invention designed to project their fears and insecurities onto fellow human beings with black skin. "White Americans do not believe in death," he once speculated, "and this is why the darkness of my skin so intimidates them." Racism, then, at bottom was the whites' way of coping with their own human limitations, a resort to labeling that masked a fundamental failure of empathy. As Baldwin put it in "My Dungeon Shook," the introductory section of *The Fire Next Time* (1963), all racial stereotypes demean their authors, not their victims. "The details and symbols of your life," he told his black readers, "have been deliberately constructed to make you believe what white people say about you. Please try to remember that what they believe, as well as what they do and cause you to endure, does not testify to your inferiority but to their inhumanity and fear. . . . You can only be destroyed by believing that you are what the white world calls a *nigger*."

In Baldwin's reversal of the conventional categories, what made

America truly exceptional was not its boundless democratic vision but the limited range of its interior horizons; not its inspiring egalitarian ideals but its failure to acknowledge that whites were living a lie. But there was also more than a trace of Myrdal's liberal optimism in Baldwin's formulation, especially in his confidence that racial equality was America's inevitable destiny, and his periodic use of the word *love* to describe the eventual biracial outcome.

Baldwin presents a problem for the more militant black voices of our day, much as he did for those of his own day, because he was able to inhabit both sides of what we have called the Jeffersonian legacy and never dismissed the visionary side as merely mythical, though his emphasis was always on the hypocrisy and willful blindness of the prevailing darker side. In the end, Baldwin could never fit comfortably into political categories or racial camps, finding all such labeled locations too constricting for his all-encompassing soul. As we grope about for guidance on our pockmarked racial landscape, perhaps his most disarming advice is to read more fiction in order to expand the range of our imaginations. While Ta-Nehisi Coates is the militant voice of the moment, Baldwin is a man for all American seasons, the Jeffersonian legacy come to terms with its darker side, as Jefferson himself never could.

One final forecast. We should expect a major backlash to wash over us as we approach the middle of this century. For a truly historic change is already baked into the demographic profile of the United States, a change that can be predicted with as much scientific certainty as warming in the atmosphere. In or about 2045, the white population will become a statistical minority. Because whites will continue to hold the balance of power politically and economically, ample opportunities will present themselves for demagogues to stoke fears of a looming apocalypse. Indeed, voices in this vein are already audible in such slogans as "Make America great again" and "Take our country back."

The multiracial future that Jefferson always feared, then, is already visible on the horizon. The positive way to put it is that covert racism is likely to surge primarily because racial interaction will be increasing, and "the arc of the moral universe" will be moving upward another increment. The historical way to put it is that every expansion in the meaning of "We the people" has been a struggle, residual prejudices may disappear but never die, and the ongoing battle for racial equality remains the longest, most challenging struggle in American history.

CHAPTER 2

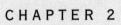

Equality

John Adams

In every society known to man an aristocracy has risen up in the course of time, consisting of a few rich and honorable families who have united with each other against both the people and the first magistrate.

John Adams, A Defence of the Constitutions
of the United States *(1787)*

. . .

You and I ought not to die, before We have explained ourselves to each other.

John Adams to Thomas Jefferson, 15 July 1813

Coming to terms with John Adams has always been a complicated negotiation. His impeccable revolutionary credentials mark him as a candidate for the top tier within that "band of brothers" we capitalize and mythologize as Founding Fathers. Indeed, a plausible case could be made that no American founder other than George Washington did more to make the American Revolution happen. But as he predicted, there is no memorial to Adams on the Mall or Tidal Basin, and his profile is not to be found on Mount Rushmore or our common currency. Somehow he seemed fated to become the Prodigal Son of the revolutionary generation, the founder almost determined to undermine our iconic expectations, most predisposed to wander off script in ways that violated the central story line that posterity wanted to hear.[1]

Part of what we might call the Adams Problem is the sheer volume and unfiltered candor of his correspondence, which replicated the unburdened, take-no-prisoners character of his conversation. "Have mercy on me Posterity," he shouted near the end, "if you should ever see any of my Letters." Unlike Washington, who instructed his wife to burn all their correspondence, Adams and his beloved Abigail kept and preserved their nearly twelve hundred letters. And while Washington's diary dutifully recorded the weather, Adams's diary was often about the storms surging through his own soul.

He much admired what he called Washington's "gift of Silence" but acknowledged that the gift was not in him, and if permitted a glimpse of the future, he could only smile in bemused envy at the fact that there are no words on the Washington Monument. While the other prominent founders were auditioning for roles as proper Roman stoics, Adams actually preferred to be cast as Sancho Panza, riding across the American landscape on a mule while admonishing his betters for tilting at windmills. Who else among his distinguished colleagues, if asked to declare an opinion on the hereafter, possessed the temerity to pronounce that "if it could be revealed or demonstrated that there is no future state, my advice to every man, woman, and child would be, as our existence would be in our own power, to take opium"?[2]

As the modern edition of the Adams Papers has marched forward at a stately pace, such colorful irreverence has attracted the interest of historians and scholars more prepared than their predecessors to appreciate the one founder who defied the iconic stereotype in such singular style. The prediction made by Charles Francis Adams, who published the first edition of his grandfather's collected works, appears to be coming true over a century and a half after he made it: "We are beginning to forget that the patriots of former days were men like ourselves . . . and we are almost irresistibly led to ascribe to them in our imaginations certain gigantic proportions and superhuman qualities, without reflecting that this at once robs their character of consistency and their virtues of all merit."[3]

The emerging affection for flawed founders has, in fact, found its hero in Adams, as the very vivacity, contrarian mentality, and striking candor that once burdened his reputation now buoy it to heights that accord with his actual achievements as a statesman. My own contribution to the recent Adams resurgence ended with a modest proposal and a wink: the construction of an Adams memorial on the Tidal Basin, "done in the classical style and situated sufficiently close to the Jefferson Memorial that, depending on the time of day and angle of the sun, he and Jefferson might take turns casting shadows across each other's facades."[4]

My point, which will be the burden of the following pages, is that the recently recovered relevance of Adams should extend beyond our newfound appreciation of his bracingly honest, all-too-human personality. Adams has become relevant for our time because he is the only prominent founder who anticipated the emergence of an embedded version of economic inequality in American society, a prophecy that seemed so bizarre and thoroughly un-American to most of his contemporaries that it served as evidence for the charge that he had obviously lost his mind. As Gordon Wood, the distinguished historian of the early republic, so nicely put it: "For too long and with too much candor he [Adams] had tried to tell his fellow Americans some truths about themselves that American values and American ideology would not admit." As a political thinker, not just as a fully revealed personality, Adams is in vogue for the very reasons he was previously dismissed.[5]

Rather than go back and search through Adams's long career to find the origins and eventual evolution of his distinctive way of thinking about what he called "the illusion of equality," let us begin at the end, where we can encounter the core idea fully formed in his correspondence with Thomas Jefferson. This makes logical if not chronological sense, since Jefferson epitomized the mentality that Adams regarded as illusory, so the dialogue of their twilight years, which has justifiably achieved classic status as the literary capstone of the founding era, contains the clearest expression of the underlying issues at stake. It also helps that Adams was an inherently dialectical thinker who mobilized his intellectual arsenal most fully in opposition, in this case in response to Jefferson's embodiment of the received wisdom of the day. He was throwing down the gauntlet to Jefferson when he observed, "You and I ought not to die, before We have explained ourselves to each other."[6]

━━◆━━

Between 1812 and 1826 Adams and Jefferson exchanged 158 letters, of which Adams wrote 109. The fact that they died on the same day in 1826, which happened to be July 4, and the fiftieth anniversary of American independence, has always seemed too providential to be true, the kind of event that no novelist would have dared make up. The correspondence also casts an elegiac spell, as we watch two elder statesmen playing the role of philosopher-king, looking back from very different perspectives at the history they had made and that in turn made them. It is clear from the start that there are two fundamentally different temperaments at work: Jefferson more controlled, self-protected, less invested; Adams more candid, flamboyantly expressive, and compelled to search out the edgy borders of their famous friendship. A video of their dialogue would have Jefferson standing erect, arms folded against his chest in his customary posture of stately composure, Adams pacing back and forth in frenzied animation, periodically stopping to pull at Jefferson's lapels, incapable of holding a pose.

For our purposes, however, the temperamental contrast, while beguiling and psychologically revealing, is less important than the different mentalities in play, most especially the different ways they understood and processed the meaning of the revolution they had both fought and wrought. Benjamin Rush, the Philadelphia physician and revolutionary gadfly who brought them together, put it succinctly: "I consider you and [Jefferson] as the North and South Poles of the American Revolution. Some talked, some wrote, and some fought to promote and establish it, but you and Mr. Jefferson thought for us all."[7]

For over a century, starting with Herbert Croly's landmark critique of the Jeffersonian political tradition, *The Promise of American Life* (1909), the major debate at the center of the American political tradition has been depicted as an argument between Jefferson and Alexander Hamilton, the former the most articulate advocate for agrarian America, the latter for the fully empowered national government along the lines of the New Deal. This political pairing has the virtue of modern-day relevance, but it would have struck most members of the revolutionary generation as bizarre. In the political firmament of their time, Adams and Jefferson were the two juxtaposed stars, while Hamilton was the brilliant comet that raced across the horizon, then disappeared.

More relevantly, the Adams critique of Jefferson operates at a much deeper level of intellectual and ideological sophistication, involving nothing less than a wholesale rejection of what he regarded as the following illusions of the French Enlightenment: the unfounded belief in the preternatural wisdom of "the people"; the naïve assumption that human beings are inherently rational creatures; and the romantic conviction that American society was immune to the class divisions so prevalent in Europe. The political differences between Adams and Jefferson are too multifaceted to be captured in the conventional categories of "liberal" and "conservative." What we must negotiate is the distinction between a realist and an idealist, a pessimist and an optimist, a skeptic and a believer. Both men were rock-ribbed American patriots, though diametrically at odds over the likely shape of America's future.

The central dynamic of the correspondence followed an episodic pattern. Each man would try to remain diplomatic, preferring safe topics like the aging process, or the strange characters they had to suffer in public ceremonies as president. Then Jefferson would inadvertently mention one of the volatile issues and thereby touch off a round of verbal airbursts from Adams, which momentarily illuminated their ideological differences. One such occasion was actually triggered by Jefferson's use of the word *ideology*.

Adams's first instinct was to make a joke. "What does it mean?" he asked. "I was delighted with it, upon the Common Principle of delight in every Thing we cannot understand. Does it mean Idiotism? The Science of Non compos Menticism? The Science of Lunacy?" He went on for several sentences in this jocular vein, eventually concluding that *ideology* was one of those French words that must pay an import duty if Jefferson wished to use it in America.[8]

Then Adams suddenly turned serious. He remembered that it was when he and Jefferson were serving together in prerevolutionary Paris that he had first encountered this strange term. They were both listening to French philosophers spin their utopian webs in what Adams called "the school of folly." It now suddenly dawned on him that Jefferson's entire style of political thinking was "much indebted to the invention of the word IDEOLOGY." This was very much a French way of thinking about politics, a systematic way of going wrong with confidence by confusing what one could imagine—human perfectibility, social equality—with what was possible in the world. He was essentially accusing Jefferson of embracing attractive dreams, molding them into an *ideology,* then reading the world through that tilted prism.

One dimension of the Jefferson dream that Adams singled out for special ridicule, a central delusion in "the school of folly," was his enshrinement of "the people" or "the mighty Wave of public opinion" as an infallible source of political wisdom. This struck Adams as the secular version of the divine right theory promulgated by medieval kings and popes: "I wish that Superstition in Religion exciting Superstition in Politics . . . may never blow up all your benevolent and philanthropic Lucubrations," he warned Jefferson, "but the History of all Ages is against you." He reminded Jefferson of the mobs that gathered around the presidential mansion in 1799 to urge war with France, a popular course of action that Adams refused to follow: "I have no doubt you was fast asleep in philosophical tranquility, when ten thousand People, and perhaps many more, were parading the Streets of Philadelphia."[9]

By citing this example, Adams was lifting the lid on a Pandora's box of painful memories that he knew full well Jefferson shared. While his larger agenda was to document the inherently ephemeral character of popular opinion, his decision to disregard the overwhelming popular appetite for war with France in 1799 was the defining decision of his presidency. And that decision almost certainly cost him reelection the following year to none other than the man receiving this letter. In effect, Jefferson's ascendance to the presidency was a direct consequence of Adams's insistence on resisting the political pressure of a momentary majority, instead sacrificing his prospects for a second term in order to avoid a war that was simultaneously unnecessary and misguided.

The clear implication of his presidency, at least as Adams saw it, was that leadership necessarily entailed *not* listening to the voice of "the people" when it ran counter to the abiding interest of "the public," which the president had a moral obligation to defend even more forcefully when it was unpopular. (In Adams's political universe, the very fact that he had lost the presidential election of 1800 to Jefferson was the surest sign he had done the right thing.) Adams had no trouble endorsing the Lockean doctrine that all political power derived from "the people." But he could never bring himself to think about popular sovereignty in the reverential fashion that Jefferson embraced with such intoxicating assurance. "The fundamental Article of my political Creed," he declared quite defiantly, "is that Despotism, or unlimited Sovereignty, or Absolute Power is the same in a popular Assembly, an Aristocratical Counsel, an Oligarchic Junto and a single Emperor."[10]

Adams realized that this creedal statement was heretical in the Jeffersonian political universe, where it was inherently impossible for "the people" to behave despotically. He was attempting to disabuse his old friend of the same kind of magical thinking that had permitted medieval theologians to conjure up miracles. There was in fact no surefire source of political omniscience on this side of heaven, and making "the people" into just such a heavenly creature was a preposterous perpetuation of an alluring illusion about kings long since discredited by Jefferson himself in his indictment of George III in the Declaration of Independence. Indeed, if you wanted to know where such illusions about the infallibility of "the people" led, you only needed to follow the bloodstained trail of the French Revolution, which moved through massacres at the guillotine to its inevitably despotic destination in Napoleon.

The next word to trigger an Adams explosion was, somewhat strangely, Jefferson's apparently harmless reference to *grief,* when he observed: "I wish the pathologists then would tell us, what is the use of grief on the economy, and of what good is it the cause?" He was obviously making the sensible point that wallowing in grief was not a good way to pursue one's happiness. But Adams proceeded to deliver a long lecture on "the uses of grief," a strange subject on which he claimed to be one of America's greatest experts. Grief, he explained, was not just a futile form of sorrow, as Jefferson implied. It was a potent emotion that "sharpens the Understanding and Softens the heart," driving many of the great men in history to "habits of serious Reflection." The furrows depicted in portraits and statues of the Greek and Roman heroes, Adams observed, "were ploughed in their Countenances by Grief."[11]

Jefferson tried to drop the subject: "To the question indeed on the Utility of Grief, no answer remains to be given. You have exhausted the subject." But Adams was just getting started. In addition to the "uses of grief" must be added the equally important "abuses of grief," all documented with references to the classics and to Christian iconography. Grief, it turned out, was a many-sided and many-splendored emotion that Jefferson needed to understand if he wished to grasp the irrational energy driving most of human history. It was true, Adams acknowledged, that "Reason holds the helm," but more true that "the passions are the gales." The awkward segue into the meanings of "grief" was really an opening wedge to lift the lid on the bottomless storehouse of human emotions against which, so Adams insisted, human reason had no chance: "Our Passions possess so much metaphysical subtlety and so much overpowering Eloquence, that they Insinuate themselves into the Understanding and the Conscience and convert both to their Party. . . . It would seem that human Reason and human Conscience, though I believe there are such things, are not a Match for human Passions, human Imaginations, and human Enthusiasms."[12]

There was no way for Adams to know that, almost a century later, Sigmund Freud would put labels on the same psychological ingredients he was describing, calling them id, ego, and superego. There was also no way for Adams to know that Jefferson had once written a love-sick elegy, entitled "Dialogue Between the Head and Heart," in which the powers of the heart were privileged. (He was under the spell of his infatuation with Maria Cosway, who was described by contemporaries as "a golden-haired, languishing Anglo-Italian.") The irrational side of human nature, then, was not terra incognita for Jefferson, and a few scholars have written whole books on his sentimental soul.[13]

But it needs to be noticed that the dismissive attitude toward grief that launched the Adams onslaught was characteristically Jeffersonian behavior. When an unpleasant or upsetting event threatened to disrupt his domestic circle, Jefferson's standard response was to advise all concerned to put it out of mind. Unlike Adams, he never kept a diary of his interior dialogue, perhaps because he did not have one, perhaps because he regarded introspection as self-indulgent. Even the aforementioned "Dialogue," though clearly designed as a testament to his throbbing heart, was contrived in its very cogency, meaning that ultimately the head prevailed. As a result, the Adams argument on behalf of the emotions as the driving force in shaping the course of human history did not fit into any of the preferred Jeffersonian categories, which emphasized the very qualities—harmony, control, reason— that Adams described as overmatched. Jefferson chose not to engage

Adams on such an inherently chaotic playing field, but instead waited for Adams to exhaust himself, then eventually moved on to another topic more suitable for an exchange.

He did not need to wait long. This time the loaded term was *aristoi*, Greek for "the best." And once again it was Jefferson who inadvertently triggered another Adams eruption, this time generating a spirited dialogue between the two patriarchs that has justifiably achieved the status of a classic conversation about the meaning of equality for the revolutionary generation:

> The same political parties which now agitate the U.S. have existed thro' all time. Whether the power of the people, or that of the *aristoi* should prevail, were questions which kept the states of Greece and Rome in eternal convulsions. . . . To me it appears that there have been party differences from the first establishment of governments, to the present day. . . . Every one takes his side in favor of the many or the few.[14]

This was the essential Jeffersonian formulation that carried enormous rhetorical appeal, for it depicted all political history as a clash between popular majorities and despotic elites, an eternal conflict that Americans would come to describe as the abiding quarrel between democracy and aristocracy. It was a simple but not simplistic story line that possessed the incalculable advantage of providing moral certainty in the "forces of light versus the forces of darkness" mode.

Adams's first instinct was to agree with Jefferson's basic distinction. "Precisely," he replied to Jefferson: the clash between "the few and the many" was "as old as Aristotle." But then he began to complicate Jefferson's categories. As Adams recalled, the *aristoi* was a subject that Jefferson had urged him to write about when they were serving together in Paris, and he claimed that he had been writing on the subject ever since, "the only problem being that I have been so unfortunate as never to make myself understood."[15]

His chief heresy appeared to be a direct refutation of Jefferson's most famous words, namely that "all men are created equal." Perhaps in some lofty humanistic sense that was true; that is, equal as fellow members of the human race. But in all worldly ways, Adams insisted that inequality was the natural condition of mankind. Why? Because "Inequalities of Mind and Body are so established by God Almighty in the constitution of Human Nature that no Art or policy can ever plain them down to a level." Adams then went on a colorful tirade against the illusion of social and economic equality, arguing that he had "never read Reasoning more absurd, Sophistry more gross in proof of the Athanasian Creed, or Transubstantiation, than the subtle labors to demonstrate the Natural Equality of Mankind." And it followed from this less comforting self-evident truth that the *aristoi* or aristocracies always were and always would be a permanent fixture in all societies on earth, including the aspiring republic called the United States that they both helped to bring into being.[16]

Unlike the earlier Adams tirade against "grief," this salvo struck at the soul of Jefferson's fondest convictions, so it could not pass unnoticed. But after acknowledging that this was one issue on which he and Adams were diametrically opposed, Jefferson's first instinct was diplomatic: "We are both too old to change opinions," he observed, "which are the result of a long life of inquiry and reflection." Best, then, to avoid a confrontation and allow this disagreement to pass, as he put it, like the proverbial wave under the ship.

He quickly changed his mind, however, as it dawned on him that it was possible to rescue common ground with his long-lost friend by making two distinctions. First, he suggested that the Adams argument about inequality was true for Europe, where feudal privileges, inherited titles, and more limited economic opportunities created conditions that sustained class distinctions. In America, on the other hand, the elimination of primogeniture and entail and the existence of an unspoiled continent meant that "everyone may have land to labor for himself as he chooses," so enduring elites were unlikely here.

Second, Jefferson distinguished between the "natural aristocracy," based on virtue and talent, and the "pseudo aristocracy," founded on "wealth and birth, without either virtue or talents." The Adams strictures against aristocracy, he suggested, were really warnings about the pseudo aristocracy, which Jefferson agreed was "a mischievous ingredient in government, and provision should be made to prevent its ascendancy." Given the favorable laws and the abundant land of America, it was reasonable to expect that "rank and birth, and tinsel-aristocracy will finally shrink into insignificance." The result should be a roughly equal, middle-class society blissfully bereft of European gaps in wealth and embedded social distinctions.[17]

Adams found neither of Jefferson's arguments persuasive. To be sure, there were no moats or castles and what Jefferson called "tinseled aristocrats" of the feudal sort in America. But there were the merchant class of New England and the great planter families of the Chesapeake. Those elites, however, were mere symptoms. "No Romance could be more amusing," he chided Jefferson, than his belief that the United States would prove the exception to the dominant pattern of economic inequality throughout recorded history, as if human nature itself had been magically transformed in the migration from Europe to America. "After all," he observed, "as long as Property exists, it will accumulate in Individuals and Families. . . . I repeat, so long as the Idea and existence of PROPERTY is admitted and established in Society, accumulations of it will be made, the Snow ball will grow as it rolls."[18]

He then cautioned Jefferson, "Your distinction between natural and artificial Aristocracy does not appear to me well founded." He moved from caustic condescension to playful jest: "Now, my Friend, who are the *aristoi*? Philosophy may Answer 'The Wise and the Good.' But the World, Mankind, have by their practice always preferred 'the rich and beautiful and well born.' " Even philosophers, he chided, when

marrying their children, "prefer the rich and handsome and th
descended to the wise and the good." There were "five Pillars of Aristocracy," he concluded, "Beauty, Wealth, Birth, Genius, and Virtues.
Any one of the three first can, at any time, overbear any one or both
of the two last." But it would never become an equal contest that could
be measured, because the qualities Jefferson regarded as artificial and
those he regarded as natural were always mixed together inside the
individual personality, then again within society, in blended patterns
that defied Jefferson's geometric dissections—yet another case of
"ideology" transforming the messy realities of the world into reified
categories that existed only in his imagination.[19]

Jefferson did not respond, preferring to permit the conversation to shift toward less contentious topics: the character of Napoleon; Plato's metaphysical murkiness; whether medicine would ever
become a science. The debate over the *aristoi,* in fact, proved to be
the last extended argument in the correspondence, as both patriarchs,
even the ever combustible Adams, chose to subordinate their political
and intellectual differences to the recovery of their famous friendship.
In 1818, when asked by a curious observer how he felt about that man
from Monticello, Adams embraced a policy of total amnesty. "He is
the last & oldest of my confidential bosom friends," he explained, "let
party faction and politics say what they will."[20]

Only one sensitive subject threatened to disrupt their mutual desire
to go out as charter members of the "band of brothers," and that was
the French Revolution, which came up by accident in 1816. But Jefferson averted an argument by making a huge concession. "Your proph-
ecies proved truer than mine," he acknowledged to Adams, "and yet
fell short of the fact, for instead of a million, the destruction of 8 or
10 millions of human beings has probably been the effect of the convulsions. I did not, in [17]89 believe they would have lasted so long, nor
have cost so much blood." What's more, as Jefferson recalled, Adams
had predicted that Great Britain would eventually win the competi-
tion for European supremacy with France, and the recent defeat of

Napoleon at Waterloo had proved him right. Adams recognized that Jefferson was making a major concession, since their different perspectives on the French Revolution had been a dominant source of disagreement during the party wars of the 1790s. "I know not what to say of your Letter," he wrote, "but that it is one of the most consolatory I have ever received."[21]

While he was prepared to acknowledge that history had confirmed the Adams prediction about the French Revolution, Jefferson felt no need to make any conciliatory statement about the Adams prediction that social and economic inequality would afflict the American republic. Indeed, for the next half century, for as long as the American economy remained primarily agrarian and western land remained available for settlement, it also remained plausible to speak of a Jeffersonian America in which his egalitarian vision retained a measure of credibility. The history that would eventually confirm the Adams assessment had not yet happened.

The correspondence with Jefferson permitted Adams to articulate his main arguments against Jefferson's vision of social and economic equality as the natural condition in the United States, but the diplomatic etiquette both correspondents felt obliged to observe—Adams, to be sure, less consistently—precluded full disclosure of what Adams called "my system." The urge to recover the friendship trumped the desire to probe their differences more deeply. Indeed, if Jefferson had been able to control the agenda, there would have been no exposure of differences at all.

It so happened that, at the same time he was writing to Jefferson, Adams received a six-hundred-page manuscript entitled *An Inquiry into the Principles and Policy of the Government of the United States*. The author was John Taylor, a disciple of Jefferson who had served in the Senate while Adams was vice president. "Taylor was an eternal talker," Adams recalled, "the greatest talker I ever knew, excepting George the Third." Apparently Taylor had been spending his retirement on his plantation in Caroline County, Virginia, reading and arguing with the three-volume work Adams had written in the 1780s under the title *A Defence of the Constitutions of Government of the United States of America.* "I thought my books as well as myself were forgotten," Adams joked to Jefferson, "but behold! I am to become a great man in my expiring moments." The thirty-two letters Adams wrote to Taylor, in order, if you will, to defend his *Defence,* became the full exposition of the "system" he had been unable to provide in his correspondence with Jefferson.[22]

The *Defence* was very much a product of the 1780s. Adams had been appointed America's first minister to the British court in 1784. (Given Adams's leading role in promoting American independence, appointing him to that critical post was regarded by the British press as a defiant gesture, akin to appointing Martin Luther as the first minister to the Vatican.) Apart from ceremonial duties, Adams found himself denied access to relevant officials in the British ministry and therefore with little to do. He decided to use his time reading widely in Scottish, French, and Italian sources—he even taught himself Italian to read Machiavelli in the original—in order to compose a treatise aimed at an American audience currently preoccupied with framing state constitutions and, by 1786, contemplating the prospects for what became the Constitutional Convention. It was a propitious moment, and Adams, who justifiably regarded himself as one of America's leading constitutional thinkers, was heartsick at missing it.

What became the *Defence,* then, was his way of projecting, in absentia, his influence across the Atlantic, thereby helping to secure the revolution he had done so much to launch. "The people in America have now the best opportunity and the greatest trust in their hands that Providence even committed to so small a number since the transgression of the first pair," Adams observed. But he wanted to underscore the decidedly secular character of this crucial enterprise, which would occur on this earth and not in the Garden of Eden: "It will never be pretended that any persons employed in this service had interviews with the gods, or were in any degree under the inspiration of heaven."

(In fact, just such mythical pretenses almost inevitably dominated the histories of the Constitutional Convention.) He himself was not praying but reading David Hume, Adam Smith, Jean-Jacques Rousseau, and Niccolò Machiavelli.[23]

Adams began with the assumption, by then broadly shared among American political thinkers, that the old revolutionary faith in public virtue so prevalent in the 1770s was inadequate as a basis for political stability now that independence was won. "The best republics will be virtuous," Adams acknowledged, "but we may hazard a conjecture that the virtues have been the effect of the well ordered constitution rather than the cause." Most of the *Defence* was devoted to a description of just what such a well-ordered constitution should look like. No surprise, the tripartite model that Adams had first proposed in his *Thoughts on Government* (1776), subsequently adopted in most of the state constitutions, was the proper framework: an elected executive, bicameral legislature, and independent judiciary.

Within that familiar framework, however, Adams veered off in two distinctive directions. The executive, whom he called "the first magistrate," was in the Adams scheme a de facto elected monarch who possessed veto power over the legislature that could not be overturned by a two-thirds majority. When critics accused him of harboring fondness for a European-style king based on his long residence in Paris and London, Adams rejected the charge by noting that his executive would occupy an elected rather than a hereditary office, and that he had proposed the same executive powers in his draft of the Massachusetts Constitution in 1779. He clearly believed that many Americans had overlearned the lessons of '76, thereby viewing any robust exercise of executive power as monarchical. As he joked to Jefferson, "I am no king killer merely because they are kings—poor creatures they know no better—they believe sincerely and conscientiously that God made them to rule the world." No criticism could budge him from the belief that only a strong executive, "who had the whole nation before him," could provide the stability required in a large republic. He was the earliest advocate for what twentieth-century historians have called "the imperial presidency."[24]

His other conspicuous deviation concerned the role of the Senate and the distinctive way he thought about it. His initial fear—in truth, his utter dread—was that his American colleagues in Philadelphia would opt for a single-house legislature, an idea made popular by French philosophers like Turgot and endorsed by no less than the author of *Common Sense,* Thomas Paine, as well as by Benjamin Franklin. Adams regarded such an idea as the embodiment of another fatal illusion so popular among the Paris salon set, namely that "the people" was a harmonious whole, so all one needed to do was gather their elected representatives together in one place and let them govern. His fears proved unfounded, since there was a clear consensus at the Constitutional Convention that the legislature should be bicameral, though not for the reasons that so preoccupied Adams.

The debate with Jefferson over the *aristoi,* it turned out, concerned issues that he had been brooding about for some time. In *Defence* he articulated his position most forcefully and clearly. "In every society known to man," he claimed, "an aristocracy has risen up in the course of time, consisting of a few rich and honorable families who have united with each other against both the people and the first magistrate." There were very few universal principles in the Adams political universe, but this was one of them. All societies eventually produced social and economic elites that, left unchecked, achieved political domination at the expense of everyone else. Although Jefferson probably did not remember it, Adams had alerted him to their differences on this score in December 1787: "You are afraid of the one, I, the few."[25]

Indeed, in the Adams scheme or "system," the obsessive American fear of monarchy was misguided, not just because all republics needed strong executive leadership but even more because the prevailing pattern throughout history was for monarchs to defend the bulk of the citizenry against all-powerful oligarchies (from the Greek, meaning rule by "the few"). "The executive is the natural friend of the people," Adams wrote, "and the only defense which they or their representatives can have against the avarice and ambition of the rich and distinguished." As a result, most Americans were aiming their political guns in the wrong direction, blazing away at "the one" while the dominant danger came from "the few." And much like gravity in nature or the current in a river, the relentless pressure toward oligarchy was an ever present danger that demanded constant attention from all branches of government.[26]

If Adams's analysis of the age-old *aristoi* problem was perceptive, even profound, his proposed solution was odd, even bizarre. He described the Senate as the political chamber in which to place the aristocrats, an arrangement, he claimed, "that is to all honest and useful instincts, an ostracism." This strange solution probably came from his reading of John Louis de Lolme, a Swiss writer whose *The Constitution of England* suggested the scheme, which was obviously a rationale for the English House of Lords. The truly weird suggestion that electing America's aristocrats to the Senate was a way of *limiting* their influence should probably be seen as a measure of Adams's desperation. He was searching for an answer to what he regarded as the central problem of political science. The inadequacy of his answer only exposed his exasperation at the intractability of the problem.[27]

<hr />

The central argument of John Taylor's long-winded critique of *Defence,* apart from specific disagreements about the power of the presidency and the role of the Senate, was to claim that Adams's entire way of thinking about politics was hopelessly anachronistic and fundamentally un-American. Taylor felt the freedom to say outright what Jefferson had only implied; namely that the very categories of the Adams thought process—the one, the few, the many—were relics of the ancient and medieval world that had been blown to pieces by the very revolution he had helped to foster. To be sure, Jefferson had hinted at this point by citing the elimination of feudal traditions like primogeniture and entail. But Taylor went further to claim that the American Revolution had ushered in a wholly new era in modern history in which words like *aristocracy* were offensive irrelevancies no longer allowed in the egalitarian vocabulary.

Taylor's extension of the Jeffersonian argument in this sweeping fashion prompted Adams to extend his own critique of this new American "ideology" of equality. "That all men are born to equal rights is true," Adams acknowledged, thereby endorsing Jefferson's famous formulation in the Declaration of Independence. But to believe that "all men are born with equal powers and faculties and equal influence in society . . . is as gross a fraud as ever was practiced by monks, by Devils, by Brahmins, by priests of the immortal Lama, or by the self-styled philosophers of the French Revolution." Moreover, the very belief that Americans had somehow discovered the ultimate answer to mankind's eternal quandaries and were now poised to establish heaven on earth was a delusion that deserved to be ranked alongside the fables about the Holy Grail and the fountain of youth. "We may boast that we are one, the chosen people," he warned, "and we may even thank God that we are not like other men, but, after all, it would be but flattery, delusion, the self-deceit of the Pharisee."[28]

Adams also felt more disposed with Taylor than Jefferson to mention an awkward irony: How could it be that a slave-owning Virginian with a huge estate was lecturing the son of a New England farmer about social and economic equality? After observing that Taylor had married into the Tidewater elite, "obtaining both an amiable consort and a handsome fortune," Adams stuck in the knife. "If you complain that this is personal," he observed, "I confess it and intend it should be personal, that it might be more striking to you." Taylor, in short, was just the kind of privileged aristocrat that Adams was talking about, one who also bore the additional burden of overseeing a plantation of enslaved blacks whose very existence contradicted his rhapsodies about America as the land of equality.[29]

Finally, Taylor had devoted a lengthy section of his book to one subject that Jefferson had not seen fit to mention, what he intriguingly called "finance capitalism." Like most members of Virginia's planter class, Taylor was heavily in debt to British bankers, and he had embraced the conviction that banks were places you sent your money to disappear based on some principle of magic called compound interest. Bankers, he firmly believed, were diabolical swindlers who manipulated interest rates to make "a minority of [the] nation rich and potent, at the expense of the majority, which it makes poor and impotent." Taylor's view of banks as snakes in the American Eden that must be exterminated found favor a few years later when Andrew Jackson targeted them for removal along with the Native Americans east of the Mississippi. Many years later, with the ascendance of the Populist movement, Taylor's pages on banking made his book a minor classic in the agrarian tradition.[30]

It was wholly plausible for Taylor to assume that Adams disagreed with him about banks. After all, he was a New Englander, a Federalist, and he had even overseen the debate concerning Alexander Hamilton's proposal for a National Bank in the Senate during his vice presidency. But as Adams was quick to inform him, no one hated banks more than he did, and his denunciations of banks as "engines of inequality" were more colorful than anything Taylor ever wrote. "Our whole banking system I ever abhorred," he thundered, "I continue to abhor and shall die abhorring," adding that his dying regret would be to exit life in a "bebanked, bewhiskied, and bedollared nation." It was clear that both men viewed the profits of bankers as inherently immoral, in part because they made huge amounts of money without doing any productive labor themselves, in part because they transferred wealth from the middling and poorer classes into the hands of the already rich.[31]

Both Adams and Taylor, then, viewed banks as worrisome new features on the economic landscape of the early republic. For Taylor they were "our new aristocracy of paper and patronage," while Adams regarded them as "an Aristocracy as fatal as the Feudal barons, too impregnable a Phalanx to be attacked by anything less than disciplined Roman Legions." In that sense, they were both respond-

ing to the institutional agents of an emerging capitalist economy with
some combination of suspicion and horror. But they then proceeded
to move in diametrically different directions when diagnosing how to
solve the banking problem.[32]

Taylor was one of the first to articulate the sectional perspective
of the agrarian South as the victim of a northern banking conspiracy
sanctioned by the federal government, in effect an unholy alliance between capital and government. (His mystical depiction of agrarian
values was thoroughly Jeffersonian both in its nostalgic celebrations
of the yeoman farmer and in its convenient obfuscation of the fact
that the planter class south of the Potomac did not fit neatly or at all
into the pastoral picture.) Taylor's solution was to liberate the agrarian economy from financial manipulation by severing all connections
between banking and the federal government.

While Adams agreed that banks were essentially gambling casi-
nos that accelerated the most unequal features of the marketplace,
he believed they performed a valuable role in establishing credit and
stabilizing the currency. In that sense, banks were emblematic of all
aristocracies, that is, dangerous but indispensable. "An attempt to
annihilate them," he warned, "would be as romantic an adventure as
any in Don Quixote," which was close to saying that they were too
big to fail. Rather than sever the connection between banks and the
federal government, he thought that all banks should be public institutions placed under the control of Congress: "My own opinion has
invariably been that there ought to be one Bank in the United States,
and that a National Bank with a branch in each state. . . . This ought to
have been a fundamental Article in the Constitution." If Taylor's views
on banks foreshadowed the Jacksonians and the Populists, Adams's
views anticipated the Federal Reserve Board of the Progressives and
the banking regulations of the New Deal. This was all in keeping with
his two rock-ribbed convictions: the new financial aristocracy, like all
aristocracies throughout history, could not be killed but must be controlled; and the invisible hand of the marketplace required the visible
hand of government to regulate its inevitable excesses.[33]

One could make a compelling case that Adams was a lifelong contrarian, so that his antagonistic posture toward Taylor, as well as his more modulated conflict with Jefferson, constituted the continuation of a pattern that first entered the public record in 1770, when he agreed to defend the British soldiers on trial for perpetrating the Boston Massacre. While true enough, this explanation obscures the deeper contrarian instinct exposed in the correspondence with Jefferson and Taylor, which took the form of an outright rejection of their belief in American exceptionalism, especially the heartfelt conviction that social and economic equality was the new natural order in the United States, and the corresponding corollary that government regulation of the marketplace was an unnecessary disruption of that natural order, which became the defining feature of the liberal tradition in the nineteenth century. Ironically, the very reasons Taylor cited to accuse Adams of irrelevancy in his own time make him relevant in ours, for by clinging to his classical categories—the one, few, and many—Adams anticipated the structural inequality and plutocratic politics of both the first Gilded Age and our own. His heresy has become our prophecy.[34]

What we might call the contrarian principle is our best guide through the vast regions of the Adams soul, since we can safely assume that he will prove most relevant when he is most irreverent. His correspondence with Benjamin Rush (1806–12) is one obvious location, loaded as it is with colorful eccentricities delivered in a Mad Hatter style and, most intriguing, devoted to a discussion of their mutual dreams. "Dream, you know, is a mighty Power," he observed to Rush. "It is not shackled with any rules of Method in Arrangement of Thoughts. Time, Space and Place are annihilated and the free independent Soul darts from Suns to Suns, from Planets to Planets to all the Milky Way, quicker than rays of light." Closely connected to his critical assessment of "ideology" as a delusional version of human reason was his belief that the engine driving all human ambitions, including the quest for wealth, was located in what Freud called the subconscious mind. The term *Age of Reason* always struck Adams as a laughable label.[35]

Another prime candidate for scrutiny is the marginalia in Adams's books. Even a cursory glance at his personal collection of about three thousand volumes, currently housed in the Boston Public Library, reveals a treasure trove of commentary that provides one of the clearest windows into his thinking as a political philosopher. Adams did not just read books, he battled them. Much as he needed a Jefferson or Taylor to focus his contrarian temperament, books became the fixed objects against which he did his mental isometric exercises.[36]

Apart from marginal epithets—Rousseau was "a coxcomb and satyr," Voltaire "a liar and complete scoundrel," Condorcet "a fool, and mathematical Charlatan"—Adams wrote out commentaries as if he were engaged in a heated conversation with the author. For example, when he encountered Abbé Mably's endorsement of community ownership of private property in *De la législation,* he scribbled, "Stark mad," then amplified his criticism with this suggestive remark: "The Abby has not seen the true source of the passions. Ambition springs from the desire for esteem and from emulation, not from property." His more positive comments on books by David Hume and Adam Smith, most especially Smith's *The Theory of Moral Sentiments,* suggest that Adams found more to admire in the Scottish than the French Enlightenment, primarily because the Scots tended to emphasize the psychological foundation of economic and political power; in short, to make the emotions, not reason, the driving force in human history.[37]

This was an assumption that Adams had been harboring his entire life. Its seminal source was his own soul or psyche, where in his diary entries as a young man he discussed the "raging bulls" that drove him to levels of vanity and ambition he routinely regretted but could seldom control. His only published account of the psychological roots of his "system" appeared in 1790, in a series of newspaper articles subsequently collected as a book entitled *Discourses on Davila*. If *Defence* argued that the United States would create its own social and economic aristocracy and thereby make a mockery of all Jeffersonian presumptions of equality, *Davila* attempted to explain the motivations that drove the American elite to acquire vast amounts of wealth in such ostentatious displays of superiority.[38]

He introduced the main theme of *Davila* with a fable. There was once an admirable young man who fell on hard times and became a pauper. He and his faithful dog were seen begging for food, which the young man always shared with his dog. As he approached starvation, his friends urged him to stop sharing with his dog in order to avoid his own death. But the pauper refused to do so, asking rhetorically, "Who will love me then?" This plaintive question, Adams observed, "is the key to the human heart, to the history of human life and manners, and to the rise and fall of empires." The bedrock human passion in the Adams scheme went deeper than the quest for wealth, which served only as a means to the ultimate goal, the need for attention and affection. As his tale of the starving pauper was designed to illustrate, the deepest human drive was the irrational need to be noticed and loved.[39]

Adams quoted several long passages from Adam Smith's *Theory of Moral Sentiments,* at times making *Davila* into a mere commentary on the great Scottish philosopher's psychological observations on the mentality that accompanied the arrival of the market economy. This was typical of Adams's frenzied mode of composition, which in its excited incoherence seized whatever sources were at hand, and thereby embodied the very irrational style it sought to study, making *Davila* an inherently unsystematic explication of his "system." The great insight he took from Smith's treatise was that while the new aristocracy of the modern world would be based on wealth rather than inherited bloodlines, the psychological imperatives of commercial societies would be driven by the same passions for distinction that animated the aristocracies of old, and would benefit from the same emotional urge for conspicuous displays of extravagance that royal families had enjoyed in the medieval world. The crucial Adams contribution was to recognize that Smith's analysis of the irrational urges driving the new commercial aristocracy would prove even more pronounced in the United States, where there were no vestiges of the old-style aristocracy to offset wealth as the primary measure of elite status.

As a result, the new American elite would be a "moneyed aristocracy" with an even more avaricious appetite to set themselves apart with flamboyant displays of excessive wealth in the form of extravagant estates, sumptuous dinner parties, and more material possessions than they could possibly need. "Riches force the opinion on man that he is the object of the congratulations of others," Adams wrote. "His imagination expands, and his heart dilates at these charming illusions. His attachment to his possessions increases as fast as his desire to accumulate more; not for the purposes of utility, but from the desire of illustration."[40]

The new American aristocracy, then, would be simultaneously powerful but pathetic, for it was attempting to purchase affection with currency that would never fetch much in the only emotional exchange that mattered. "Why do men affront heaven and earth to accumulate wealth, which will forever be useless to them?" Adams asked rhetorically. It was *"because riches attract the attention, consideration, and congratulations of mankind."* Looking backward, the Scottish philosophers had helped Adams to recognize the psychological dynamic he had encountered in New England Puritanism, which emphasized the futility of amassing wealth as a way of persuading oneself, and others, that salvation was assured. Looking forward, Adams was anticipating Thorstein Veblen's doctrine of "conspicuous consumption" in his *Theory of the Leisure Class.*[41]

The timing of *Davila* is also revealing, coming as it did in the wake of Adams's most embarrassing performance as vice president, when he made a fool of himself by insisting on extravagant titles for the American president, to include such pufferies as "His Majestic Mightiness." As silly as it seemed, his underlying motives represented his effort to enhance the honorific status of prominent public offices in order to provide incentives for an honorable form of public service that would help offset a purely plutocratic oligarchy. In the absence of the digni-

...d distinctions, he proposed to gales of laughter from the gallery in the Senate, the only distinctions that would remain were distinctions based on wealth. After suffering humiliation in what the press called "the titles debate"—pundits labeled him "His Rotundity"—Adams began drafting the essays that became *Davila*, perhaps as a form of therapy but also to provide a more comprehensive explanation of the motives driving America's new aristocracy of wealth, which he was hoping to harness for public service with honorable titles more valuable than mere money.[42]

— ⋙⋘ —

In *Davila*, Adams never used the word *capitalism*. (Nor, for that matter, did Adam Smith in *The Wealth of Nations*.) But he did describe the emerging American nation as a "commercial republic" in which the quest for material rewards in the marketplace would dominate and define what subsequent generations meant by "pursuit of happiness." (Jefferson had intended something different.) It followed that wealth could become the distinguishing characteristic of the American aristocracy for the foreseeable future and, like all aristocracies in European history, would use its powers to wrest control over political institutions in order to serve its own interests and agenda. That is what happened in the late nineteenth century during the first Gilded Age, and it has now happened again in the early twenty-first century during our updated version of the same embedded plutocracy.

Adams's crystal ball was always history, which he regarded as a "lamp of experience" that shed light on previous patterns of human behavior from which he could select analogous episodes relevant to the decision at hand. On military matters, his favorite historian was Thucydides. For political lessons, he preferred Tacitus, Sallust, and Machiavelli. His chief sources on economic questions were the Scottish thinkers, chiefly David Hume and Adam Smith.

Whereas Jefferson searched the past for abiding or even eternal principles, Adams looked for patterns and paradoxes. "I have read in a book that Alexander did much good," he recalled wryly to one friend, "and in another book that Caesar did great work, and in others that English liberties were all owing to Cromwell, and I believe all these paradoxes." He was as interested in repeated examples of ignorance or patterns of political blindness as he was in demonstrations of impressive insight, and he was most attentive when they were mixed together in one man or movement. If history were a massive text, he acknowledged that much depended on finding the proper page to study, so that the best method was to develop a large memory bank of possible sources that could be called up when a crisis demanded seasoned wisdom. There was a consensus among his fellow founders, fully endorsed by Jefferson, that Adams had accumulated the richest memory bank of them all.[43]

Adams believed that entrenched economic inequality would create a political oligarchy in America because that was the relentless pattern throughout European history, documented beyond doubt or dispute by classical and modern chroniclers whom he was fully prepared to cite until readers surrendered from exhaustion. And he saw no reason to believe that the United States would prove an exception to that pattern. "There is no special providence for Americans," he wrote in *Defence*, adding that "Riches, Grandeur, and Power will have the same effect upon Americans as it has upon European minds." His defiance on this issue made Adams the most ardent opponent in the revolutionary generation of the Jeffersonian version of American exceptionalism, always poised to deploy his impeccable revolutionary credentials whenever he encountered intimations of some special, semi-sacred status for the American people or government that levitated above history's lessons and limitations.[44]

When his finely tuned antennae picked up signals that a mystical cloud was beginning to descend upon his fellow founders, transforming them into larger-than-life figures with superhuman powers, he went on record as a secular critic of all such saintly canonizations: "Don't call me 'Godlike Adams,' 'The Father of His Country,' 'The Founder of the American Republic,' or 'The Founder of the American Empire.' The titles belong to no man." He could testify from firsthand experience that no electromagnetic field had formed around the American republic or its founders, that they were all fallible creatures, deserving of respect but not reverence. As the mythology surrounding Washington grew like ivy over a statue, Adams bemoaned what he called "the pilgrimages to Mount Vernon," which had become acts of worship that made any serious study of the great man seem sacrilegious. "I consider the true history of the American Revolution & the establishment of our present constitution as lost forever," he complained. "And nothing but misrepresentation ever will be recovered."[45]

Indeed, if anything like a "true history" of his own generation was ever written, Adams argued that inspiration should come from a painting by Rubens that he had once viewed in Antwerp. It depicted Jesus in the midst of the twelve apostles, "leaning familiarly on the shoulder of the beloved disciple [John], and distinguishing him from all the other eleven by some peculiar marks of attention and kindness." But the truly revealing feature in the painting was the reaction of all the other apostles, especially Peter, "transported with rage, eyes bulging out of his sockets, lips seeming to quiver and teeth clenched so that you are apt to fancy you hear them grit against each other." Here was a picture of human jealousy and rivalry that drove all mankind throughout history, including the most prominent members of the revolutionary generation.[46]

But if Peter's face in the Rubens painting were applied to Adams himself, his campaign to shatter the statues in the new American pantheon becomes an illustration of his own seething anger and palpable jealousy at not being given his proper place among the icons. In that sense, he appreciated the irrational motives that drove all aristocracies throughout history because he was a striking example of the boundless ambition he was describing. If ever charged with the offense, he would have pleaded guilty, his only defense being that, unlike Jefferson, he knew it.

In the Adams scheme, all societies produced aristocracies, and all aristocracies were motivated by the same elemental passion to distinguish themselves from their peers, though that primal urge assumed different shapes in different historical contexts. His prognosis for the American future was a plutocratic aristocracy that distinguished itself by accumulating wealth—accurately anticipating the "captains of industry" that dominated the Gilded Age. His own generation, on the other hand, had sought distinction by pursuing fame rather than fortune, which was a higher standard in the Adams pecking order, though he was quick to insist that the quest for fame was just as irrational and ungovernable as the other emotions. "We must still remember," he cautioned, "that this passion, although refined by the purest moral sentiments and intended to be governed by the best principles, is a passion still, and therefore like all other human desires, unlimited and insatiable."[47]

He was acknowledging that his own patriotic motives, as well as those of his prominent peers, were rooted in unconscious regions of the soul that defied rational rules of conduct. "For what folly it is!" he declared. "What is it to us what shall be said of us after we are dead? Or in Asia, Africa, or Europe while we are alive? There is no greater possible or imaginable delusion. Yet the impulse is irresistible." Like some primordial instinct, the lust for fame was simply there, perhaps driven by the need to deny one's mortality by living on in the memory of posterity. Whatever its origins, Adams could testify that it had been the driving force in his life, perhaps first exposed as a very young man, when he stood before the mirror to practice oratorical gestures in the style of Cicero.[48]

While Adams vehemently rejected the Jeffersonian version of American exceptionalism, he had no difficulty recognizing that the American Revolution had presented his generation with an exceptional opportunity to satisfy their quest for fame. Such opportunities appeared only once every few centuries, he noted, when nations were being founded or great crises that shaped the future course of world history came to the surface. These rare historical moments called forth the deepest reservoir of human ambition, the most ferocious form of the passion for distinction. "This is the tribe," he observed, "out of which proceed your patriots and heroes," who otherwise would have lived and died in relative obscurity. Though Adams was at pains to repudiate the mythology already forming around his fellow founders, he endorsed the fact that they had all enjoyed the good fortune to come of age in special circumstances that were unlikely to come again in the foreseeable future.[49]

This did not mean that future generations would achieve distinction and recognition solely by accumulating wealth. In his hierarchy of human emotions, Adams ranked the quest for fame as more potent and enduring than merely material distinction in the marketplace. He expected that a small percentage of the wealthiest Americans would seek a higher level of satisfaction by trading their private fortunes for public visibility in philanthropic ventures that offered the greater promise of secular immortality. Adams anticipated the appearance of Andrew Carnegie and John D. Rockefeller during the first Gilded Age, as well as Warren Buffett and Bill Gates in ours. Because fame trumped fortune in the emotional sweepstakes, Adams predicted that wealth would never completely overwhelm commonwealth. There was, in effect, a built-in incentive implanted in the human personality that ensured a modest redistribution of wealth.

⋅⋅⋅⊰✦⊱⋅⋅⋅

How far beyond that modest level Adams was prepared to go is difficult to know. He is distinctive within the revolutionary generation for calling attention to the fault line that ran through the middle of the Jeffersonian creed, which presumed the compatibility and coexistence of equality and freedom. Adams insisted that the freedom to pursue one's happiness in the marketplace essentially ensured the triumph of inequality in American society. And that argument, in retrospect, is the chief source of his relevance for our ongoing debate about economic inequality, since it exposes the illusion that equality is the natural order that can be recovered by a "reset" of the economy, or that the victims of income stratification have no one to blame but themselves.

We can say with confidence that Adams rejected the socialistic solution, which he encountered among the radical French philosophers in prerevolutionary Paris. He correctly predicted that any effort to do away with private property would only create an impoverished society of paupers within an oppressive totalitarian state. Indeed, he held firmly to his belief in the property qualification to vote even after it became unpopular. The specific reforms he proposed to constrain aristocratic domination in his own day—isolate the elite in the Senate, create honorific titles to offset the allure of wealth—were as grossly inadequate then as they are now.

Nevertheless, as we attempt to grapple with the ongoing failure of our current economy to distribute wealth in accord with our egalitarian expectations, it is useful to have the Adams legacy at our disposal. For he strips our inquiry of burdensome market-based illusions and thereby helps us to frame our analysis more historically and realistically. Once you realize that equality is the exception, not the rule, in a capitalistic society, the question changes. It is not "How can we free the marketplace from government regulations to increase productivity?" It is instead "How can we free ourselves from illusions about the free market in order to assume a more equitable distribution of wealth?" Not for nothing did Adams insist that Massachusetts was more than a mere state but a commonwealth.

He invites us to think about the meaning of the word *republic*, which comes from the Latin meaning "public things." Do we still believe, as he did, that there is a "public interest" beyond the reach of markets and majorities of the moment? Are we a society composed of winners and losers, givers and takers, or is there some larger status we share more collectively as citizens? These are the questions he posed in his own cantankerous way for posterity, which now, more than ever, is us.

Our Gilded Age

There are two things that are important in politics. The first is money. I can't remember what the second is.

Mark Hanna (1898)

. . .

During the 1970s, a handful of the nation's wealthiest corporate captains felt overtaxed and overregulated and decided to fight back. . . . Their ambitions were grandiose—to "save" America as they saw it, at every level, by turning the clock back to the Gilded Age before the advent of the Progressive Era.

Jane Mayer, Dark Money *(2016)*

The vexing problem of economic inequality in the United States has one redeeming feature: there are few deniers. Unlike global warming, the growing gap between rich and poor has become a recognized reality in twenty-first-century America, and it carries in its wake truly disarming implications that violate the seminal truth on which the country was founded. To be sure, when Thomas Jefferson asserted that "all men are created equal," he was not speaking or thinking economically. But when he identified "the pursuit of happiness" as a God-given, inalienable right, he enshrined equality of opportunity as a permanent fixture in the American Creed.

And fifty-nine years later, when Alexis de Tocqueville identified "equality of condition" as the distinguishing feature of America's emerging democratic society, he was announcing the birth of a new and more inherently egalitarian society destined to destroy and displace the aristocratic and hierarchical structure of the European world. Unlike modern-day economists or social scientists, Tocqueville was not fond of charts or graphs, but a graphic description of the revolutionary transition he described would have looked like this:

What we see in this picture is the emergence of a middle-class society in which wealth is widely shared rather than concentrated at the top. And this new arrangement provided the economic foundation for the first nation-size democracy in the world. Indeed, the entire democratic edifice rested atop a set of economic and demographic conditions almost designed to make a mockery of Marx's looming prophecy of class warfare by empowering a middle class with a vested interest in sustaining the existent order. Jefferson himself acknowledged that, even in America, there would always be "the few and the many." But only in the United States—and this became the economic nucleus of American exceptionalism—the political domination of the many followed naturally from the economic hegemony of a middle-class majority.

And therein lies the most unnerving implication of the recent increase in economic inequality. The incentive system of American democracy can survive the existence of a permanent underclass as long as it remains a statistical minority. But the erosion of the middle class is unacceptable and inexplicable because it destroys the functional faith that any hardworking citizen can expect to enjoy a fair share of the American pie. Larger pieces can go to a fortunate few, as long as the many get the bulk of the pie to slice up among themselves.

Since 1980, this implicit bargain has broken down. As a result, American history has somehow veered off course in an un-American direction. Over two centuries ago John Adams predicted this would happen, and it did during the late-nineteenth-and-early-twentieth-century era called the Gilded Age.* Now it is happening again. Graphically, the American diamond is becoming the old European triangle.

‑‑ ⚎ ‑‑

While the causes and consequences of this ominous trend remain controversial, the growing disparity in wealth is undeniable. According to what is called the Gini index, a crude but venerable measurement of economic inequality that the Census Bureau has used since 1947, the United States has a higher level of income inequality than any other democracy in the developed world. In effect, as the size of the economic pie has grown over the last fifty years, larger slices have increasingly gone to a smaller segment of American society. The richest 10 percent currently own nearly 60 percent of the wealth. And the further up the social pyramid you go, the more unequal the distribution becomes: the top 1 percent now earns about 30 percent of total income; the top .1 percent earns more than 10 percent. Between 1972 and 2012, after adjusting for inflation, the average income for most Americans declined by 13 percent; it rose by 153 percent for the top 1 percent. The old cliché about a rising tide lifting all boats has been untrue for nearly the last half century. It now lifts only yachts, and the most expensive yachts have been floating further upward on a veritable tsunami of wealth.

Thanks to the exhaustive research of two European economists, Anthony Atkinson of Great Britain and Thomas Piketty of France,

---

*The term *Gilded Age* was coined by Mark Twain in a novel of that title in 1873, coauthored by Charles Dudley Warner. It was meant to describe an American society with a glittering surface of gold that concealed a corrupt core. Historians use the term to characterize an era when the most influential figures were not presidents but corporate leaders—Andrew Carnegie, Cornelius Vanderbilt, John D. Rockefeller—and elected officials took their orders from them. Our second Gilded Age replicates both the plutocratic politics and the high level of economic inequality of the first. In terms of the American Dialogue, the values of capitalism take precedence over the values of democracy and trump the right to pursue happiness for all but the favored few.

there is a fact-based consensus concerning the past hundred years. The chart below might be entitled "The Second Coming of the Gilded Age." In the middle years of the twentieth century, as the chart shows, economic inequality went into a steep decline and then leveled off. Economists have called this the Great Compression because wealth once again became concentrated in the middle ranks of American society. America's most influential economist at the time, Simon Kuznets, argued that the more equitable distribution of wealth represented a new but abiding pattern, as the industrial economy became more mature, education more widespread, and the state played a more redistributive role (i.e., the highest tax bracket averaged 75 percent). But what Kuznets described as the new order turned out to be a temporary aberration. Income inequality increased on a steady path starting in the late 1970s, and by 2008 it had reached the same historical high point achieved in 1928. The Great Compression had been replaced by the Great Divergence—a term journalists began to deploy as shorthand to describe the unexpected arrival of a second Gilded Age in twenty-first-century America.

Hindsight, the historian's chief interpretive tool, reveals that the more egalitarian era from 1930 to 1980 was not, as Kuznets believed, the recovery of the American norm but rather an interlude between

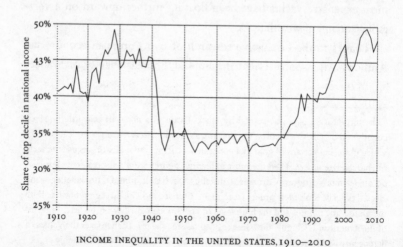

INCOME INEQUALITY IN THE UNITED STATES, 1910–2010

the dominant norm of economic inequality once the American economy industrialized. Kuznets formulated his generalizations about the course of American economic history during the Great Depression, World War II, and the outset of the Cold War, when the federal government's management of the economy and the pro-worker policies of the New Deal reigned supreme, effectively enforcing a redistribution of wealth based on a public agenda that took precedence over the unregulated laws of the free market.

The salient fact is that the Great Convergence during the middle decades of the twentieth century, which Kuznets celebrated as "the new normal" and that most senior citizens in the twenty-first century fondly recall as the Golden Age, was in fact an anachronistic interlude largely dependent upon government policies enacted during national and international crises, then continued by both political parties in the 1950s and 1960s. In effect, the New Deal and Great Society programs ameliorated the unequal impact of industrial capitalism on the distribution of wealth.

—◆—

There are two overlapping explanations for what happened to generate the dramatic increase in income inequality during the last quarter of the twentieth century and beyond. The first focuses attention on policy changes—that is, political decisions that removed regulations on the free market and reduced taxes on the rich. The second emphasizes changes in the postindustrialized economy that were a product not of policy choices but rather of structural shifts generated by technology, globalization, and what economists call "financialization."

The chief piece of evidence for the primacy of the structural explanation, thoroughly documented in the landmark studies by Piketty and Atkinson, is that the advanced economies of Europe are also experiencing a slightly muted version of the same increase in inequality as the United States. While globalization has vastly expanded the size of the marketplace, thereby increasing potential customers exponentially, it has simultaneously expanded the labor pool, thereby allowing corporations to move labor-intensive jobs to low-wage markets in Asia and Latin America and to significantly reduce the leverage of labor in negotiating salaries and benefits. And while technology has essentially eliminated distance for most forms of communication and distribution, thereby reducing costs for consumers, it has also replaced factory workers with machines and robots, producing a discernible job shift from manufacturing to the service sector, where salaries and benefits are lower. These shifts in the tectonic plates of the global economy have simultaneously depressed wages and inflated corporate profits not just in the United States but in all advanced societies.

Meanwhile, most of the yachts on the rising tide are moored in the harbors of finance located in New York, London, and Hong Kong. The emergence of the financial sector tracks the increase in economic inequality almost perfectly, and the top 1 percent, even more the top .1 percent, is dominated by investment bankers, hedge fund managers, and private equity managers, joined by a sprinkling of CEOs who on average make three hundred times more than the workers they employ. (The top ten hedge fund managers make more than all the kindergarten teachers in the United States.) The rhetorical juxtaposition of Wall Street and Main Street, it turns out, is not just a political cartoon. The industrial moguls of old made steel, ships, and railroads. The super-rich in the second Gilded Age mostly manage and make only money, and this is happening throughout the developed world.

If we confine our focus to the United States, the chief strength of the policy-based explanation for economic inequality—the argument that its causes are chiefly conscious choices rather than impersonal forces—is both obvious and simple: in the 1980s the federal government stopped doing what it had been doing for the preceding half century to offset the inherently unequal distribution of wealth by the free market. More specifically, the highest tax bracket was almost halved, from an average of 75 percent to 39 percent; the minimum wage remained fixed at levels set in the early 1970s; multiple loopholes in the tax code were added to protect high incomes and inherited wealth; the voiding of the Glass-Steagall Act (1933) in 1999 eliminated most federal regulations on investment banking; and the *Citizens United* decision (2010) by the Supreme Court removed all restrictions on corporate giving to political candidates, thereby forging the link between an economic oligarchy and a political plutocracy. Once again the infamous words of Senator Mark Hanna, uttered during the first Gilded Age, echoed through the halls of Congress: "There are two things that are important in politics. The first is money. I can't remember what the second is." Incoming members of Congress were advised to allocate their priorities accordingly, devoting over half their time to fund-raising.

There is no need to choose between the structural and policy explanations for ascending levels of income inequality, since the two obviously overlap and interact. In sum, globalization and technology dramatically increased the inherent inequalities in all market economies, and just when those structural changes began to take hold in the late 1970s, the United States chose to adopt policies that exacerbated the social and economic consequences of the postindustrial marketplace. More specifically, at precisely the moment when the progressive tax policies and federal regulations of banks and corporations put in place by the New Deal became even more essential to offset increased disparities in wealth, the federal government during the presidency of Ronald Reagan repudiated the underlying assumptions of the New Deal.

In doing so, Reagan broke with two Republican predecessors, Dwight Eisenhower and Richard Nixon, both of whom tacitly endorsed the fiscal policy of FDR as a necessary and permanent presence on the American political landscape. Reagan became the most eloquent voice for a political narrative that depicted the federal government as a domestic version of the Evil Empire. This conservative story line echoed the antigovernment message of Barry Goldwater twenty years earlier, though anyone with a longer historical lens could locate the origins of the New Right in the old liberalism of agrarian, preindustrial America, whose patron saint was no less than Thomas Jefferson. In the original Jeffersonian version, sovereignty resided in the individual soul, not in the collective society, and all efforts to impose federal control over the economy—Alexander Hamilton was the chief villain—were tyrannical second comings of British imperialism, which the American Revolution had supposedly banished forever. Not for nothing did Reagan begin his presidency by declaring that "we should pluck a flower from Thomas Jefferson's life and wear it on our soul forever."

If ideas were timeless stars in the American sky, then embracing the antigovernment side of the Jeffersonian legacy would have made historical sense. But Jefferson himself acknowledged that his deepest political convictions would become irrelevant once the United States moved past its agrarian phase, that is, when the continent was fully settled, factories replaced farms, and most people lived in cities. All these developments occurred between 1890 and 1920, after which Jeffersonian America became a lost world.

In his Commonwealth Club Address (1933), delivered just after winning the presidency, Franklin Roosevelt cited these demographic and economic changes as the primary reason why Americans needed a New Deal. Only enhanced government power at the federal level could offset the economic imbalances fostered by large corporations, manage a huge industrial economy, and redistribute wealth in order to ensure that ordinary workers shared in the bounty. In sum, the Jeffersonian depiction of government as an alien presence had served its purpose but outlived its time. This positive profile of government as "us" rather than "them" became received wisdom in mainstream American politics for the next fifty years. The central Adams insight, namely that the free market required regulation for capitalism to coexist with the egalitarian expectations of democracy, was firmly in place.

From either a historical or a philosophical perspective, the emergence in the 1980s of a New Right movement based on a demonic view of government seems strange. For it required a massive dose of amnesia to blot out the considerable benefits that had accrued to two generations of the American population over the preceding half century, and it required a radically revisionist view of American history to depict the Federal Reserve Board, Social Security, and Medicare as illegitimate aberrations that must somehow, like most of the twentieth century, be revoked. And as already mentioned, the timing of Reagan's conservative agenda was especially unfortunate, coming as it did just when globalization and technology were amplifying the inequities of a postindustrial marketplace and the chief weapon to mitigate the escalating inequities suddenly became unavailable.

It makes more sense to explain Reagan-era conservatism not as a coherent political philosophy, but more pragmatically as a successful effort to dismember the New Deal coalition by deploying the antigovernment message to attract three otherwise disparate constituencies to the Republican banner: first, southern whites opposed to the civil rights legislation that dismantled Jim Crow policies in the states of the former Confederacy; second, evangelical Christians disenchanted by the *Roe v. Wade* (1972) decision that legalized abortion rights for women; third, corporate executives opposed to the progressive tax structure and federal regulation of the industrial and financial economy.

The corporate constituency, an old Republican stalwart, was most crucial because of the nearly limitless resources it was prepared to provide for the antigovernment agenda. In one sense, nothing more profound was at work than the privileged class protecting its privileges. But as the number of millionaires and billionaires multiplied in the globalized economy, the amount of disposable wealth also increased exponentially and flowed disproportionately toward conservative causes as well as candidates. Jane Mayer has documented in considerable detail the successful campaign conducted by corporate executives in the fossil fuel industry, orchestrated by Charles and David Koch, who financed a vast network of think tanks, media outlets, and political action committees that gave the antigovernment agenda a commanding presence in the national conversation.

The infusion of what Mayer has called "dark money" into an orchestrated effort to demonize the federal government coincided with a dramatic shift in popular opinion already occurring for reasons unrelated to any conscious campaign by the corporate class. Polls conducted in the early 1960s indicated that between 70 and 80 percent of the American population viewed the federal government favorably, answering yes to the question "Do you trust the government of the United States?" By the mid-1970s these numbers were almost exactly reversed and have remained overwhelmingly unfavorable ever since.

Three midcentury events combined to generate the change, each for different a reason: the Vietnam War, which disenchanted younger Americans, especially on the left; the civil rights movement, which alienated older white residents of the former Confederacy; and the Watergate scandal, which spread cynicism toward Washington's corrupt culture that cut across several demographic categories. In addition, a generational shift was occurring as memories of the Great Depression and World War II faded.

Despite these favorable historical winds, the dramatic success of the New Right in wresting control of America's long-standing debate over the role of government was quite remarkable. "Their ambitions were grandiose," as Mayer observed, "to 'save' America as they saw it, at every level, by turning the clock back to the Gilded Age before the advent of the Progressive Era." Historically, the idea that it is possible to erase nearly a century of American experience is bizarre, akin to the midlife dream of returning to one's youth. Politically, the Gilded Age is a strange candidate for paradise, burdened as it is with images of Robber Barons feasting at Delmonico's in self-indulged splendor, the millionaires' club of wholly bought-and-sold congressmen, and a reigning ideology called Social Darwinism that depicted entrenched poverty and permanent economic inequality as conditions sanctioned by some combination of God's will and Nature's laws.

On the other hand, if you were corporate titans like the Koch brothers, who grew up in a family with close ties to the John Birch Society, you viewed FDR's New Deal as a pale imitation of Stalin's totalitarian gulag. The Gilded Age was the American Eden before the Fall. The death of America's middle-class dream was only collateral damage in the war for the freedom of the fortunate few to pursue their happiness without government interference or regulation. In this extreme version of capitalist theology, any federally sponsored policy of income redistribution was heresy. The emergence of a permanently stratified American society represented a welcome return to the natural order when the Captains of Industry ruled the earth.

—◆—◆—

Looking back over the full span of American history, the debate regarding the proper role of the federal government has been a central feature in the ongoing American Dialogue since our origins as the first nation-size republic. It was the core conflict during the 1780s, in the debate at the Constitutional Convention between defenders of the Articles of Confederation and advocates for a more fully empowered federal government. That argument continued in the Great Debate of 1787–88 between Federalists and Antifederalists, a debate won by the Federalists and enshrined in the historical record ever since in the Federalist Papers, which, as its name suggests, represented the pro-government, winning side of the argument.

No such thing as the Antifederalist Papers was ever published during the Great Debate, though historians and constitutional scholars have assembled collections of pamphlets and speeches from the state ratifying conventions that thoroughly document the antigovernment argument, which had roots in the natural rights section of the Declaration of Independence as well as in the arguments colonists hurled at Parliament and George III to justify secession from the British Empire. (In 1861 the Confederate States of America repeated those arguments to justify their secession from the Union.) The seminal source for the antigovernment ideology of the New Right today is the Antifederalist tradition. The most eloquent defender of that legacy at the founding was Jefferson, who insisted till the end that the true "spirit of '76" was incompatible with federal authority over domestic policy. Jefferson went to his grave believing that the United States was a union of sovereign states, a coherent confederation, not a nation-state.

Our modern-day political categories of liberal versus conservative do not translate neatly in the world of the American founding, but we are still living within an argumentative framework the founders established over the proper role of government. The American Dialogue is an ongoing conversation between the two sides in that argument. The passionate and at times vitriolic debate in the 1790s between Federalists and Republicans exposed the deep disagreements between the two sides of the revolutionary generation. Washington, Adams, Hamilton, and John Marshall led the Federalist pro-government side against Jefferson and the recently converted Madison for the Republican opposition. The great beauty of the Adams-Jefferson correspondence (1812–26) was its seamless connection of both legacies, making it an elegiac embodiment of the American Dialogue, the original version of our ongoing argument about government as "us" or "them." Only the argument between those choices, not one or the other, captures the full meaning of the founders' legacy.

We currently inhabit a second Gilded Age in which the active interplay within that dialogue has almost completely disappeared because belief in a prominent role for government has been placed on the permanent defensive, in part because one side enjoys the advantage of a very large and expensive megaphone that amplifies its message. As a result, mainstream politics is trapped in a one-sided conversation, a muted version of the American Dialogue bereft of the energy and conflict-driven dynamism possible only with full engagement of both sides of our founding principles. Adams predicted this outcome because, in the Adams scheme, aristocracies throughout history always created oligarchies that then mobilized their economic power to unbalance the political equation.

Until some semblance of balance is restored, there is no realistic hope for reducing our unacceptable levels of economic inequality, which are certain to increase as technology makes most forms of manual labor anachronistic and globalization deepens the divide between winners and losers in the global marketplace. Nothing less is at stake than the survival of the American Dream as embodied in a robust middle class that becomes the beneficiary, not the victim, of the new global economy. Without a role for government, the American Dream becomes a realistic prospect only for the favored few.

John Adams tried to tell us that outcome was virtually inevitable over two centuries ago. The two Republican presidents enshrined on Mount Rushmore, Abraham Lincoln and Theodore Roosevelt, both insisted that the federal government was the ultimate arbiter of our common fate. Franklin Roosevelt, the greatest Democratic president, declared that the federal government was responsible for enforcing a social contract in which the right to pursue happiness included the right to a job. Something is not only missing but terribly wrong when these voices are absent from our national conversation. To switch the metaphor, at present there is a thumb on the right side of the political scale that renders a balanced argument true to the long-standing legacy of the American Dialogue currently beyond our reach.

CHAPTER 3

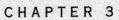

Law

James Madison

Never have I seen so much mind in so little matter.

Eulogy, Richmond Enquirer, *July 1, 1836*

In the same way that practicing Christians trace their abiding truths back to the Bible, practicing judges in the United States trace their versions of the truth back to the Constitution. How to interpret these hallowed texts is, of course, a matter of considerable disagreement, though the conviction that there is a preferred earthly place where one can find the truth revealed is apparently an irresistible human impulse with origins that go back to the Delphic Oracle. And just as there are fundamentalists on the Christian side of this interpretive tradition, there are originalists on the judicial side, both groups insisting that our lives in the present must be guided by principles embedded in language written long ago and in the intentions or meanings of the authors of those sacred, or semi-sacred, words.

Fortunately, we know much more about the authors of the Constitution than about the authors of the Bible. And so, if we try to take the doctrinal assumption of the originalists seriously, there is a rich historical record to consult in order to recover the mentality of the men who wrote the Constitution and its important epilogue, the Bill of Rights. The obvious place to start is the late 1780s, when the Constitution was still in the process of being born, and the obvious person to focus on, the central player in the story, is James Madison.

When it comes to James Madison, however, appearances are often misleading, sometimes downright deceptive. He is unquestionably a prominent member of the founding generation but does not seem to fit the iconic mold. "Little Jemmy Madison," as he was called, was a diminutive creature, about five feet two inches tall and 120 pounds. He was a frail and sickly young man, forever lingering on the edge of some fatal ailment, frequently confessing to family and friends that he was haunted by intimations of his own mortality. His classmates at the College of New Jersey (Princeton) acknowledged that he was the smartest of their lot, but they also predicted that he would never amount to much—perhaps a career librarian or schoolmaster—because of his short duration. As it turned out, Madison outlived every member of his Princeton class and all the leading figures of the revolutionary generation, observing near the end, "Having outlived so many of my contemporaries, I ought not to forget that I may be thought to have outlived myself."[1]

This discrepancy between appearances and reality also emerges if we bring Madison into focus at a pivotal moment in his long public career. It is February 1787, and he is seated alone at his desk in drafty one-room quarters reserved for bachelors on the southern tip of Manhattan. He is biding his time because—a recurrent problem— the Confederation Congress lacks a quorum, and as a member of the Virginia delegation, he is far away from friends and family back home at Montpelier.

He is apparently doing a pedantic version of what we would call therapy, scribbling in his highly compressed handwriting a sixteen-page history of all the political confederations that came and went over the last thousand years of European history, which he entitled "Notes on Ancient and Modern Confederations." It was a boringly repetitive little essay, because the same thing happened over and over again: whether it was one of the Greek, Italian, Dutch, or Germanic confederations, they all came together against a common enemy, then eventually dissolved into civil wars, anarchy, and political oblivion.

Madison's tedious immersion in the historical record was obviously designed to document the inherently transitory character of the confederation as a political framework. He was apparently consoling himself about the looming collapse of the Confederation Congress as one of those inevitable and eminently predictable developments that neither he nor anyone else could prevent. He was looking back at the European past to identify political patterns that would help him understand what was happening to the current American confederation of states, which was on the verge of dissolution. If there were any doubts about his intentions, they disappear once he began to draft an equally tedious diagnosis of the recent American experiment with republican government under the Articles of Confederation, entitled "Vices of the Political System of the United States."[2]

Once again, however, appearances are deceptive. While it is true that Madison was frustrated by the increasingly dysfunctional character of the Confederation Congress in the early winter of 1787, his study of European confederations was not just a pedantic exercise, and "therapy" was not only a word he never would have recognized but also a mental posture alien to every fiber of his personality. He was not wasting his brainpower on indulged thoughts about the inevitable end of the American confederation. He was more like a lawyer preparing his case for a new kind of American government that would allow the infant American republic to avoid all the pitfalls that befell its confederated predecessors. We are witnessing not the end of one story so much as the start of another.

We know this because we possess the advantage of hindsight. For we now recognize that Madison was beginning the most creative and consequential chapter in his lengthy public career. He would soon orchestrate the agenda for the Constitutional Convention, manage the ratification process as Publius alongside Alexander Hamilton in the Federalist Papers, lead the all-important ratification debate at the Virginia Convention, then single-handedly draft the Bill of Rights. Given the huge political issues at stake, which involved nothing less than a fundamental change in the meaning of the American Revolution, what we might call "Madison's Moment" between 1787 and

1789 just might constitute the most brilliant political performance in American history.[3]

—+—≍+≍—+—

Madison's "Vices of the Political System of the United States" reads like an indictment of the Articles of Confederation because that's what it was. But it was also a catalog of his own experience over the past five years, when he went through a grueling and gradual transformation from a provincial Virginian to a dedicated nationalist. It happened in the crucible of specific crises: the states had refused to honor their tax obligations during the war and their pledge to fund veterans' pensions after the war; they had refused to cooperate on internal improvements like roads and canals and had even imposed domestic tariffs on one another; they had encroached upon federal authority to sign separate treaties with various Indian tribes, essentially stealing Native American land; the Confederation Congress had failed to pass a 5 percent duty on imports, in effect deciding to renege on the $40 million foreign and domestic debt; and all debates about foreign policy were riddled by local, state, and regional interest blocs, making it impossible for Congress to speak with one voice in the international arena.[4]

Tracking Madison's political evolution from Virginian to American in the early 1780s can be a tedious exercise that risks getting lost in the thicket of extraneous details. While he supported the creation of a national bank, for example, he did so only to finance the war debt, not to establish a permanent institution to manage the national economy. (Like most Virginians, Madison regarded banks as places where you sent your money to disappear.) Or to take another example, while he embraced the argument that the western land acquired in the Treaty of Paris (1783) was a national trust that must be overseen by the Confederation Congress, he insisted that Virginia's claims to the Northwest Territory must be honored and that Kentucky statehood was a matter to be decided by the Virginia legislature.[5]

These lingering vestiges of Madison's Virginia allegiances were only way stations on the road to his emerging national orientation, but they are worth noticing for what they reveal about the way his mind worked. Despite his scholarly demeanor, he was an intensely political creature whose best thinking occurred within contested political arenas, rather than, like Jefferson, in solitary sessions at his desk. Two congressional debates in late 1782 and early 1783—the failure to pass the impost and the refusal to fund pensions for veterans—carried him over the line. Until then, Madison's goal had been to make the government under the Articles of Confederation work. Afterward he regarded the Articles as a hopelessly dysfunctional political arrangement that must be revised or, better yet, replaced. As he put it in January 1783, "The Idea of erecting our national independence on the ruins of public faith and national honor must be horrid to every mind which retained either honesty or pride."[6]

Over the next two years Madison's pessimistic predictions kept coming true. The simple fact was that some semblance of an American union had held together, but barely, to win the war. Once the war ended, however, all the political forces became centrifugal, as the states retreated into their own more proximate and provincial bailiwicks, delegates elected to the Confederation Congress either refused to serve or to show up, and the Congress itself became a traveling circus, moving from Philadelphia to Princeton, to Trenton, to Annapolis, and then to New York. Madison knew that political reform of some sort was essential. "The perpetuity & efficacy of the present system cannot be counted on," he lamented. "The question is, in what mode & at what moment the experiment for supplying the defects are to be made. The answer to this question can not be given without a knowledge greater than I possess of the temper & views of the different states."[7]

If our core concern is to recover Madison's mentality as it evolved prior to the Constitutional Convention, at this stage he had become a complete convert to a more fully empowered federal government with authority over the states; but he did not know how to implement that fundamental shift in sovereignty, since all foreseeable efforts to achieve that transformation ran afoul of the very state and local interests they were designed to subordinate.

In the fall of 1786 two unrelated events occurred that, taken together, provided a solution to Madison's dilemma, though both in richly ironic ways. The previous spring the Confederation Congress had endorsed the calling of a special convention in Annapolis to consider commercial reform, presumably to end the current state-based system in favor of a more unified trade policy. Madison confided to Jefferson that the proposed Annapolis Convention represented only a small step in the right direction, then added, "To speak the truth, I almost despair even of this."[8]

Madison's fears proved well founded. The Annapolis Convention, which met on September 11, proved a fiasco. Only five states showed up, so the first and only act of business that Madison and the other commissioners could perform was to move for adjournment. But then, in an act of utter audacity, the commissioners issued a statement—drafted by Alexander Hamilton—recommending that the Confederation Congress call "a future Convention which would enlarge the mandate beyond commerce," with the goal of "rendering the constitution of the Federal Government adequate to the exigencies of the Union." In order to allow sufficient time for preparation, the proposed convention should be scheduled in Philadelphia for the second Monday in May 1787. It was as if a young mountain climber, having failed to scale a local hill, announced that he would next climb the highest peak on the continent.[9]

Proposals for some kind of convention to reform the government under the Articles had been floating through Congress for several years but had never mustered sufficient support even to come up for a vote. What changed the political chemistry in the late fall of 1786 was an outbreak of violence in western Massachusetts that came to be called Shays's Rebellion. The Shaysites were farmers, many veterans of the Continental Army, who were protesting mortgage foreclosures and tax increases imposed by the Massachusetts legislature in Boston, which they linked to the arbitrary taxes imposed by Parliament twenty years earlier. A generation of historians has tended to describe Shays's Rebellion as the earliest manifestation of the Populist movement, but subsequent scholarship has more persuasively seen it as the last act of the American Revolution.[10]

Safely ensconced in Paris, Jefferson called it "a little rebellion." But press reports vastly exaggerated the size of the insurrection, claimed that the rebels were poised to march on Boston, even had plans to join with their compatriots in Vermont, then secede from the United States, probably enjoying British support from Canada. The watchword for those predisposed toward apocalyptic scenarios was *anarchy*, the collapse of the American confederation leading to civil war between the states and then, as Madison himself predicted, the breakup of the union into two or three regional confederacies.[11]

All of a sudden, the bizarre proposal that had emerged from the Annapolis Convention did not seem so strange at all. Somehow the total failure of one attempt at reform was now interacting with the melodramatic hysteria surrounding a local uprising of aggrieved farmers to create political momentum for a cause that Madison had previously presumed unattainable. He immediately went into high gear in the Madisonian mode: lobbying delegates at the Confederation Congress to endorse the recommendation from the Annapolis Convention for a convention in Philadelphia; introducing a bill in the Virginia legislature to elect a delegation to such a convention even before it was officially approved; and opening up a correspondence with George Washington to lure him back to public life as one of the Virginia delegates, a bold move calculated to lend legitimacy to the gathering in Philadelphia that would almost ensure that it did not repeat the Annapolis embarrassment.[12]

In one of his several letters to Washington, Madison found himself making an ingenious argument, politically calculated to touch what Abraham Lincoln later called "the mystic chords of memory," which played a tune that Washington knew by heart, even though it seemed to defy all the conventional wisdom currently embodied in the state-based system under the Articles. For we need to remember that the American colonies had declared their independence as sovereign states, so that any shift in sovereignty from the state to the federal level was a repudiation of "the spirit of '76." Madison made the opposite case, arguing that such a shift in sovereignty represented a rescue of the revolution rather than a betrayal of its core principles:

> We can no longer doubt that the crisis is arrived at which the good people of America are to decide the solemn question, whether they will reap the fruits of that Independence and of that Union which they have cemented with so much of their common blood, or whether by giving way to unmanly jealousies and prejudices, or to partial and transitory interests, they will renounce the auspicious blessings prepared for them by the Revolution, and furnish its enemies an eventual triumph over those by whose virtue & valor it has been accomplished.[13]

There were profound implications to his new political posture, for Madison was insisting upon a fresh understanding of what the American Revolution meant if it was to live up to its name. American history was headed in one direction in the 1780s, and he sought to change that direction by transforming the American confederation to a nation-state. Madison's chief goal in the early months of 1787 was nothing less than to orchestrate a second American Revolution, which he regarded as the proper fulfillment of the first. In order to make that happen, the looming convention in Philadelphia had to succeed, so all his mental power was focused on fashioning a strategic plan that would maximize that possibility. He was determined to ensure that no delegate to the Constitutional Convention would be as fully prepared as, so he still styled himself, James Madison, Junior.

If God was in the details, Madison would be there to greet him upon arrival. The all-important, indeed essential, detail in Madison's preconvention strategy was George Washington, who instantly transformed a highly problematic enterprise into an intriguing political possibility. Madison had first met "His Excellency" at Mount Vernon in the fall of 1785, at two conferences focusing on improving navigation on the Potomac. Like everyone else who first encountered Washington, Madison was duly impressed, though for reasons beyond Washington's towering presence.

For Madison discovered that Washington had already made the transition from Virginian to American that he was still negotiating. Washington's conversion had occurred during the eight years he had served as commander in chief of the Continental Army, when he developed a caustic and critical attitude toward Congress and state legislatures for failing to provide money and men for the war effort, then sending his soldiers home as beggars without pensions rather than as heroes. Moreover, his criticism of the state-based government under the Articles continued after the war. "I do not conceive we can long exist as a nation," he warned, "without having lodged some power which will pervade the whole Union in as energetic a manner as the authority of the different state Governments extends over the several States." Washington did not need to be persuaded that the Articles must be revised; he was already convinced that they should be altogether replaced.[14]

The courting of Washington began seriously in December 1786 and continued through the following spring, assuming the character of a relentless campaign against Washington's multilayered defenses. The most impregnable wall was his deep-seated commitment to retirement beneath his proverbial vines and fig trees at Mount Vernon. "Yet having happily insisted in bringing the ship into port and having been fairly discharged," he pleaded, "it is not my business to embark again on a Sea of Troubles."[15]

There was both an avowedly political and deeply personal dimension to Washington's reticence. On the political side, he had surrendered his sword at Annapolis in a highly symbolic scene—Washington was an impresario of exits—that the American press likened to the retirement of Cincinnatus. Washington relished the classical comparison and embraced its implications; namely, once gone, the American Cincinnatus could never come back.

On the personal, even emotional side, the great barrier was a keen sense of his limited duration. The phrase he frequently used, "gliding down the stream of life," was a way of referring to his recognition that few males in the Washington line lived beyond their fifties, so he was much closer to the end than the beginning. As he put it to his beloved Lafayette: "I was a short lived family—and might soon expect to be entombed in the dreary mansion of my fathers—These things darkened the shade & gave a gloom to the picture, but I will not repine—I have had my day." He did not believe there was room in his story for yet another chapter.[16]

Madison chose not to make a frontal assault on Fortress Washington, preferring skirmishes on the flanks. For example, Washington had argued that there was no way he could travel to Philadelphia in early May, since he had already apprised the Society of the Cincinnati that he could not make a meeting there at the same time; his rheumatism was also acting up; and his aging mother was dying of cancer. Madison expressed his sympathy for Washington's justifiable excuses, then added that the larger issues at stake were so paramount that he alone could decide "whether the difficulties which you enumerate ought not to give way to them."[17]

Washington received a similar letter from Edmund Randolph, governor of Virginia, notifying him that the legislature had unanimously chosen him to head the list of the Virginia delegation to the Philadelphia convention. Randolph sounded the old revolutionary drumbeat: "For the gloomy prospect still admits one ray of hope, that those who began, carried on & consummated the revolution, can yet rescue America from impending ruin." Madison adopted a more indirect approach, advising Washington that he could withdraw his candidacy at some future date, but for now "having your name at the front of the appointments is a mark of the earnestness of Virginia." At the same time that he urged Washington to delay a decision, Madison began

making inquiries to arrange Benjamin Franklin's availability to pre-
side over the convention if Washington, in the end, backed out.[18]

Meanwhile, still floating in the crack that Madison had kept open,
Washington reached out for advice from two trusted veterans of the
Continental Army. Henry Knox, his old artillery commander, thought
that the prospects for a successful convention were remote, that Washington had less to gain than to lose by participating, and therefore he
should not budge from Mount Vernon. David Humphreys, a former
aide-de-camp currently serving as Washington's private secretary,
reiterated Knox's argument, emphasizing the stain on Washington's
legacy if the convention failed. Humphreys then added the intriguing insight that if by some miracle a national government emerged
from the deliberations at Philadelphia, Washington would almost certainly be chosen to head it, thereby ending his retirement forever. By
March 1787 Washington appeared convinced. "In confidence I inform
you," he wrote to Knox, "that it is not, at this time, my purpose to
attend."[19]

As it turned out, the phrase "at this time" proved most revealing,
since it left Washington vulnerable until later in March, when Madison
provided his state-by-state canvass of the delegates selected to attend
the looming convention. Exactly how Madison acquired this information is difficult to fathom, since newspaper coverage did not appear
for several weeks. Most likely Madison used his perch in New York to
interview members of the Confederation Congress about the votes in
their respective state legislatures, a nose-counting exercise that most
of Madison's peers disdained but that came to him naturally, indeed
was becoming a core feature of the Madison mode. What he found and
immediately shared with Washington was that, with the exception of
New York, which would be stacked with opponents to any change in
the Articles, and Rhode Island, the reliably eccentric state that would
boycott the whole business, the convention would be evenly divided
between moderates who wanted to revise the Articles and radicals
who wanted to replace them altogether.

This information, which proved accurate, transformed the previous political calculus, making the prospects for fundamental change at least imaginable. When Washington shared this news with Knox, the trusted confidant reversed his advice. "But were an energetic and judicious system to be proposed with Your Signature," Knox now argued, "it would be a circumstance highly honorable to your fame in the present and future ages; and doubly entitle you to the glorious republican epithet—the Father of Your Country."[20]

By late March, then, the great prize was almost in hand. Washington informed Madison that he was willing to lead the Virginia delegation to Philadelphia, but on one condition. Madison must promise that he "adopt no temporizing expedient, but probe the defects of the Constitution to the bottom, and provide radical cures, whether they are agreed to or not." This was a huge request, since it meant that Madison was agreeing to violate the mandate of the Confederation Congress, which had charged the convention merely to revise the Articles, not replace them with an entirely different government.[21]

In April Madison concurred with Washington's demands. "Radical attempts, although unsuccessful, will at least justify the author of them," he observed, "since anything less would only delay the collapse of the union into a series of regional confederations." He had been harboring a radical strategy all along, and now Washington's insistence made it the centerpiece of his final preparations for the convention. "I am afraid you will think this project, if not extravagant, absolutely unattainable and unworthy of being attempted," he wrote to Edmund Randolph. But now nothing would suffice other than a complete shift in sovereignty from the state to the federal level.[22]

This was a pivotal moment in Madison's life and the course of American history, for it established Madison's political agenda in the month preceding the Constitutional Convention and thereby allowed him to focus his thinking more sharply. Though never trained as a lawyer, he thought like one, and now he could prepare his case knowing that his client was a fully empowered federal government, while the hostile witnesses that he would need to cross-examine were those old-style revolutionaries like Samuel Adams and Patrick Henry, who regarded such a dramatic change as the second coming of British tyranny.

Madison's best thinking occurred within clearly defined political contexts in which the intellectual parameters were already settled. He was less adept at defining the borders of the political landscape—that was Jefferson's specialty—than in functioning with considerable and conspicuous mental agility within those borders. This put a premium on sheer preparation and deftly manipulating the evidence to fit a pre-ordained conclusion. If you knew where history needed to head, and now he did, it was much easier to lead the way.

He began with the assumption, broadly shared, that the proper model for a national government was the tripartite structure originally proposed by John Adams in *Thoughts on Government* (1776), then subsequently adopted in most of the state constitutions. That meant a bicameral legislature, an elected executive, and an appointed judiciary. The very fact that the Articles did not follow this model was the clearest evidence that they were not intended to function as a government. And lurking beneath that intention was the assumption, also broadly shared, that republican governments worked only in small geographic areas no larger than the former colonies, now states. From the start, Madison recognized that this assumption, which had venerable origins in the great Montesquieu's *Spirit of the Laws* (1748), had to be challenged and rendered obsolete. For unless and until that was done, any national government was inherently incompatible with the republican principles of the American Revolution.

The concentrated thinking that Madison did in late March and April 1787 is recoverable in his correspondence with Washington, Randolph, and Jefferson (in code), as well as in the final notes he made in "Vices." He insisted on a total transfer of authority from the state to the federal level: "Let the National Government be armed with a positive & complete authority in all cases where uniform measures are necessary As in trade & C & C." These last abbreviations presumably referred to foreign policy, especially treaties, and fiscal policy, especially taxes, though Madison's vagueness also exposed his recognition that specificity ran risks. The same combination of boldness and reticence shaped his case for vastly expanded executive power, which was absolutely necessary for an energetic federal government, he believed, but ran against the potent prejudices against monarchy. "The supremacy of the whole in the Executive department," he acknowledged, "seems liable to some difficulty," because any robust expression of executive power conjured up patriotic protests against George III.[23]

Nevertheless, he thought that the overlearned lessons of 1776 must not prevent an elected chief executive from focusing the energies of the new government. Madison went so far as to insist that the executive should "have a negative in all cases whatsoever on the Legislative Acts of the States as the K. of G.B. [King of Great Britain] heretofore had." This was a direct reference to George III's assertion of veto power over all colonial legislation, a proposal loaded with political dynamite and therefore the strongest, almost intentionally provocative expression of his all-or-nothing strategy.[24]

There were two additional proposals that Madison regarded as nonnegotiable because they eliminated the last vestiges of any state-based claim to authority. The first was his argument that representation in both branches of the legislature be based on population. The ridiculous idea that Rhode Island should have equal representation with Virginia had been dramatically exposed several times over and now needed to die a quiet death. The second proposal called for the ratification of any constitution to emerge from Philadelphia by conventions called specifically for that purpose rather than by the state legislatures. This implied that the new government was sanctioned by the people at large rather than the states, a political assertion of more than symbolic significance.

Finally, Madison knew that he needed some kind of answer to the argument that any nation-size republic was too large to work because republics, by their very nature, could impose political control only over small populations and areas. In effect, he turned this small-

republic argument on its head, claiming that a larger and more populous society generated "a greater variety of interests, of pursuits of
passions, which check each other . . . so an extensive Republic ame-
liorates the administration of a small Republic."[25]

Because this counterintuitive idea, developed more fully in Federalist 10, has become famous as the earliest expression of a pluralis-
tic vision of American politics, much ink has been spilled attempting
to discover where Madison got the idea. The most likely sources of
inspiration were the Scottish philosophers, chiefly David Hume and
Adam Smith, especially the latter's *The Wealth of Nations* (1776),
which posited a self-regulating principle in the marketplace that Madison transposed to political interest groups. Even if correct, however,
this explanation invariably becomes a conversation about Madison as
a political philosopher, which misconstrues the context in which his
mind was working at the time. He was a political strategist preparing
his case for the great debate to come in Philadelphia. He knew what
he needed to disarm his looming critics and proceeded in his tightly
focused mode to find it wherever he could.[26]

Madison's intense preparation was designed to equip him for
the debates at the Constitutional Convention, but chance and circumstance magnified the impact of his homework. Ever diligent, he
arrived in Philadelphia on May 3, eleven days before the convention
was scheduled to start. The rest of the Virginia delegation, including
the all-important Washington, trickled in by May 17, but the lack of
a quorum due to severe rainstorms up and down the Atlantic coast
delayed the opening session for over a week, leaving time for multiple
meetings at local taverns where Madison lobbied his fellow Virginians
to support his radical strategy. They were joined by two Pennsylvania
delegates, Gouverneur Morris and James Wilson, both of whom, it
turned out, also favored replacing rather than revising the Articles.

The result of their deliberations was the fifteen-point Virginia Plan,
which embodied everything that Madison wanted: a tripartite government; a bicameral legislature with representation in both branches by
population; ratification by special conventions; and a slightly watered-

down version of his executive veto over all state laws. In the absence of any comparable proposal from moderate delegates, when the Constitutional Convention officially met on May 25, the Virginia Plan would command the field by default. Madison's agenda became the convention's agenda. With Washington in the chair and the radical agenda in the proverbial saddle, all of Madison's wildest dreams were coming true.[27]

As it turned out, and as the next fifteen weeks of debate in the East Room of the Pennsylvania State House revealed, the first days of the convention were the high point for Madison's radical agenda. It was all downhill from there. If we ask our recurring question—what were Madison's intentions at the start of the Constitutional Convention?— the answer is quite clear: to replace the Articles with a truly national government that shifted authority from the state to the federal level in a decisive and uncompromising fashion. It soon became clear that Madison's preferred goal was politically impossible.

—— ═╪═ ——

Between May 25 and September 17, 1787, a total of fifty-five delegates met in the same seminar-size room where the Declaration of Independence had been debated and signed, thereby at least symbolically signifying the connection between American independence and nationhood. For two reasons Madison merits serious consideration for the title "Father of the Constitution": first, his Virginia Plan set the agenda for the convention; second, he kept the fullest record of the debates, providing subsequent generations with the authoritative account of what is, by almost any reckoning, the most consequential political deliberation in American history. The spiritual haze that surrounded the Constitutional Convention for over a century—words like *providential, sacred,* and *miracle* dominated the early histories— are wholly understandable, given the irresistible urge for emerging nations to link their origins with godlike heroes and mythical legends that defy merely human understanding.[28]

It therefore seems almost sacrilegious to notice several incontrovertible and inconvenient facts. There was never a moment when all fifty-five delegates were present—Madison, of course, made every session—because the sense of melodrama that we bring to the occasion was not present for most delegates. While the Declaration of Independence eventually garnered unanimous support, only thirty-nine delegates signed the Constitution, because nationhood remained considerably more controversial than independence. The outcome was dependent on the state-based voting procedure established at the beginning, which essentially ensured that the small states could block any proposal for representation based on population; as a result, eloquence was less determinative than entrenched interests, and Madison's radical agenda for a complete conversion from confederation to nation was doomed from the start. For that matter, and for the same structural reasons, neither side could get what it wanted, and all "original intentions" fell victim to compromises best embodied in the Great Compromise that made representation in the House by population and in the Senate by state (July 16).[29]

Madison regarded the compromise as a devastating defeat. In conjunction with the failure of his ultranational proposal for federal jurisdiction over all state laws, which was dead on arrival (June 7), the principle of outright federal sovereignty over the states had been soundly rejected. Writing in code to Jefferson in Paris, Madison confessed that his hopes for a fully empowered national government had been blasted away. "I hazard an opinion," he lamented, "that the plan should it be adopted will neither effectively answer the national object nor prevent the local mischiefs which everywhere excite distrust agst the state government." He had not been able to keep his promise to Washington that only a wholly national solution would be acceptable. He might have added that when he unfurled his counterintuitive argument about the greater stability of large republics (June 6), no one seemed to have the vaguest idea of what he was talking about.[30]

It is clear, at least in retrospect, that Madison was reacting emotionally. He might just as easily have recognized that half a loaf was better than none at all; that his own insistence on a radical agenda had pushed the argument for American nationhood further than it would otherwise have reached; that he had won the battle for ratification by specially called conventions; and perhaps most panoramically, that the creation of a hybrid government that was partly national and partly federal was a great step forward.

But it was not what he, or anyone else for that matter, had originally wanted, and no principled posture on either the radical or the moderate side could garner the votes to win outright. Washington, ever the realist, and more capable in the aftermath of the convention of assessing the fruits of their labor, apprised his beloved Lafayette that, given the diversity of opinions present, "it was the best that could be obtained at the time." Benjamin Franklin conjured up one final spasm of preternatural wisdom, echoing Washington but more elegiacally: "Thus I consent, Sir, to this Constitution because I expect no better, and I am not sure it is not the best."[31]

Madison was initially incapable of such equanimity. In late September he went back to New York, prepared to cast his final vote in the Confederation Congress, which would send the newly minted Constitution to the state ratifying conventions. At this stage he was convinced that the document was fatally flawed and that ratification, if it should succeed, would provide only a temporary fix. He had done his best; his fellow nationalists had all done their best. But they had failed.

Hamilton, on the other hand, was not predisposed to allow the prospect of failure to cross his mind. On the last day of the convention, he made a plea for unanimity on the final vote. As Madison recorded in his notes, "No man's ideas were more remote from the plan than his were known to be." But despite profound reservations, Hamilton asked rhetorically, "Is it possible to deliberate between anarchy and convulsion on one side and the chance of good to be expected from the plan on the other?"[32]

It took six weeks for Madison to muster an equivalent resolve. By late October personal appeals from Washington to assume leadership of the looming debate over ratification in Virginia could not be ignored. (A request from Washington was a de facto command and represented a neat reversal of Madison's recruitment of Washington the previous spring.) In November Hamilton, conveniently living a block away in New York, extended an offer for Madison to join him and John Jay in writing a series of essays under the pseudonym Publius, aimed at the New York ratification convention and entitled the Federalist Papers. Madison was back on board.

Initially he regarded his role as primarily strategic—that is, to plot a course of action that maximized the prospects for influencing the voting blocs within each state. This was Madison in his familiar nose-counting mode, a talent that he had exhibited so proficiently before the Constitutional Convention, now deployed across a larger canvas of twelve states and more than sixteen hundred delegates. Extensive newspaper coverage of what was being called "The Great Debate" made his task somewhat easier, even though a reliable count pro and con was maddeningly difficult because each state was different and divided into local coalitions that defied any coherent principle of preference.

His early estimate was that the New England states could be counted in the safe column, except for Rhode Island, "whose folly and fraud," he observed caustically, "have not finished their career." The middle states looked reasonably safe—Maryland, New Jersey, Delaware easily, and Pennsylvania as long as Philadelphia held strong against the western counties. New York would be very difficult because of Governor George Clinton's patronage influence upstate, though the rumor mills suggested that New York City and its environs might threaten to secede if the Clintonites succeeded in blocking ratification. Virginia, the largest and most important state, was leaning pro but was too close to call, and it carried a momentum factor into the overall calculation, influencing voting patterns in the Carolinas and Maryland.[33]

There was another momentum factor that Madison made the centerpiece of his strategy. According to Article VII, nine states needed to ratify for the Constitution to go into effect. (Technically, this was illegal, since the Articles required a unanimous vote for amendments, but the Confederation Congress silently endorsed the lower bar when it sent the Constitution to the states.) By a happy coincidence the most problematic states, chiefly Virginia and New York, came near the end of the ratification sequence. This shaped Madison's "get to nine" strategy, which envisioned a strong push to reach the magic number, and as he put it, "the tardy remainder must be reduced to the dilemma of either shifting for themselves or coming in without any credit for it." In effect, once nine states ratified, all debates in the remaining states became meaningless, although Madison acknowledged that it was difficult to imagine any American government without Virginia.[34]

Finally, there was one piece of Madison's strategic plan that was wholly improvisational and that emerged after debates began in the early state ratifying conventions. It soon became clear that a sizable group of delegates in several states preferred a middle option, meaning a movement to "ratify with amendments," which became an attractive alternative to an up-or-down vote on the Constitution. Madison pressured his contacts in all states where amendments became part of the debate to accept *recommended* amendments but oppose any *mandatory* changes. The prospects for ratification became much more likely once a clear vote of aye or nay became the only option. This tactical victory, achieved on the fly, was Madison's major accomplishment as a hands-on political operative of unparalleled agility. How he managed to persuade delegates at the state conventions that mandatory amendments would be interpreted by the Confederation Congress as a nay vote has never been explained.

Then, in the late fall of 1787, Madison came to a realization that dramatically affected his understanding of what he and the other delegates in Philadelphia had actually done. The realization came gradually, in the midst of planning for the looming debates in the Virginia and New York ratifying conventions, but its political implications transcended the pragmatic goals of his strategic agenda. Put simply, Madison recognized that the Constitution would have stood no chance whatsoever of being ratified if his radical vision of unequivocal federal sovereignty had prevailed. And this recognition then led him to a counterintuitive insight every bit as provocative as his argument for the greater stability of a large or extended republic; namely, there was no single source of sovereignty in the new Constitution. What he had initially regarded as the great failure at the Constitutional Convention—the coexistence of federal and state claims to authority—was, albeit inadvertently, in fact the great achievement.[35]

This was an interpretation of the new Constitution with far-reaching political and philosophical implications, for it not only defied the classical assumption—as old as Aristotle—that every government must have one supreme and final source of authority, but also transformed the Constitution from a clear blueprint for a nation-size republic to a framework for debate in which arguments about federal versus state sovereignty would continue forevermore. Indeed, argument itself became the abiding solution, and ambiguity the great asset that ensured the argument could never end, making the Constitution an inherently "living document" that successive generations would interpret in light of changing historical circumstances.

Madison did not reach this conclusion freely or willfully. It was, in fact, forced on him by the opponents of ratification in the state conventions, who described the proposed federal government as a "consolidation." This was a loaded term previously used against the British ministry to mean a concentrated source of political power that, once in place, devoured the liberties of all citizens in a relentless display of unstoppable avarice, corruption, and tyranny. The prowess of the "consolidation" argument, which had quasi-paranoid dimensions, derived from its association with the hallowed opposition to British imperialism. Thus Madison needed to counter it in order to blunt the charge that the advocates of ratification were imposing a domestic version of the British leviathan so recently and dramatically destroyed.[36]

The first sign of Madison's shift in thinking occurred in late January 1788, in three essays written for the Federalist Papers, where he took up the charge of "consolidation." His major argument was that the charge was unfounded because sovereignty had *not* been transferred from the state to the federal level in the proposed Constitution. Instead, the states retained many of the functions they enjoyed under the Articles, to include representation in the Senate, control over selection of electors in the Electoral College, and final authority over the ratification of both the Constitution itself and all subsequent constitutional amendments.

In previous descriptions of the division of jurisdiction between federal and state governments, he had emphasized "the clear line of demarcation" granting the federal government "primary responsibility for General purposes," leaving the states to perform functions he described as "subordinately useful." Now the line itself was blurry, and the new emphasis was on the persistent role of the states, especially when it came to domestic policy. In some of his earlier remarks Madison had also hinted at the possibility that the Supreme Court might be the ultimate arbiter of constitutional disagreements, but now he seemed to suggest that each branch of the government would decide such questions for itself. The watchword for the new Constitution, he insisted, was not "consolidation" but "diffusion."[37]

Madison's fullest explanation of his new interpretive posture toward the Constitution came at the Virginia ratifying convention in Richmond five months later. Once again, he was responding to criticism that the new federal government rode roughshod over the venerable authority of the states, a position now argued with considerable passion by Patrick Henry, the greatest orator of the age. Henry had no doubt that Madison was defending the creation of "one consolidated empire in America . . . whose features, Sir, appear to me horribly frightful."[38]

In response, Madison repeated the arguments he made in the Federalist Papers about the limits imposed on federal power and the hybrid character of the proposed Constitution. "It is in a matter unprecedented," he claimed, "it stands by itself. In some respects it is a government of a federal nature; in others it is of a consolidated nature." He added that the phrase "We the people" referred not to the people composing one great body but to the people living and voting in thirteen separate sovereignties. This was a huge concession on Madison's part, and a complete reversal of the nationalist position he had championed in Philadelphia the previous summer.

But in the same way that the debates at the Constitutional Convention were resolved by compromises that no one, Madison included, found fulfilling, the debates over ratification forced modifications in Madison's version of how the document should be understood. All of which throws a cloud of confusion over all pursuits of the original meaning of the document itself, in part because his position kept shifting, in part because the shifts were not voluntary changes of mind but rather mandatory adjustments to changing political circumstances. In that sense, Madison's claim that the Constitution should be regarded as a "living document" was an accurate description of his own evolution as one of its most dedicated defenders.[39]

The same pragmatic mentality propelled him through the final stages of his most creative phase, the drafting of the Bill of Rights. While a strong case can be made for Madison as "Father of the Constitution," there are other plausible candidates for the title, chiefly Gouverneur Morris. Moreover, Madison lost most of the debates he considered crucial. But no such qualifications apply to the title "Father of the Bill of Rights." Madison drafted the original list of rights single-handedly, and while the House and Senate reshuffled his words, and the states refused to ratify two of his proposed amendments, it is fair to say that the original ten amendments now called the Bill of Rights were a thoroughly Madisonian creation.[40]

Our pursuit of the historical Madison, then, should conclude with a final focus on his thought process in the spring and early summer of 1789. Two things had changed since the end of the ratification debates: first, Patrick Henry had used his influence over the Virginia legislature to block Madison's election to the Senate but could not prevent his election as a representative to the House; second, Madison had become a more conspicuous star in the American political firmament, no longer regarded as the behind-the-scenes operative counting noses and massaging egos. Washington asked him to draft his inaugural welcome to the Congress; then the House, unaware of Madison's confidential role, asked him to draft the response, making the initial exchange of political pleasantries a case of Madison writing to Madison.[41]

He was on record, throughout the ratification process, asserting that a Bill of Rights was unnecessary, chiefly because the federal government possessed only enumerated powers, and explicit guarantees of personal rights were superfluous, since they were already embedded in the state constitutions. Moreover, assembling a list of rights could be dangerous, he had argued, because such a list might not prove sufficiently comprehensive. The more prosaic truth was that the delegates in Philadelphia had not provided a Bill of Rights primarily because by September 1787 they were exhausted and wanted to go home. As the debates in the ratifying conventions made clear, this was a huge mistake, which many critics of the Constitution cited as its most glaring weakness.

Jefferson weighed in from his perch in Paris, also arguing that the absence of a bill of rights was a fatal flaw in the document because it performed the essential function of defining what government could *not* do, thereby creating a permanent zone where individual rights could roam free of surveillance or restriction by kings, judges, or legislators. Madison disagreed with his friend and mentor, suggesting that Jefferson's problem was his misguided fear that the primary threat to individual rights came from government. That was true in Europe, Madison argued, "but in our Governments the real power lies in the majority of the community," so the real threat came "from acts in which the Government is the mere instrument of the major numbers of the constituents." As a result, Madison insisted that "a bill of rights, however strongly marked on paper, will never be regarded when opposed to the decided sense of the public." All bills of rights in the state constitutions, he observed, were only "parchment barriers" that were routinely ignored "by overbearing majorities in every state," most especially in Virginia, "where the Declaration of Rights has been violated in every instance where it has been opposed to a popular current."[42]

Jefferson and Madison were clearly looking at the question of individual rights through different ends of the telescope. Madison's view made no sense within a Jeffersonian universe because Madison presumed that the great danger came from popular majorities, which Jefferson found unimaginable. It is also clear that Madison did not yet embrace the role of the Supreme Court as an ultimate arbiter of either the Constitution or the Bill of Rights. All of which, as Madison saw it, made the whole question of a bill of rights superfluous. "I have never thought its omission a material defect," he declared, "and I have not viewed it in an important light."[43]

By January 1789, however, soon after his election to the House, Madison had changed his mind, or at least changed his political agenda. "It is my sincere desire," he vowed, "that the Constitution ought to be revised, and that the first Congress meeting under it ought to prepare and recommend to the States for ratification, the most satisfactory provisions for all essential rights, particularly the rights of conscience in the fullest latitude, the freedom of the press, trials by jury, security against general warrants, etc." Not only that, but he would personally undertake the task of preparing the list for congressional approval. Obviously, something had changed.[44]

It was not Madison's dismissive attitude toward the Jeffersonian idea of a bill of rights as the American version of Magna Carta. He never abandoned his belief that popular opinion would easily overwhelm any mere listing of individual rights. What changed was his enhanced appreciation of all those states, Virginia included, whose reservations in the form of recommended amendments to the Constitution made them lukewarm supporters of the new government. He had experienced such reservations firsthand during his congressional campaign in Virginia, where he came under enormous pressure to promise that he would support at least some of the forty amendments proposed by the opposition at the Virginia ratifying convention. More ominously, he worried that Antifederalist leaders like Henry and Clinton would play on the doubts of the disaffected to revive their idea of a "second convention," which was only a disguised attempt to undermine the hard-won victory in the ratification debates. As he put it to Jefferson, perhaps a bill of rights would conciliate the faint of heart and "extinguish opposition to the system, or at least break the force of it by detaching the deluded opponents from their designing leaders."[45]

He offered a more diplomatic version of his motives in a subsequent speech in the House:

> It cannot be a secret to the gentlemen of this house, that notwithstanding the ratification of this system of government by eleven of the thirteen United States [Rhode Island and North Carolina remained outliers], yet there is a great number of our constituents who are dissatisfied with it; among whom are many respectable for their talents, their patriotism, and for the jealousy they have for their liberties. There is a great body of the people falling under this discription. . . . We ought not to disregard their inclination [but rather] conform to their wishes, and expressly declare the great rights of mankind secured under this constitution.[46]

In truth, Madison did not believe that any effort to "declare the great rights of mankind" in the Constitution would make any appreciable difference in expanding the range of freedom for American citizens. His intention in the spring of 1789 was to maximize support for the new government and outflank those opponents—Patrick Henry was the chief culprit—who hoped to undermine it. He regarded the Bill of Rights less as a philosophical statement than as a political tactic.

Madison's political agenda dictated the way he went about drafting the Bill of Rights in March and April 1789. The list of prospective amendments he compiled was drawn from the Virginia Constitution and the pool of amendments recommended by the ratifying conventions in those states where the margin of victory was provided by reluctant supporters. There were nearly two hundred recommended amendments, but many were duplications, leaving a residue of about one hundred—depending on how you count—from which to choose.

As Madison worked through the possible candidates for inclusion, he tended to prefer the standard set of rights already enshrined in the state constitutions. The major ones included the right of free speech, a free press, freedom of religion, freedom from unwarranted searches and seizures, the right to a jury trial within a reasonable period of time, and the explicit presumption—declared in the Articles—that powers not delegated to the federal government were reserved for the states. As a result, the Madison list represented a codification of rights based on the previous thirty years of American history, most especially the lessons learned in opposing the policies of the British ministry in the run-up to the Declaration of Independence. What has come to be regarded as a set of timeless truths was, in fact, a distillation of the political experience of the revolutionary generation.

The special status the Bill of Rights has enjoyed over the ensuing years is in large part a function of its placement as a separate document, in effect an elegiac epilogue to the Constitution. But that is not what Madison originally intended, which was to insert amendments into the text. "There is a neatness and propriety in incorporating the amendments to the Constitution itself," he explained, "so that the amendments are interwoven into those parts in which they naturally belong." If he had succeeded in doing what he planned, the long and still ongoing debate in the Supreme Court concerning federal jurisdiction over the states based on the Bill of Rights would be moot. But partly because the editorial task of corkscrewing the added amendments into the Constitution proved a daunting task, and mostly because, as Roger Sherman of Connecticut pointed out in the subsequent debate in the House, Madison's preferred scheme would have altered the document the framers in Philadelphia had signed without their authorization, he was forced to abandon the effort. The net result was to feature the Bill of Rights as a codicil rather than bury it within the original text. Despite its conspicuous location at the end, the first ten amendments did not receive a separate title as the "Bill of Rights" until Franklin Roosevelt popularized the term in the 1930s.[47]

The list Madison proposed to the House in May 1789 consisted of nine amendments. The House unbundled several of his composite paragraphs to produce seventeen amendments, which the Senate rebundled to twelve, ten of which were ratified by the states in 1791. It is only a slight exaggeration to regard the debates in the House and Senate as a reshuffling of the cards that Madison had dealt them. And since our overarching goal is to recover Madison's mentality, now in the final stage of its most creative contribution, the obvious focus should be his original list of amendments and the editorial process he used to distill the much longer list of recommended amendments to his final nine. Many of his choices, as noted, were obvious repetitions of rights already articulated in state constitutions that embodied the political principles learned during the conflict with British imperial policy in the 1760s and 1770s. But there were three choices he made that defy the obvious pattern and therefore merit special scrutiny.

First, he dropped altogether an amendment to regard federal tax requests as voluntary rather than mandatory. Each state suggested a different scheme whereby the state and federal governments might negotiate their differences, but the central idea was to blur the sovereignty question on the essential question of taxation. Since this amendment struck at the heart of the union by threatening to render permanent the fiscal chaos under the Articles, Madison simply ignored it. The most outspoken critics of the Constitution took Madison to task for failing to include this amendment, arguing that it exposed his true intention, which was to appease the maximum number of voters in the Congress and state legislatures by making the minimum number of concessions. And that, in truth, was precisely Madison's goal.

Second, Madison proposed an amendment of his own that no state had recommended: "No state shall violate the equal rights of conscience or the freedom of the press, or the trial by jury in criminal cases." Madison was attempting to implement his conviction that the most serious threats to individual rights would come from the states, not the federal government. So here we have another instance in which Madison endorsed federal jurisdiction over the states to protect individual rights in a manner that the Supreme Court did not recognize until the 1930s. Indeed, Madison claimed that "this is the most valuable amendment on the whole list." But the Senate deleted it for the same reason Madison valued it so highly: it was a conspicuous projection of federal authority over the domestic policy of the states.[48]

Third, five states had recommended an amendment calling for the prohibition of a standing army on the grounds that it had historically proven to be an enduring threat to republican values. Many critics of the Constitution were deeply troubled by language in Article 1, Section 8 describing the powers of Congress to "provide for the common Defense and general Welfare of the United States." Two specific provisions were regarded as ominous projections of federal jurisdiction over the militia-based military establishments of the states: first, giving Congress the authority "to raise and support armies," despite the caveat that "no Appropriations of money to that Use shall be for a longer term than two years"; second, granting Congress the power "to provide for calling forth the Militia to execute the Laws of the Union, and suppress Insurrections and repel Invasions." In the Virginia ratifying convention, Madison had been forced to listen as Patrick Henry conjured up apocalyptic scenarios in which the Virginia militia were ordered out of the state to support military operations in faraway places that citizens of the Old Dominion considered misguided deployments in foreign countries.

One of the recommended amendments Virginia submitted for consideration in 1788 reflected Henry's concern on this score, drawing on language contained in the Declaration of Rights in its own state constitution: "The people have a right to keep and bear arms; that a well-regulated militia composed of the body of the people trained to arms is the proper national, natural, and safe defense of a free state. That standing armies in times of peace are dangerous to liberty, and therefore ought to be avoided." Madison clearly had Virginia's recommended amendment on his desk and in his mind when he drafted the following words: "The right of the people to keep and bear arms shall not be infringed; a well armed and well regulated militia being the best security of a free country; but no person religiously scrupulous of bearing arms shall be compelled to render military service in person."[49]

During the debate in the House, Elbridge Gerry of Massachusetts solidified his reputation as a revolutionary gadfly by envisioning the sudden conversion of the citizenry to the Quaker faith whenever war loomed. His protestations led to the deletion of Madison's clause endorsing conscientious objector status. For unspecified reasons, the Senate reversed the first two clauses in Madison's draft, which grammatically clarified the rationale for the right to bear arms, thus the Second Amendment: "A well regulated militia, being necessary to the security of a free state, the right of the people to keep and bear arms, shall not be infringed."

By nodding toward a primary role for the militia, Madison had appeased some of his Antifederalist critics, but he had not satisfied those like Henry who wanted an unambiguous statement that the state legislatures, not the Congress, enjoyed sovereign control over their own citizenry in times of war. Creating ambiguity, in fact, was the centerpiece of Madison's political agenda. During the debates over ratification that ensued in the House and Senate, as well as in those state legislatures that kept a record, considerable attention focused on a current proposal from Secretary of War Henry Knox, calling for a professional army of unspecified size, which opponents described as a violation of the Second Amendment.

In 1792, soon after the first ten amendments were ratified, Congress passed the Militia Act. It required every able-bodied white male citizen between the age of eighteen and forty-five to enroll in a state militia. It also required them to purchase a gun as well as a complete outfit of equipment essential to perform their military duties, thereby making gun ownership not an individual right but a legal obligation. For those disposed to unpack the Second Amendment for the original meaning of "bear arms," it has collective implications that lead not toward the right to own a gun, but toward mandatory national service. In that sense, both Madison and the critics he sought to appease were living in a world forever lost to us.[50]

—✦—

Although what we have called "Madison's Moment" ended in 1789, his life continued for another forty-seven years and featured two dramatic reversals of the constitutional positions he had taken earlier. The first occurred in the 1790s, when he performed a breathtaking turnabout to oppose Alexander Hamilton's fiscal program, especially the National Bank, and in 1799 authored the Virginia Resolutions, which echoed the arguments for states' rights that Patrick Henry had made so eloquently at the Virginia ratifying convention and that Madison had so deftly opposed. Then, during the Nullification Crisis (1828), he backtracked again, rejecting any association with the secessionist arguments of John C. Calhoun, in which Calhoun cited the Virginia Resolutions as the bedrock precedent for his claim of state sovereignty. Secession, Madison insisted, was not what he had ever had in mind.[51]

In some larger historical sense, Madison remained consistent, since the dominant pattern of his intellectual life was to release his creative energies in response to specific crises that history presented, always poised to shift his position to accommodate what the evolving political context required. He regarded such shifts not so much as contradictions as political adaptations of principle to changing conditions. This, it turned out, perhaps not so coincidentally, just happened to be the adaptive genius of the Constitution itself.

Immaculate Misconceptions

When a case comes to me, I don't do whatever I feel like doing, I have a standard. That standard is what would the people at the time the Constitution was enacted have said.

Antonin Scalia, Speech at the University of Fribourg,
March 8, 2008

. . .

Some men look at constitutions with sanctimonious reverence, and deem them, like the ark of the covenant, too sacred to be touched. . . . We might as well require a man to wear still the coat which fitted him when a boy, as civilized society to remain under the regimen of their barbarous ancestors.

Thomas Jefferson to Samuel Kercheval, July 12, 1816

For most of American history, the Supreme Court only infrequently stepped forward to redefine the American political landscape in decisive and dramatic fashion. And interestingly, the two most conspicuous occasions both involved the great American dilemma of race.

In *Dred Scott v. Sandford* (1857) the Supreme Court overturned two federal laws, the Missouri Compromise (1819) and the Compromise of 1850, to rule that freed slaves could never become citizens and that the federal government had no authority to limit the expansion of slavery in the western territories. Chief Justice Taney based his opinion on his interpretation of the intent of the framers of the Constitution, an interpretation that Abraham Lincoln vehemently challenged in his Cooper Union speech (1860). Taney's implicit motive was to offer a legal resolution of the politically insoluble problem of slavery, in effect endorsing its anomalous persistence within the American republic. Nevertheless, *Dred Scott* helped to make the Civil War virtually inevitable. And primarily for that reason, it is generally regarded by historians and legal scholars as among the worst Supreme Court decisions in American history.

Almost a century later, in *Brown v. Board of Education* (1954), the Supreme Court struck down the legal justification for racial segregation of schools in *Plessy v. Ferguson* (1896). The *Brown* decision had expansive implications in several senses: legally, it further extended the application of the Bill of Rights to the states, in this case finding that school segregation violated the Fourteenth Amendment; politically and socially, it made the Supreme Court an agent of change by placing segregation on the permanent defensive at a time when a clear majority of the white citizenry in the American South were reluctant to accept the inevitability of racial integration.

Unlike those in *Dred Scott*, however, the justices in *Brown* did not rest their verdict on the intentions or language of the framers, acknowledging that the original meaning of the Fourteenth Amendment with regard to segregated schools was at best problematic. Instead, they cited evidence based on several recent sociological studies, concluding that segregation by race in schools was inherently discriminatory. Again, unlike *Dred Scott*, subsequent American history has endorsed the wisdom of *Brown*, which is generally regarded as the landmark Supreme Court decision of the twentieth century because it launched the movement for a racially integrated American society.

If only in retrospect, the *Brown* decision signaled a shift in the political templates by which the Supreme Court became the dominant branch of the federal government in determining the direction of

American domestic policy. None of the original framers of the Constitution could have imagined this development, save perhaps Alexander Hamilton, who glimpsed it in Federalist 78, where he recognized the power of the judicial branch to rule on the legality of state and federal legislation; or perhaps John Marshall, who as chief justice established the principle of "judicial review," whereby the Supreme Court became the ultimate arbiter of the Constitution, thereby elevating the judicial branch of government to coequal status with the legislative and executive branches.

But if you read the debates among the delegates at the Constitutional Convention, then read their prescription for judicial power in Article III of the Constitution, it becomes clear that the last thing the thirty-nine signers of the Constitution wanted was for the Supreme Court to become supreme. They presumed that that status belonged to Congress, and a majority thought that each branch of the government should and could decide the scope of its own authority. The last place they preferred to place sovereignty over the document they drafted that summer in 1787 was the Supreme Court, the most unrepresentative branch of the government and the most removed from the wellspring of ultimate authority called "the People."

⊷ ⚊⚌⚊ ⊷

The judicial revolution launched by *Brown* proceeded in a liberal direction for nearly thirty years. The liberal wave was based on the belief that federal judges were interpreting a "Living Constitution" that obliged them to adjust its meaning to evolving standards of justice. Landmark decisions in this liberal tradition envisioned the American founding as a truly creative moment that rejected the medieval values that had shaped European history for over a thousand years, replacing them with laws that vested unprecedented rights in individual citizens. The evolutionary expansions of those rights, including the elimination of the property requirement to vote, the ending of slavery, and the inclusion of women and African Americans as enfranchised citizens, were, according to this way of thinking, all logical and necessary extensions of human rights enshrined in the Declaration of Independence and codified in the Bill of Rights.

Two iconic figures in American history endorsed this expansive interpretation. Although Abraham Lincoln challenged the conclusion in *Dred Scott* by arguing that most of the framers of the Constitution were on the record as opposing slavery and its extension, he also based his repudiation of slavery on the belief that Jefferson's words in the Declaration of Independence, not the Constitution, defined the moral agenda and the creedal convictions of the revolutionary generation. "All honor to Jefferson," he wrote, "to the man who, in the concrete pressure of a struggle for national independence by a single people, had the coolness, forecast, and capacity to introduce into a merely revolutionary document, an abstract truth [i.e., that all men are created equal], and to embalm it there, that to-day and in all coming days, it shall be a revoke and a stumbling-block to the very harbingers of reappearing tyranny and oppression."

The seminal source for the belief in a "Living Constitution" is none other than Jefferson himself. The messy truth is that a diligent reader of the letters and documents written by the most prominent founders can find pretty much what he or she is looking for, but Jefferson's testimony near the end of his life possesses a resonance and relevance difficult to ignore:

> Some men look at constitutions with sanctimonious reverence, and deem them, like the ark of the covenant, too sacred to be touched. They ascribe to the men of the preceding age a wisdom more than human, and suppose what they did to be beyond amendment. I know that age well; I belonged to it, and labored with it. It deserved well of its country. . . . But I know also that laws and institutions must go hand in hand with the progress of the human mind. . . . We might as well require a man to wear still the coat which fitted him when a boy, as civilized society to remain under the regimen of their barbarous ancestors.

Under the light shone by these impeccable sources, the liberal agenda of the Supreme Court proceeded apace through the 1960s and into the 1970s. Landmark rulings expanded the rights of criminal suspects, affirmed that all electoral districts must reflect the principle of "one man, one vote," and broadened the definition of free speech. The two most consequential (and controversial) decisions involved the right to privacy, a right that only the most inventive justices could discover in the language of the Constitution. In *Griswold v. Connecticut* (1965) the court struck down a law prohibiting the sale of contraceptives on privacy grounds. And in *Roe v. Wade* (1973), building on the privacy principle declared in *Griswold*, it affirmed a woman's right to abortion during the first trimester. The prevailing assumption of this liberal agenda was that there was an ongoing American Dialogue between the founding and the present in which judges on the Supreme Court were required to translate the original language of the founders in order to accommodate the evolving standards of justice over time.

Perhaps, given the back-and-forth pattern of American politics, a conservative reaction to the liberal wave of judicial activism was inevitable. At any rate, an assault on the liberal belief in the "Living Constitution" began in several law schools, chiefly the University of Chicago. The new judicial doctrine was called "originalism." The founding father of the new creed was Robert Bork, an undergraduate and law student at Chicago whose core idea was that the true meaning of the Constitution, which he believed had been perverted by liberal judges with their expansive agenda, resided in the original intentions of the framers.

Originalism was very much a product of the curricular culture at the University of Chicago, where mandatory reading of the Great Books was a long-standing tradition, and close study of ancient Greek and Roman texts purportedly provided unique access to the classical origins of Western civilization. Bork's doctrine of originalism embraced the same text-based model and the same classical assumptions, though for Bork the core text became the Constitution and the fountainhead of eternal wisdom became the founding era. Seen in this light, originalism was an intriguing if somewhat eccentric school of thought, likely to enjoy some measure of influence in the classrooms and corridors of elite law schools, then fade into the middle distance when the next fashionable theory came along.

What rescued originalism from that customary fate was its utility as a weapon in the ongoing war between liberals and conservatives on the bench and beyond. In three specific ways, originalism was a godsend to conservative opponents of the liberal triumph embodied in those Supreme Court decisions stretching from *Brown* to *Roe* and the legislative legacy of the New Deal. First, originalism provided a seminal source of philosophical authority that placed all advocates of the "Living Constitution" on the permanent defensive by stigmatizing their interpretations as latter-day impositions of their political agenda, while originalists posed as detached students of the pristine values embedded in the document itself. Second, originalism was an avowedly conservative judicial doctrine with radical potential, for all those liberal precedents now on the books and protected by the conservative principle *stare decisis* (i.e., let the decision stand) became vulnerable, because they violated the original meaning of the Constitution, which trumped all subsequent decisions by mere mortals on the Supreme Court. Third, the appearance of originalism in the early 1970s coincided with the emergence of a highly orchestrated and fully financed corporate campaign by the New Right to wrest control of the national debate over the power of the federal government from liberals, who had dominated the debate for the past half century.

Jane Mayer has chronicled that campaign in *Dark Money* (2016), which identifies Lewis Powell, a Richmond attorney and soon-to-be Supreme Court justice, as the unlikely architect of the conservative strategy that would enjoy such resounding success over the ensuing decades. In a long memorandum entitled "Attack on the American Free Enterprise System" (1971), Powell laid out his blueprint for "guerrilla war" to capture the citadels of liberal influence in academia, the media, and the courts. It began with a steady flow of money from the wealthiest members of the corporate elite, which would then be funneled through philanthropic foundations—thus "dark money"—to newly created think tanks explicitly committed to conservative or libertarian principles. Over the next decade, the Heritage Foundation, the American Enterprise Institute, and the Cato Institute became the institutional embodiments of Powell's strategy. In 1982 a $5 million start-up grant from the Olin Foundation created the Federalist Society at Yale as a network for conservative law students, lawyers, and judges. The legal principle binding its members together was originalism.*

A pivotal moment in the conservative surge occurred in July 1985, when Attorney General Edwin Meese delivered an address before the American Bar Association. Meese endorsed the doctrine of original intent, which he also called "original meaning," describing it as a truly detached approach to jurisprudence, vastly preferable to the inherently politicized, judge-oriented philosophy of previous liberal courts, and therefore the proper criterion for all subsequent nominees to the Supreme Court by the Reagan administration.

The conservative wave in fact represented a continuation of the judicial activism of the previous liberal wave, this time driven by a conservative agenda. Both the liberal court under Chief Justice Earl Warren and the conservative court under Chief Justice John Roberts

---

*There is a range of originalist opinion within the Federalist Society, which now boasts a roster of more than 40,000 members at 150 law schools. All Republican-appointed justices on the Supreme Court are members. The definition of originalism has shifted from "original intentions" to "original meanings," which in practice expands the targeted group of seminal sources from the 55 framers in Philadelphia and roughly 1,600 delegates at the ratifying conventions to the entire citizenry in 1787–88, about 800,000 souls. This change avoids dependence on the most prominent founders, who almost to a man denounced being mythologized, and it also creates a sufficiently large pool of "original meanings" to ensure that assiduous law clerks can find whatever they are looking for. Whether the rationale is "intentions" or "meanings," the core claim of all originalists is that contemporary standards of justice cannot take precedence over the values, convictions, and ideas that prevailed when the Constitution was written and ratified.

contributed to the expansion of judicial power at the expense of the legislative and executive branches of the federal government. Both embraced judicial philosophies granting the Supreme Court almost unlimited power to alter or subvert long-standing legal precedents and social mores.

The devotees of a "Living Constitution" could plausibly find reasons to expand a woman's right to choose, make health care a right of citizenship, and reject all state laws prohibiting gay marriage. Ardent originalists could plausibly find both *Roe* and *Brown* unconstitutional, as well as all New Deal legislation that empowered the federal government to regulate the economy in redistributive ways, to include Social Security. Indeed, it had become received wisdom that the single most consequential power of the presidency was now the power to nominate judges to the Supreme Court.

The political direction of the conservative court became clear in three controversial decisions during the first decade of the twenty-first century. In *Bush v. Gore* (2001), the new conservative majority read the tea leaves of a baffling Florida statute in such a way as to award the presidency to George W. Bush, the only time in American history that the Supreme Court had exercised that power. In *District of Columbia v. Heller* (2008), the majority opinion by Justice Antonin Scalia, the most outspoken originalist on the court, overturned two centuries of legal precedents to find that the Second Amendment sanctioned the right to bear arms except in the rarest of circumstances. And then in *Citizens United v. Federal Election Commission* (2010), this time overturning a century of precedents, the court found that all federal restrictions on corporate giving to political campaigns were unconstitutional violations of the First Amendment right to free speech.

Taken together, or perhaps taken one after the other, the liberal and conservative waves of lawmaking gave the Supreme Court a conspicuous place of prominence in our political culture. It came at a price. For most of American history, the court had enjoyed special status as the one branch of government that levitated above the hurly-burly of partisan politics in some transcendent realm reserved for demigods.

The Supreme Court, in effect, enjoyed the same kind of privileged treatment that was accorded the founding generation. In both cases a kind of electromagnetic field surrounded the judges on our highest court and the political elite that was "present at the creation." One of the most seductive appeals of the originalist persuasion was the claim to derive its judicial insights from founders who allegedly enjoyed privileged access to eternal truths. After all, why ascribe such enduring significance to the original words or intentions of the framers if you did not regard them, or the historical moment in which they lived, as semi-sacred?

Both deifications were always illusions, though extremely useful ones. For the same bundle of reasons that most mortals need to believe in eternity, most new nations require mythical heroes. Similarly, it is comforting to believe that all controversial and divisive political questions can be sent to a trusted tribunal composed of godlike judges who possess a preternatural affinity for the truth.

Whatever useful purposes such illusions might have once served, over the past half century the scholarship on the founders and the blatantly political character of the Supreme Court makes them untenable. To repeat, the American founding, most especially the drafting and ratification of the Constitution, was always a messy moment populated by mere mortals, whose chief task was to fashion a series of artful political compromises. And the Supreme Court had never floated above the American political landscape like a disembodied cloud of heavenly wisdom. It always was a political institution comprised of human beings with no special connection to the divine. Both illusions were now exposed as childish fables.

→ ⚞ ←

In the ongoing debate between advocates of a "Living Constitution" and originalists, several mitigating factors prevent the most extreme version of each doctrinal position from coming into play. The vast majority of Supreme Court decisions do not involve significant constitutional issues with vast historical consequences, and in many of those cases the votes are often unanimous opinions that defy doctrinal adjudication. There is also an unspoken understanding among judges on both sides of the political divide that the court should only rarely impose its verdicts in opposition to widespread public opinion, though both *Brown* and *Citizens United* are exceptions to this rule. For example, liberals were predisposed to wait for a sufficient number of lower court decisions on gay rights before ruling on that controversial question. And conservatives recognize that it would be politically dangerous to deploy their originalist arguments against *Brown* or a case questioning the constitutionality of Social Security.

That said, there is a fundamental difference between the two sides of this judicial debate. The liberal devotees of a "Living Constitution" are transparent about their political agenda, but the conservative originalists are not. While the judicial doctrine of the originalists was explicitly designed as a weapon to overturn liberal precedents, its core claim is its assiduous political detachment. At least on the face of it, that claim is incompatible with the series of one-sided decisions made by the conservative majority in the twenty-first century. This was the reason why the usually understated Justice William Brennan described originalism as "arrogance cloaked as humility."

＊━━◄◆►━━＊

The fullest illustration of the originalist approach in its purest form is the decision by Justice Antonin Scalia in *District of Columbia v. Heller* (2008). Scalia, the most outspoken advocate for the originalist doctrine on the Supreme Court, described *Heller* as his magnum opus, "the most complete originalist opinion that I have ever written." *Heller* was indeed a landmark decision that overturned two centuries of legal precedents to find that the Second Amendment recognized the right to bear arms as an individual right on a par with the right to free speech.

The case could have been decided on narrower, less expansive grounds. Joseph Heller was a security guard who wanted to bring his handgun home for self-defense but was prohibited from doing so by restrictions on handguns imposed by the District of Columbia, which included mandatory trigger locks. But Scalia and other conservative members of the court were in fact looking for an opportunity to expand the interpretation of the Second Amendment. The decision to hear the *Heller* case represented a recognition that the legal opportunity to achieve that goal had arrived. Assigning the majority opinion to Scalia ensured a verdict for the originalist persuasion.

Context is crucial. *Heller* was not some surprising airburst in the night but the culmination of a decades-long campaign orchestrated and funded by the National Rifle Association (NRA) to make gun ownership a right of citizenship. In that sense, *Heller* was to the conservative cause what *Brown* was to the liberal cause. Just as the NAACP waged a long legal and political battle against racial segregation that culminated in the Supreme Court decision that ended segregation by race in public schools, the NRA waged a similar and more heavily funded campaign to remove all legal restrictions on the right to purchase, own, and carry guns. Both *Heller* and *Brown* represented the final triumph in a long-standing, well-disciplined, highly organized struggle that both the NAACP and NRA knew could end only at the Supreme Court.

In retrospect, given what the NRA was up against, the speed of its successful campaign is stunning. Throughout the 1960s, polls showed that between 50 and 60 percent of Americans favored an outright ban on handguns. Moreover, judicial opinion on the Second Amendment was considered "settled law," meaning that all the legal precedents, most recently synthesized in *U.S. v. Miller* (1939), found that the right to bear arms in the Second Amendment was conditional upon service in the militia and therefore did not constitute a nearly unlimited individual right. When Chief Justice Warren Burger, a conservative appointed by Richard Nixon, was asked if the Second Amendment guaranteed open-ended access to guns, he expressed amazement: "This has been the subject of one of the greatest pieces of fraud, I repeat the word 'fraud,' on the American public by special interest groups that I have ever seen in my lifetime."

But the political templates were already shifting, thanks in part to relentless pressure from NRA spokesmen but mostly because the new-found right to bear arms coincided with the libertarian agenda of the New Right, subsidized by the unprecedented flow of money provided by the Koch brothers and their conservative think tanks. As early as 1980, the Republican platform proclaimed its conversion: "We believe the right of citizens to keep and bear arms must be preserved. Accordingly, we oppose federal registration of firearms." A year later Senator Orrin Hatch, chair of the Judiciary Committee, announced the new Republican dogma that "the Second Amendment sanctioned an individual right to keep and carry arms."

As the ideological message of the New Right moved from the fringe to the center of the Republican Party, the more expansive version of the Second Amendment became the acid test for the antigovernment agenda. The great fear in this rendering was that government agents were coming to take your guns. By 2008, on the eve of the *Heller* decision, a Gallup poll showed that 73 percent of the citizenry believed the Second Amendment "guaranteed the right of Americans to own guns." By then it had become rude to notice that the words on the plaque at NRA headquarters—"the right of the people to keep and bear arms shall not be infringed"—had deleted the preceding clause about service in the militia.

One wing of the conservative campaign to capture public opinion focused its efforts on the law schools. In the 1990s the NRA paid three lawyers nearly $1 million to write thirty articles for law reviews, all designed to generate an alternative body of legal scholarship. Unlike historical journals, where submissions must undergo peer review, law school publications are run by students, so there is no editorial screening provided by academic professionals in the field. The result was a new wave of legal and historical scholarship of dubious accuracy, multiple misquotations, and sometimes comical conclusions that its advocates began to call the "Standard Model." The term described a set of shared historical distortions that soon began to invoke, then to celebrate, an unambiguous right to own guns.

Within this new historical universe, for example, the English Bill of Rights (1688) purportedly declared that all Englishmen enjoyed the right to bear arms. In fact, the Glorious Revolution restored the right to bear arms to Protestants with wealth "suitable to their conditions," a right previously denied by James II. It also became received wisdom that the Second Amendment was in part motivated by bitter memories of British patrols going house to house during the American Revolution, disarming potential rebels. But there is no record of any such confiscations of muskets ever occurring before or during the war. Patrick Henry became a new hero, and the NRA paid $1 million to endow a chair in his name at George Mason Law School with a plaque quoting Henry's famous words: "the great object is that every man is armed." Unfortunately, Henry never said that. The misquotation comes from a speech in which Henry was complaining about the excessive cost of arming a large militia. Nor did Henry ever say, as some publicity for the endowed chair claimed, that "they want to take away your guns." At the Virginia ratifying convention he did say, reportedly to gales of laughter, "They'll take your niggers from you."

By the time Antonin Scalia and his law clerks began to draft what became the majority opinion in *Heller*, public opinion on the meaning of the Second Amendment had shifted dramatically. Thanks to the orchestrated efforts by the NRA, with an able assist from the bottomless coffers of libertarian philanthropists and their think tanks on the New Right, a more expansive understanding of the Second Amendment had become the new political orthodoxy. Within the Republican Party it was now an unquestionable article of faith. And even Democratic candidates for national office were required to skirt the edges of the gun issue. Moreover, an impressive body of new evidence had been deftly planted in the legal scholarship that was now available for harvesting by assiduous law clerks with a clear set of marching orders.

If that is the proper context for understanding the *Heller* decision, the ironies abound. For while Scalia went to his grave devoutly believing that *Heller* was the ultimate expression of his originalist philosophy of jurisprudence, it was in fact an excellent example of the principle of a "Living Constitution," the very approach he denigrated and despised. Reva Siegel of Yale Law School was the first to point out the irony of it all by noticing that the argument made in *Heller* depended almost entirely on legal evidence generated in recent decades and, most blatantly, on the shift in popular opinion toward gun ownership over the same time. The deeper truth, which Scalia had devoted his entire career to denying, was that all judges, like all historians, cannot escape the fact that they are viewing the past through the prism of the present. And *Heller* represented the judicial version of a new understanding of the Second Amendment, albeit an understanding achieved in a deftly orchestrated fashion. In that sense, all judges, Scalia included, are invariably and inevitably interpreting a "Living Constitution," because they are rendering their opinions as living, breathing residents of now.

That said, it was in fact possible to render an originalist interpretation of the Second Amendment in *Heller*. There is no need to conjure up such an opinion because Justice John Paul Stevens wrote it in his impassioned dissent. "The Second Amendment was adopted to protect the right of the people of each of the several states to maintain a well-regulated militia," he declared.

It was a response to concerns raised during the ratification of the Constitution that the power of Congress to disarm the state militias and create a national standing army posed an intolerable threat to the sovereignty of the several states. Neither the text of the Amendment nor the arguments advanced by its proponents evidenced the slightest interest in limiting any legislature's authority to regulate private civilian uses of firearms. Specifically, there is no indication that the Framers of the Amendment intended to enshrine the common-law right of self-defense in the Constitution.

With a few minor caveats, Stevens's opinion accurately summarizes what Madison and his fellow founders thought they were doing when

they wrote and ratified the Second Amendment. It is somewhat misleading to claim they were concerned that Congress wished "to disarm
the state militias." The concern was rooted in the fear that a national
army would render militias irrelevant. What Stevens described as "the
common-law right of self defense" also suggests a clear principle of
individual rights only problematically present in the eighteenth century. Nevertheless, the Stevens opinion correctly synthesized the historical evidence in a way that recovered the original meaning of the
Second Amendment as it was understood by the authors and the larger
audience of readers and listeners at the time. It is the originalist opinion of the Supreme Court in *Heller.* The problem, of course, is that an
originalist opinion did not permit the more expansive understanding
of the Second Amendment that a long-standing member of the NRA
named Antonin Scalia, soaked in the evidence it had so diligently
assembled, could find credible.

— ·=·=·· —

This collision between Scalia's originalist convictions and his political
agenda helps explain why his opinion in *Heller* is so difficult to follow,
indeed seems almost designed to create a maze of labyrinthian path-
ways that crisscross, then double back on one another like a road map
through *Alice in Wonderland.* For Scalia was committed to providing an originalist reading of a historical document whose words and
historical context defied the conclusion he was predisposed to reach.
If *Heller* reads like a prolonged exercise in legalistic legerdemain, or
perhaps a tortured display of verbal ingenuity by an overly assiduous
Scrabble player, that is because Scalia's preordained outcome forced
him to perform three challenging tasks: to show that the words of the
Second Amendment do not mean what they say; to ignore the historical conditions his originalist doctrine purportedly required him to
emphasize; and to obscure the radical implications of rejecting completely the accumulated wisdom of his predecessors on the court.

Scalia began his opinion in *Heller* by distinguishing between what
he called the "prefatory clause" and the "operative clause" of the Sec-

ond Amendment. He then declared that "the former does not limit the latter grammatically but rather announces a purpose." It soon became clear that this distinction was a verbal version of judo with more than acrobatic implications, for it redefined the syntax of the Second Amendment. The words "A well regulated Militia, being necessary to the security of a free state" were transformed into a merely rhetorical overture. In Scalia's parsing of the text, the militia requirement imposed no limitations on "the right of the people to keep and bear arms." The fact that announcing a purpose explicitly imposed limiting conditions was lost in translation. The Scalia version of the Second Amendment, much like the plaque at NRA headquarters, lopped off the militia requirement as an irrelevant prologue, leaving only the individual right to bear arms as the full and true meaning of the amendment. The game is essentially over at the very start in *Heller*, for with this singular act of editorial magic, the stated rationale for bearing arms disappears.

There was still the nettlesome question of context, chiefly Madison's motives for drafting the Second Amendment, the debates and revisions made in the House and Senate, then the ratification debates in the state legislatures. A good deal of potential trouble lay along that path, since the militia question and the fear of a standing army, sometimes referred to as a "select militia," dominate the historical record. Scalia handled this inconvenient evidence with a dismissive wave of the hand: "The Second Amendment's drafting history [was] of dubious interpretive worth."

A slightly less cavalier attitude emerged when Scalia confronted the precedents that *Heller* was overturning. These were four previous Supreme Court rulings on the Second Amendment. The most recent, *U.S. v. Miller* (1939), reaffirmed the conclusion reached in the three earlier cases, that the right to bear arms was not an individual right but rather a right dependent on service in the militia. Although Scalia's argument in *Heller* was a direct refutation of what had previously been considered "settled law," he devoted seven pages to a review of his Supreme Court predecessors before reaching the extraordinary conclusion that "none of the Court's precedents forecloses the Court's interpretation." Scalia clearly needed to believe that he was operating within the bounds of *stare decisis,* even though he clearly was not.

Heller goes on for many pages, making it one of the longer majority opinions in Supreme Court history. Scalia obviously realized that he was creating his masterpiece, and his zealous clerks provided him with a massive amount of historical evidence he could not resist quoting at length. Many of the citations are drawn from English and American dictionaries of the period, though the analysis wanders well beyond the founding era to the Civil War and its aftermath for reasons never explained. The prose becomes tedious, even tortured, as when the phrase "the right to bear arms" is parsed to explain the separate meanings of "right," "bear," and "arms."

He was determined to demonstrate that the crucial phrase had more than a merely military meaning. His researchers found that the state constitutions of Pennsylvania and Vermont explicitly mentioned "self defense" as a rationale, primarily because backwoods residents in those states needed their muskets to fend off Indian attacks. That was all Scalia needed to clinch his point, the proverbial exception that proved the rule. A database survey of the published correspondence for the eight most prominent founders revealed that they used the words "bear arms" 150 times, on all occasions referring to service in the military. To be fair, not that it would have made any difference, the survey was not available at the time Scalia wrote *Heller.*

···◄≡►···

Scalia was not a historian and never claimed to be. But as the preeminent proponent for originalism as a judicial doctrine, he claimed to base his interpretations of the Constitution on historical grounds, which for originalists entailed recovering the mentality and language of the framers on their own terms in their own time. Whether he knew it or not, this commitment imposed a disciplinary standard of attempted detachment and an analytical framework in which a preferred outcome must not be permitted to dictate the research agenda.

Scalia's opinion in *Heller* openly and unapologetically violated those core convictions of the historian's craft. He began with the presumption that the right to bear arms was a nearly unlimited individual right, assembled evidence to support that conclusion, and suppressed or dismissed evidence that did not. Nor did he attempt to conceal what he was doing. Indeed, he subsequently called attention to the intellectual agility and debater-like skills required to make his case. The problem that Scalia faced in *Heller* was that the preponderance of historical evidence went against his case, which was all the more reason why he was so pleased with his acrobatic performance.

Scalia's methodology in *Heller* is a textbook example of what constitutional scholars have called "law office history," which assumes that the suppression of evidence harmful to your client is not only permissible but professionally obligatory. This assumption is built into the adversarial framework of the American legal system itself. Even judges are required to fit their verdicts into one of two categories, in Supreme Court cases to accept or reject the argument of the plaintiff. Historians are not required to think in such binary terms. And their "on the one hand, on the other hand" judgments, or paradoxical conclusions that fit both sides or neither side of an up-or-down verdict, are the earmarks of their commitment to detachment. While Scalia's lawyer-like reasoning process in *Heller* is tolerated, accepted, even admired by many legal scholars, professional historians view it quite differently, regarding it as a flagrant violation of the canons of their craft.

From the historian's perspective, *Heller* is most revealing for what it exposes about originalism as a judicial philosophy. It is not just that there is no single source of constitutional truth back there at the founding to be discovered. Nor is the major problem the hubris required to claim a preternatural affinity for divining the truth that no previous members of the Supreme Court have ever possessed. The great sin of the originalists is not to harbor a political agenda but to claim they do not, and to base that claim on a level of historical understanding they demonstrably do not possess.

Anyone seeking inoculation against the seductive charms of originalism need only follow James Madison on his evolutionary odyssey from 1786 to 1789. All clairvoyant visions of any singular intent or meaning of the Constitution will dissolve within the shifting contexts, unforeseen obstacles, and uncomfortable compromises of that Madisonian moment. There is, in truth, an impressive body of knowledge back there at the founding available for recovery, but only originalists genuinely interested in listening to both sides of the American Dialogue in its original version will live up to the full meaning of their own declared intentions. A few members of the Federalist Society fit that description, but the vast majority, and all recent appointees to the Supreme Court, are fixated on the antigovernment side of the dialogue.

They are deaf to the pro-government voices of John Adams, Alexander Hamilton, John Marshall, and the younger James Madison. Their one-sided version of originalism was in fact designed to impose limitations on federal authority over the marketplace and to expand the range of corporate power. That is the reason why they were appointed to the Supreme Court by Republican presidents, and the reason why their landmark decisions align almost perfectly with the conservative agenda. If a full-blooded originalist were ever appointed to the court, her or his opinions would be difficult to predict, because they would more accurately reflect the broader argumentative context of the founding era. Such a rare creature could even claim to be a thoroughly Madisonian originalist by inhabiting the multiple incarnations of Madison over his lengthy career.

At present, however, the originalist justices on the Supreme Court practice the narrower version of that doctrinal persuasion. To repeat, they would not occupy their powerful and privileged posts if they thought otherwise. This presents a serious problem, eerily reminiscent of the dilemma Franklin Roosevelt faced during his second term. At a time when America's infrastructure is aging badly, when whole regions of rural America are unprepared to compete in a globalized economy, when both the middle class and the coral reefs are eroding, a national response to those challenges will prove extremely difficult to orchestrate because a tiny group of judges will say the federal government cannot perform that role. They will express regret at the unfortunate implications of their decisions but claim that their hands are tied. The fate of 320 million Americans will be decided by five judges who, citing nineteenth-century dictionaries to translate words from an eighteenth-century document, misguidedly claim they are only channeling the wisdom of the founders.

CHAPTER 4

Abroad

CHAPTER 2

Abroad

George Washington

'Tis vain to believe that anything short of a Chinese wall will restrain land jobbers and the encroachment of settlers upon Indian territory.

George Washington to Secretary of State, July 1, 1796

. . .

Europe has a set of primary interests which to us have none; or a very remote relation. Hence she must be engaged in frequent controversies, the cause of which are essentially foreign to our concerns. Hence, therefore, it must be unwise to implicate ourselves by artificial ties in the ordinary vicissitudes of her politics, or the ordinary combinations and collisions of her friendships or enemies.

George Washington, Farewell Address *(1796)*

George Washington was the primary architect of American foreign policy in the founding era, so it makes eminent sense to make him our guide as we go back to recover whatever wisdom we can find that might help us negotiate our path forward as the dominant global power. We know at the start that the post–Cold War world has proven much messier, more challenging, and even more intractable than anyone anticipated. Perhaps the most charitable way to put it is that, despite its unrivaled economic and military power, the United

States is adrift, lacks the moral and strategic compass that guided it through the Cold War, and has begun to question the ongoing viability of its previously unquestioned role as chief defender of that elusive ideal called the liberal order. Seasoned wisdom is always a valuable commodity in diplomatic deliberations, but in the current context it has become so obviously essential, and so obviously absent, that any American version of the Delphic Oracle immediately demands and deserves our undivided attention.

Before beginning our trek back in time, however, we need to face the fact that Washington's unique status within the revolutionary generation poses an equally unique challenge. A visit to the Washington Monument exposes what we might call our Washington Problem most dramatically, for it is a monument to a monument, designed to symbolize significance beyond any human scale. There was a man named George Washington who walked the earth during the last two-thirds of the eighteenth century, but he has been transformed into an otherworldly demigod whose wisdom is silence. There are no words on the Washington Monument.[1]

The transformation from man to monument occurred during Washington's lifetime and has affected the entire historical record we seek to recover. It is no accident that Washington's diary contains little more than reports on the weather, that he ordered Martha to destroy all their letters upon his death, that there was a conspiracy of silence among members of his staff during the war, as well as his cabinet during his presidency, to keep the curtain around him closed. Even artists participated in the concealment campaign. Gilbert Stuart reported to a friend that Washington's physical features reminded him of "the wildest animal in the forest," but the Lansdowne portrait he painted depicted a statuesque icon in resplendent repose.[2]

As a result, if John Adams is the most fully revealed founder, Washington is the most fully concealed. And if Thomas Jefferson wrote the most famous tribute to self-evident truths, Washington was fated to become the singular embodiment of self-evidence, so significant that explanation was almost irreverent. We must approach Washington fully aware that there are some things we can never know, and that the man, the monument, and the mythology are so mixed together that they can never be disentangled.

One final caveat. The essence of Washington's wisdom on foreign policy is commonly considered to reside in the Farewell Address (1796). While his prescription for isolation from Europe is well known, his reasons for doing so have been forgotten, and they remain relevant reminders of what the realistic tradition in foreign policy can still teach us. The Farewell Address is really the culmination of a longer story with its origins in the postwar settlement reached in the Treaty of Paris (1783). Washington's response to the unexpected acquisition of an American empire east of the Mississippi, occupied by approximately 100,000 Native Americans, is very much worth our attention. For it raises a question that has haunted American foreign policy ever since: How can a republic, which is based on consensus, also be an empire, which is based on coercion? Or in our current context: How can a democracy function as an imperial power?[3]

There is a contradiction sitting squarely in the middle of both questions, and Washington was the first American statesman to face it. The proper place to begin our story, then, is not 1796 but 1783. Washington is preparing to disband the Continental Army, which has been encamped outside Newburgh, New York, while waiting to learn if the negotiations in Paris have officially ended the war for independence. The troops are dispirited, because it is now abundantly clear that the pensions and back pay promised them by the Confederation Congress will never be paid. The government, if it can be called a government, is broke. Washington sees fit to use the occasion to remind all concerned that these veteran troops deserve better, for they have won not only American independence but a new American empire. He delivers this message in June 1783, in his last Circular Letter to the States, which turns out to be one of the most profound political statements he ever writes. The American Revolution, he observes, was the beneficiary of two extraordinary pieces of good fortune, the first a function of time, the second of space.[4]

On the time side, the American Revolution occurred at a highly favorable historic moment, "when the rights of mankind were better understood and more clearly defined, than any former period." The term *Enlightenment* had yet to enter the political lexicon, but Washington grasped the central idea that European thinkers had created a treasure trove of new knowledge that replaced the old medieval assumptions—what he called "that gloomy age of Ignorance and Superstition"—with political principles that maximized the prospects of human freedom more fully than ever before. In effect, the blueprint for a new political architecture was almost providentially available for testing in the American laboratory. "At this period," he observed with emphasis, "the United States came into its existence as a Nation, and if their Citizens should not be free and happy, the result will be intirely their own."[5]

On the space side, Washington's vision, obviously inspired by the recent acquisition of the eastern third of North America, was even more expansive, indeed continental in scale:

> The Citizens of America, placed on the most enviable conditions, as the Sole Lords and Proprietors of a vast tract of Continent, Comprehending all the various Soils, and climates of the World, and abounding with all the necessaries and conveniences of life, are now by the late satisfactory pacification, acknowledged to be possessed of absolute freedom and Independency. They are, from this period, to be considered as Actors on a most conspicuous Theatre, which seems to be designed by Providence for the display of human greatness and felicity.[6]

There was more than a bit of magical thinking behind Washington's phrase "the Sole Lords and Proprietors," which conveniently erased Native Americans from the continental picture. Washington was fully aware that a large indigenous population inhabited those pristine forests and valleys he characterized as "a most conspicuous Theatre," and he was determined to find a way to fold them into the expanding American republic without violating the revolutionary principles on which it was founded. But for now, in the initial version of his vision, Washington chose to airbrush Indians from those western vistas that beckoned so beguilingly to the white American citizenry.

Washington was telling his fellow Americans that if independence was the great principle won in the war, the western domain was the great prize. And managing that providential gift should be the central role of American diplomacy for the foreseeable future, thereby replacing opposition to British imperialism as the focusing mechanism that bound all the states into a union. When his beloved Lafayette proposed that he take the grand tour of Europe, Washington instead asked Lafayette to join him in an American version of the grand tour of the "New Empire," starting in Detroit, then heading down the Mississippi to the Gulf of Mexico, then across the Floridas. Europe was the past; the American interior was the future.

— ❖ —

Some recovery of the eighteenth-century context is necessary to fully appreciate Washington's western message. We tend to assume that the American Revolution led naturally to American nationhood, but, quite the opposite, the end of the war eliminated the dominant motive for political cooperation among the states, which were drifting under the Articles of Confederation into local, state, and regional orbits. Washington envisioned common ownership of western lands as the gravitational field that would bind the states together as a nation rather than a mere confederation. Without the West, all political energies would become centrifugal; with the West, they became centripetal.

Our own definition of what constitutes foreign policy also needs to be revised because, assuming as we do that it refers to foreign nations like France or China, we misconstrue one of Washington's main points; namely that managing westward expansion was the central pillar of American foreign policy for as long as it took to occupy the continent. What we think of as American domestic policy was then regarded as foreign policy, under the supervision of the secretary of state until well into the nineteenth century.

Deliberately placing the Native American dilemma aside for the moment, Washington chose to focus on those features of America's new western empire that actually enhanced rather than contradicted republican values. More than a century before Frederick Jackson Turner described the western frontier as a "safety valve," Washington was telling young men without prospects to seek their future in the Ohio Valley: "If I was a young man, just preparing to begin, or even if advanced in life, and had a family to make a provision for, I know of no country where I would rather fix my habitation than in some part of that region."[7]

He extended the same invitation to European immigrants, especially those who were victims of incessant war between competing imperial powers:

My first wish is to see this plague to Mankind [war] banished from the Earth. . . . Rather than quarrel abt territory, let the poor, the needy, & oppressed of Earth, and those who want Land, resort to the fertile plains of our Western Country, to the second Land of Promise, & there dwell in peace, fulfilling the first great Commandment.[8]

In this version of American expansion, the west became an American asylum rather than an empire, indeed a refuge for those foreigners seeking to escape from the oppressive monarchies across the Atlantic.

Perhaps in response to Washington's insistence that the western domain become the centerpiece of the American political agenda, new ideas began to circulate in the Confederation Congress about the future function of the domain above and beyond its role as a source of revenue. David Howell, a delegate from Rhode Island, was inspired to envision the new empire not as a repudiation of republican values, but rather as a source of their salvation:

> The Western World opens an amazing prospect. As a national fund, in my opinion, it is equal to our debt. As a Source of future population & strength, it is a guarantee of our Independence. As its Inhabitants will be mostly cultivators of the Soil, republicanism looks to them as its Guardians. When the States on the eastern shore, or Atlantic, shall have become populous, rich and luxurious & ready to yield their Liberties into the hands of a Tyrant—*the Gods of the Mountains will save us.*[9]

This was a distinctive way of thinking that Thomas Jefferson would later embrace and deploy to rationalize the Louisiana Purchase, like Howell arguing that republican governments only flourish in agrarian societies, so that extending the westward borders of the American nation also extended the life-span of the agrarian American republic.

Finally, the most explicit attempt to demonstrate that the American empire, unlike its European counterparts, was not really imperialistic came with the Ordinance of 1784. Following Washington's advice to make the management of the domain a major priority, the Confederation Congress appointed Thomas Jefferson to chair a committee "to prepare a plan for the temporary government of the western territory." Jefferson consulted with Washington and the Virginia delegation, then drafted the following words, which, apart from the Declaration of Independence, were the most consequential he ever wrote: "The Territories so called shall be laid out and formed into States . . . and the states so formed shall be distinct Republican States and admitted members of the Federal Union, having the same rights of Sovereignty, Freedom, and Independence as the other States." He also added that neither slavery nor hereditary titles would be permitted in the new states, but Congress by a narrow vote chose to delete those recommendations. It did, however, endorse the key provision that there would be no colonies in the expanding American empire.

All white settlers who flowed over the Alleghenies were thereby assured that they would eventually become citizens, not subjects, in the new American republic, thereby creating that rarest of creatures, an anti-imperial empire.[10]

On one point, Washington insisted on a revision of the Ordinance of 1784. True to his elemental conviction about the quasi-sacred character of individual freedom, Jefferson saw no need to regulate the flow of migration over the mountains into the interior. Like a swollen stream, it should be allowed to flow freely, which in effect meant that families should pursue their happiness wherever they wished, so that new settlements would pop up like flowers wherever fertile land beckoned. It was a laissez-faire approach to American expansion.

Washington preferred a more controlled approach, what he called "compact and progressive seating," which was designed to transform the flood of settlers into a more regulated flow that assured density of occupation in discrete waves of settlements. It was not just that Washington lacked Jefferson's faith in the benign powers of individual freedom, though that was true enough. More practically, he worried that a widely dispersed westward migration would fall victim to lurking European powers, chiefly Great Britain and Spain, who would seduce isolated settlers into foreign alliances.

It was a highly realistic and cautionary vision: "The flanks and rear of the United States are possessed by other powers—& formidable ones, too," he warned. "How necessary it is to apply the cement of interest, to bind all parts of the Union together by indissoluble bonds—especially that part which lies immediately west of us, with the Middle States." A more diffused population, left to their own devices, he feared, "would in a few years be as unconnected with us, indeed more so, than we are with South America." One should not assume, as Jefferson did, that the American promise was self-fulfilling. "The Western settlers stand as it were upon a pivot," he cautioned, "and the touch of a feather would turn them any way."[11]

The result was the Ordinance of 1785, which divided the edge of western expansion into townships of thirty-six square miles, which were surveyed, sold for not less than one dollar per acre, then inhabited as the surveyors moved on to the next row. Jefferson registered his approval of this revision of his original plan, but he did so from Paris, where he succeeded Benjamin Franklin as American minister to France. The republican principle of guaranteed citizenship for all settlers remained intact, and the concentrated settlements further ensured that western territories would be folded into an expanding United States rather than stray, as colonies, into European hands.

By the mid-1780s, as a result, the infant American republic had found a way to fuse two apparently irreconcilable identities—an emerging imperial power and the first and only large-scale republic in the modern world. It would be wrong to call the United States a developing nation at this stage, because it remained a confederation, not a nation. But Washington believed, correctly it turned out, that the very act of managing its empire would literally force the state-based members of the confederation to behave collectively, thereby laying the political foundation for a nation-in-the-making.

Two features stand out in this story. First, it could never have happened without the guiding presence of a singular figure whose transcendent stature was so acknowledged that the awkward contradiction the new republic was living became, instead, a lovely paradox. And second, despite the remarkable beauty of it all, standing squarely in the middle of this seductively attractive scene was an ugly fact: namely that the entire Native American population living in the eastern third of North America was the glaring exception to everything Washington's iconic presence had made possible.

＊＊＊

Whether the Native Americans fit in the republican vision of westward expansion was clear from the start—they did not. White settlers in the new territories knew that they would eventually become full-fledged American citizens, not colonists or subjects, but most of them also assumed that Indian land was theirs for the taking. And Indian removal east of the Mississippi was the unspoken assumption for most delegates to the Confederation Congress, the only question being how it should happen.

The answer to that question became obvious in the first wave of treaties with Indian tribes negotiated and signed after the Treaty of Paris. In the treaty at Fort Stanwix (1784) with the Iroquois Confederation and the Ohio tribes, then in the treaty at Hopewell (1785) with the Cherokees, the American negotiators cited the "conquest theory" as the legal rationale for confiscating Indian land without their consent. According to this line of argument, Native Americans had no rights because they were a "conquered people" who had sided with the British in the recent war and therefore had no legal standing, so by even consulting them the American government was doing them a favor. This first version of a coherent federal policy toward Native Americans, then, was thoroughly arbitrary, wholly one-sided, and brazenly imperialistic in the European mode.[12]

This was perfectly fine from the perspective of those thousands of white settlers sweeping across the Alleghenies, who cared not a whit that revolutionary principles were being violated but instead regarded their quest for land as a natural right wholly compatible with Jefferson's words in the Declaration of Independence, namely the right to pursue their own happiness.

From the Indian side of the imperial equation, the new American policy looked and felt incomprehensible. Nearly three-quarters of the region east of the Mississippi remained Indian Country after the war, occupied by approximately thirty tribes long accustomed to regarding the land as a gift from the Great Spirit. It had never occurred to them that this expansive tract could be owned by any mortal, much less that control over it could be determined by men an ocean away, who had never hunted or even walked upon its ground, who had only written their names on a piece of parchment. Several of the surviving Native American responses to this inexplicable invasion were poignant testimonials that inadvertently called attention to the very principles enshrined in the Declaration of Independence. Consider this letter from several Cherokee chiefs, protesting violations of the Treaty of Hopewell:

> At our last treaty . . . we gave up to our white brothers all our land we could any how spare, and have but little left to raise our women and children upon, and we hope you wont let any people take any more from us without our consent. We are neither Birds nor fish; we can neither fly in the air nor live under water. Therefore, we hope that pity will be extended to us. We are made by the same hand in the same shape as yourselves.[13]

The conspicuously coercive character of its new Indian policy, most especially its unabashed imperial face, troubled some members of Congress and also drew criticism from America's most prominent citizen, now enjoying retirement beneath his proverbial vine and fig tree at Mount Vernon. A modification of the "conquest theory" then followed when the next treaty was negotiated at Fort Harmar (1789). This time the Indians were compensated for their lost land, and although the terms of the sale were obligatory, meaning that the sellers could not refuse, the exchange of money provided a veneer of consent to the negotiation.[14]

Exactly how this more indirect form of imperialism would work became clear in a letter to Congress from Philip Schuyler, a former general in the Continental Army who had extensive experience with Indian affairs during the war. The American government would negotiate treaties providing compensation with the more distant tribes,

> And then, as our settlements approach their country, they must, from the scarcity of game, retire further back and dispose of their lands, unless they dwindle comparatively to nothing, as all savages have done who gain their sustenance by the chase, when compelled to live in the vicinity of civilized people.[15]

In effect, every Indian treaty was intended as a temporary agreement, destined to be discarded once the edge of new settlements reached Indian borders. The great advantage of this approach was that it averted Indian wars because demography would do the work of armies. It was really a recipe for genocide in slow motion, and for a more gradual and palatable version of Indian removal east of the Mississippi.

By the latter half of the 1780s, then, American policy toward the Native Americans had evolved from an overt to a covert kind of imperialism. And in the Northwest Ordinance (1787), the same mixed message was effectively codified. On the one hand, the ordinance redefined the rules for establishing territories and soon-to-be states in the region between the Ohio and the Mississippi. The clear implication was that any Native American presence in the Northwest was presumed to be temporary despite treaty obligations with the Ohio tribes that said otherwise.

On the other hand, the ordinance offered a reassuring promise that American policy toward the Native Americans would always be conducted in accord with republican principles:

> The utmost good faith shall always be observed towards the Indians; their lands and property shall never be taken from them without their consent; and in their property, rights, and liberty, they shall never be invaded or disturbed, unless by just and lawful wars authorized by Congress; but laws founded on justice and humanity shall, from time to time, be made, for preventing wrongs being done to them.[16]

Given the relentless reality of the ongoing removal policy, it is difficult to avoid the conclusion that such promises of justice constituted a republican cloak over an imperialistic agenda. This was the duplicitous direction in which Indian policy was headed when Washington assumed the presidency of the United States in 1789.

Given the daunting challenge that Washington was facing, in effect to create the executive branch of the new federal government de novo, his decision to delegate most areas of domestic policy to his cabinet and focus his own personal attention on the Native American problem is revealing. Initially his motives were practical; chiefly, he feared that Indian wars would break out all along the western edge of white settlements when tribal chiefs realized that the treaties they had signed became worthless pieces of paper once the demographic wave of settlers reached Indian Country. But quite quickly he began to develop a discernibly moral perspective on the issues raised by the collision between the de facto policy of Indian removal and the values of the American Revolution.

The man who called Washington's attention to the moral implications of current American policy was Henry Knox, who had served alongside him as commander of artillery during the war for independence and was now secretary of war. The portly Knox enjoyed a sufficiently intimate relationship with Washington to tell him the unpleasant truth that the present course of American policy toward Native Americans violated all the republican principles that they had fervently believed they were fighting for.

"Indians being the prior occupants possess the right of the soil," Knox insisted, "so to dispossess them would be a gross violation of the fundamental Laws of Nature and the distributive justice which is the glory of our nation." Unless Washington found a way to effect a change in the shape and direction of foreign policy toward the Native American tribes, Knox warned that "in a short period the Idea of an Indian on this side of the Mississippi will only be found in the pages of the historians."[17]

Since Indian removal was, in truth, the unspoken goal of current American policy, albeit achieved in a way conveniently designed to obscure the imperialistic character of the enterprise, Knox was calling not only for a change in the ultimate outcome but also for a more candid acknowledgment that what they were doing to the Native Americans was just as arbitrary and morally wrong as what Great Britain had done, or tried to do, to them as American colonists. Persisting on the current course, then, "would stain the character of the nation" and, not so incidentally, become a permanent blot on Washington's revolutionary reputation that would forever diminish his historic legacy. At last, and for the first time, Washington was being asked to confront one of the central contradictions of the American Revolution, and to face rather than finesse its discomforting implications.[18]

Although most historians of Washington's presidency have rather strangely tended not to notice it, solving the Native American problem became his highest priority during his first year in office. As Washington put it to Lafayette, "the basis of our proceedings with the Indian Nations . . . shall be justice during the period in which I have anything to do in the administration of this government."[19]

During the summer of 1789, Knox and Washington worked feverishly to achieve two goals: first, to establish federal sovereignty over all state-based treaties, most especially those recently negotiated by North Carolina and Georgia; second, to identify the most appropriate tribe and tribal chief with whom to sign a model treaty that would set the standards for a new chapter in Indian-white relations more compatible with republican values. "It would reflect honor on the new government," Knox wrote to Washington, "were a declarative Law to be passed that the Indian tribes possess the right of the soil of all lands . . . and that they are not to be divested thereof but in consequence of fair and bona fide purchases, made under the authority, or with the express approbation of the United States."[20]

After several weeks of study, Knox recommended the Creek Nation as the ideal tribe to try the new approach, in part because the Creeks were the most powerful and populous tribe south of the Ohio River, and in part because the Creek chief, Alexander McGillivray, was known to be a charismatic leader who, once persuaded, possessed the authority to enforce any treaty he signed. As Knox saw it, the

Creeks should be regarded as a sovereign nation, and therefore any treaty with them was as much a matter of foreign policy as a treaty with France or Spain. This in turn meant that all Indian policy came under the authority of the executive branch, which need only obtain the advice and consent of the Senate.[21]

Washington did not know what "advice and consent" meant, and there were no precedents to guide him because the proposed treaty with the Creeks was the first such occasion to come up under the new Constitution. And so, after consultation with his cabinet, Washington decided he was obliged to appear in the Senate, taking Knox with him to explain the rationale for his new initiative on the Native American question.

The meeting on August 14 was a fiasco. No one could hear the document that Knox read, several senators requested all the background correspondence, and others questioned the choice of the Creek Nation and even whether Indian tribes should be regarded as nations. After several hours of incoherent debate, a motion was made to refer the whole matter to a committee. Washington stormed out of the session visibly perturbed, as one senator heard him murmuring, "This defeats every purpose of my coming here." He and Knox returned ten days later requesting—in effect, demanding—an up-or-down vote by the Senate without further debate, which the cowed and somewhat bewildered senators proceeded to do. This semi-comical episode became the last time an American president interpreted the term "advice and consent" to mean a meeting with the Senate rather than a written request.[22]

This awkward occasion is revealing for reasons that go beyond its constitutional consequences. The debate in the Senate clarified for the first time just what Knox and Washington envisioned as the "new model" for treaties with Native Americans east of the Mississippi. The "conquest theory" was rejected, and the policy of purchasing Indian land was revised. Now the borders of Creek country would be drawn to the satisfaction of its Indian inhabitants, and most importantly, the federal government would guarantee the sanctity of a sovereign

Creek Nation that white settlers could not violate. In effect, the "new model" envisioned the creation of a series of Native American homelands east of the Mississippi that the wave of white settlements would be required to bypass or risk removal by American troops acting to enforce federal law. In the long run, which is to say the next century, both Washington and Knox imagined the gradual assimilation of Native Americans into the union. In the short run, the goal of Indian removal east of the Mississippi was abandoned.

In order for the plan to succeed, both Washington and Knox realized that they had to win the trust of Alexander McGillivray, which turned out to be a very challenging project. McGillivray had been educated in the classics by his Scottish father, was fluent in English, Spanish, and Creek, had sided with the British during the war, and rejected in quite eloquent fashion the core assumptions of the Treaty of Paris:

> We . . . do hereby in the most solemn manner protest against any title claim or demand the American Congress may set up for or against our lands, Settlements, and hunting Grounds in Consequence of the Said treaty of peace between the King of Great Britain and the States of America, declaring that we were not partys . . . it being a Notorious fact known to the Americans, known to any person who is in any ways conversant in, or acquainted with American affairs, that his Britiannick Majesty was never possessed either by session, purchase or by right of Conquest of our Territorys and which the Said treaty gives away.[23]

Moreover, McGillivray felt no need to make any concessions to the Americans, believing as he did that the newly created American republic was a fragile experiment that was likely to collapse. And even if it survived, he could throw over five thousand Creek warriors into the field, which was more than a match for the overstretched American army on the frontier. As he saw it, the Americans needed him more than he needed them.

The first American delegation sent to confer with McGillivray in western Georgia failed completely. McGillivray brought seven hundred Creek braves with him to impress the Americans with his prowess. He found the condescending tone of the American negotiators too much to bear, and abruptly rode out with his entourage murmuring epithets about the American "puppies" and declaring that "by God I will not have a treaty cram'd down my throat."[24]

Too much was at stake for Washington to give up after one disappointment, so he dispatched a second delegation a few months later. This time the negotiators were instructed to play on McGillivray's vanity, to offer him the rank of a general in the American army at an annual salary of $1,200, and to promise that Washington himself would host him at a peace conference in the American capital of New York. McGillivray eventually relented, though there is reason to believe he saw through the personal blandishments—not for nothing was he later called "the Talleyrand of the early Southwest"—and probably intended to negotiate generous terms with the Americans that he then would parlay into more generous terms from the Spanish government. Whatever his motives, he agreed to meet with Washington that summer in New York.[25]

McGillivray arrived in New York in late July 1790, seated in a coach and trailed by twenty-six Creek chiefs on horseback, all fully feathered and resplendent in Indian dress. The seven-week trek from Creek country had been a triumphal procession. Witnesses in Georgia and the Carolinas were stunned, claiming they had never seen so many warriors whose intentions were entirely peaceful. Once in New York, McGillivray and his entourage were treated like European royalty. There was a parade past Federal Hall, where all the members of Congress came out to cheer while the Creek chiefs broke out in song that interpreters described as a tribute to brotherhood. The evening ended at City Tavern, where Washington and McGillivray exchanged toasts to a new era in Indian-white relations.[26]

For the next month McGillivray negotiated with Knox during the day and partied at night, consuming huge amounts of alcohol but amazing all observers with his apparently sober sociability. It so happened that the entire Creek delegation was housed at an inn adjoining Richmond Hill, where Vice President John Adams and his ever saucy Abigail resided. The Creek chiefs came over for dinner on several occasions and did their tribal dances around a bonfire, as Abigail put it, "singing, yelling and expressing their pleasure and satisfaction in the true Savage State. They were the first Savages I ever saw."[27]

The Treaty of New York was signed in Federal Hall on August 13. Abigail Adams, who had been made an honorary Creek with a Creek name, Mammea, was in the gallery. She watched Washington give McGillivray a gift of beads and tobacco, then shake hands Indian-style with each chief, arms locked while grasping elbows. The Creeks then formed themselves in a chorus and sang a final song that the interpreter explained was a tribute to perpetual peace. In the tortured and tragic history of Indian-white relations in the United States, this was probably the most hopeful moment.

The primary reason for the optimism was that Washington and Knox had apparently discovered a strategy that would avoid both Indian removal and Indian wars. In the Treaty of New York (1790), the Creeks were promised sovereign control over a vast tract that included what is now western Georgia, northern Florida, southern Tennessee, and most of Alabama. The federal government was legally and morally pledged to prevent white settlers from invading this new version of Creek country. And this homelands model could be applied elsewhere, creating a series of Indian enclaves east of the Mississippi.

But the ink was hardly dry on the Treaty of New York before settlers on the Georgia frontier poured across the newly established borders by the thousands, blissfully oblivious of any geographic line drawn on a map by some faraway government. The Georgia legislature brazenly defied federal jurisdiction over its western borders, claiming that all of Creek country and beyond to the Mississippi belonged to Georgia based on its colonial charter. Washington was infuriated but also helpless to stop the demographic wave. "Until we can restrain the turbulence and disorderly conduct of our own borders," he lamented, "it will be in vain I fear to expect peace with the Indians—or that they will govern their own people better than we do ours." Knox estimated that it would take five thousand American soldiers to patrol the Creek borders, and this at a time when the entire American army was less than half that size. Washington concluded that "scarcely anything short of a Chinese wall . . . will restrain land jobbers and the encroachment of settlers upon Indian territory."[28]

He and Knox had made a promise they could not keep. Indeed, Washington had invested all his enormous prestige in a just resolution of the Native American dilemma, making it the highest priority during his first term as president, but he had failed completely, and he knew it. For a man accustomed to winning all the big battles, often against the odds, this defeat haunted him to his dying days. And he was convinced that the Indian side of this American tragedy would never make it into the history books: "They, poor wretches, have no Press thro' which their grievances are related; and it is well known that when one side only of a story is heard, and often repeated, the human mind becomes impressed with it, insensibly." It took almost two centuries for history to reverse that verdict.[29]

At the time, the chief consequence of Washington's failure was to establish the Native Americans as the abiding and eventually permanent exception to the anti-imperialistic side of the American Revolution. Washington's heroic effort to avoid that fate stands as his personal testament to that anti-imperial tradition. The fact that he failed serves to expose the inability of the revolutionary legacy, even when it was still a living memory, to deter a full century of domestic imperialism.

◆→ ⊯◆⊯ →◆

Washington's second term was preoccupied by the more conventional version of foreign policy, one that looked across the Atlantic to Europe rather than westward toward those Indian tribes inhabiting the American interior. The main reason for the change in focus was the French

Revolution, a cataclysmic event that threatened to shift the tectonic plates throughout the Western world and, more immediately, lead to war between Great Britain and France for European supremacy.

It was conventional wisdom that the United States should steer clear of such European convulsions. The blueprint for an isolationist policy had first been proposed by John Adams during the summer of 1776, when the movement for American independence was still aborning. In his Plan of Treaties, Adams's chief goal was to obtain French support for the war against Great Britain, but along the way he almost incidentally sketched the outline for a more panoramic vision of America's proper posture toward the rest of the world. Put succinctly, the infant American republic should have commercial relations with all foreign nations but diplomatic relations with none. In effect, this meant independence at home should be accompanied by independence abroad, at least for the foreseeable future.[30]

Like most prominent American statesmen at the time, Washington agreed with Adams's elegantly simple formula, though with a slightly different emphasis. While Adams tended to warn against being drawn into Europe's unending controversies, Washington preferred to feature the incredible bounty available "over the mountains" in those pristine forests and river valleys he had once surveyed. But the end result was the same. The consensual centerpiece of American foreign policy was to look inward rather than outward and to avoid European entanglements at all costs.

This was easier said than done. The distinction between commercial and diplomatic relations made perfect sense in theory, but in practice the distinction dissolved during wartime, when trading partners demanded allegiance rather than neutrality. Moreover, implementing foreign policy in a republic bottomed on the principle of popular sovereignty posed unprecedented problems, because a republic was susceptible to wild swings in popular opinion that could not be ignored in the nonchalant way possible in most monarchies. As a result, foreign and domestic policy overlapped in the early American republic in ways that made long-term goals vulnerable to short-term shifts in the popular mood that were easily manipulated by political opponents with a partisan agenda. Since one of those opponents was Thomas Jefferson, Washington faced formidable criticism of his foreign policy throughout his presidency.

The international explosion that generated tremors throughout the American government was the outbreak of war between Great Britain and revolutionary France in April 1793. Washington immediately convened his cabinet and extracted a unanimous vote for a policy of strict American neutrality. A week later he issued an executive proclamation to that effect, not bothering to mention that his proclamation was an implicit repudiation of the Franco-American Treaty (1778).[31]

Washington knew better than anyone else that the war for independence could not have been won without the money and men provided by France. But that was then, and this was now. No matter that a clear majority of American citizens were, for obvious reasons, pro-French and anti-British. As Washington saw it, foreign policy must be based on a realistic appraisal of American interests, not on popular referendums or nostalgic memories of past French largesse. He issued his opinion in the form of a proclamation precisely because it sidestepped Congress, which almost surely would have been swayed by the reigning romance for all things French. If his critics condemned the proclamation as a monarchical act, and they did, so be it.

At the start of his presidency, Washington had observed that "I walk on untrodden ground." Given his prominence as the first occupant of the office, virtually every decision he made was unprecedented, but foreign policy posed the problem in its most potent form. For the specter of monarchy haunted all political conversations throughout the 1790s, making any robust projection of executive power a betrayal of "the spirit of '76." Since foreign policy required the new American nation to speak with one voice, and since Washington believed that he had been duly elected to provide that voice, he found himself living a central paradox of the early republic: what was essential for a viable and coherent foreign policy was ideologically at odds with what the infant republic claimed to stand for.[32]

The full implications of that paradox became visible in the debate over the Jay Treaty (1795), the landmark foreign policy achievement of Washington's second term. Perhaps no treaty in American history so unpopular in its own day has proved so beneficial over time. But in the crucible of the moment, the dominant reaction was that Washington's projection of executive power was both unconstitutional and misguided.

— ≡✦≡ —

If Washington's foreign policy lodestar was American neutrality, British behavior by the mid-1790s seemed designed to refract all its light. Ten thousand British troops remained stationed on the northwestern frontier in open defiance of the Treaty of Paris. From this protected perch, they proceeded to incite the Ohio tribes, generating Indian wars up and down the western border of new settlements. At the same time the British navy was scooping up American merchant ships in the Caribbean with impunity in an effort to block all American trade with France. Yet another war with Great Britain seemed imminent.[33]

In April 1794 Washington dispatched Chief Justice John Jay, one of America's most experienced diplomats, to negotiate a treaty that would remove the British troops and revive commercial relations with Great Britain. His instructions made avoiding war the highest priority, since the United States was not prepared to fight such a war, and Washington believed that several decades needed to pass before the infant republic would be ready to risk another conflict with the British army and navy.

The very idea of negotiating with the British was wildly unpopular. Although political parties as we know them did not yet exist, critics of the Washington administration, adopting the title of Republicans, began to mobilize against the Jay Treaty. Their chief organ became the *Aurora*, a Philadelphia newspaper headed by Benjamin Franklin Bache, Franklin's grandson. Bache's editorials verged on the scatological, claiming that Washington chose Jay for the diplomatic mission in order to ensure that the chief justice would be out of the country, thereby making impeachment proceedings against Washington impossible. As grounds for impeachment, Bache published a series of forged documents leaked by British officials during the war in order to undermine Washington's authority. The documents rather preposterously claimed that Washington had been a covert British spy who fully intended to betray the cause but was beaten to the punch by Benedict Arnold. It is difficult to know whether Bache or anybody else believed such lunacies, but they accurately reflected the fanatical partisanship currently at play. What has come to be called "fake news" had just entered the political and diplomatic equation.

Matters only became worse when Jay returned from London and details of the treaty were leaked to the *Aurora* and made public. On the positive side, the Jay Treaty required the removal of British troops from the frontier and committed the British to arbitrate American claims of compensation for cargoes confiscated by their navy. On the negative side, American debtors, who had owed over £4 million to British creditors—the majority Virginia planters, to include Jefferson and Madison—were required to pay what they had hoped to finesse. Most disturbing, the treaty endorsed the fact of British naval supremacy in language that gave American neutrality a British tilt. Critics could argue, and did, that the United States was accepting neocolonial status within the British Empire.

This last provision provoked the largest outcry. Both Jay and Washington were described as "closet Tories," Jay dryly observing that he could walk the entire eastern seaboard at night with his way illuminated by protesters burning him in effigy. John Adams later remembered that the presidential mansion in Philadelphia "was surrounded by innumerable multitudes from day to day buzzing, demanding war with England, cursing Washington, and crying success to the French patriots and virtuous Republicans." Washington believed that Jay had probably gotten the best terms possible, and while not all he could have hoped for, the treaty averted a misguided war and preserved economic relations with America's major trading partner. But he also recognized that, as he put it, "at present the cry against the Treaty is like that against a mad dog; and everyone, in a manner, seems engaged in running it down."[34]

In order to coordinate their opposition to the Jay Treaty, the Republicans in Congress caucused for the first time, another step toward becoming an opposition party. Leadership in the House fell to James Madison, previously one of Washington's closest confidants, who had gone over to the other side. But while Madison was referred to as "the general," Jefferson became "the generalissimo," covertly orchestrating strategy from his mountaintop at Monticello.

Jefferson had been conducting a whispering campaign against Washington for several years, the gist of which was that the grand old man was now more old than grand, in effect was becoming senile. These private thoughts remained private until April 1796, when a letter he had written to Philip Mazzei was leaked to the press: "It would give you a fever were I to name to you the apostles who have gone over to these heresies [i.e., the Jay Treaty]," Jefferson lamented, "men who were Samsons in the field and Solomons in the Council." Readers quickly recognized Washington as Samson and either Adams or Jay as Solomon. This became the opening breach that eventually caused Washington to renounce Jefferson as a duplicitous scoundrel.[35]

The problem with the Republicans' strategy, which was to block the Jay Treaty in the House, where they enjoyed a comfortable majority, was that the Constitution clearly specified that only the Senate had a say over treaties, requiring a two-thirds vote there for approval. Jefferson solved that problem by an ingenious reading of the Constitution that even Madison, who knew the document better than anyone else, could not endorse. In Jefferson's interpretation, no matter what the Constitution said, it meant that "the representatives in the House are as free as the President and the Senate to consider whether the national interest requires or gives the force of law to articles over which they have power." He went so far as to claim that he had no problem in transferring the power over treaties to the House alone "and annihilating the whole treaty making power of the executive branch."[36]

Madison regarded Jefferson's novel constitutional theory as excessive. Instead of a frontal attack on executive power, he preferred a flanking movement, arguing that certain provisions of the Jay Treaty required funding for their implementation, and the House was the proper branch to decide all money bills. This would achieve the desired result, holding the treaty hostage, without Jefferson's constitutional histrionics. But despite Madison's heroic efforts during the debate in the House, the Jay Treaty passed by a slim majority (51–48) on the last day of April 1796.

Jefferson could not believe that a treaty so unpopular could ever become law, especially since it was, as he put it, "really nothing more than a treaty of alliance between England and the Anglomen of this country against the legislature and people of the United States." He apprised his protégé James Monroe, then serving as American minister in Paris, that the defeat was primarily the result of Washington's enormous prestige, "the one man who outweighed us all in influence over the people." Monroe took Jefferson's message to heart and began instructing members of the French court to pay no attention to passage of the Jay Treaty, for it was the deranged act of a semi-senile man who would soon be gone from office. When word of this treasonable piece of treachery reached Washington, he immediately demanded Monroe's resignation.[37]

The whole episode exposed the unprecedented levels of partisanship, duplicity, and hysteria that shook Washington to the core. Although the Jay Treaty had passed, the chorus he had hoped to lead in projecting America's values to the world had turned into a shouting match in which his domestic opponents had manipulated the anti-British and pro-French sentiments in the populace to serve their own political agenda. It was more than Washington could bear. As he explained to Jay: "These things, as you have supposed, fill my mind with much concern, and with serious anxiety. Indeed, the trouble and perplexities which they occasion have added to the weight of years which have passed over me, have worn away my mind more than my body; and render ease and retirement indisputably necessary to both during the short time I have to stay here."[38]

This was his troubled state of mind, even his anguished emotional condition, when he sat down to compose what history would come to know as his Farewell Address.

Two disarming facts about the Farewell Address need to be noticed at the start. First, it was never an address delivered by Washington but rather an essay that first appeared on the inside pages of the *American Daily Advertiser,* Philadelphia's leading newspaper, on September 19, 1796, signed with ostentatious moderation, "G. Washington, United States." Second, Washington did not write it, Alexander Hamilton did. The ideas in it, to be sure, were all Washington's, but the words, or at least most of them, were Hamilton's. A veritable cottage industry developed around the question of authorship in the nineteenth century, but scholars have settled this matter beyond any reasonable doubt.[39]

Over the years the Farewell Address has levitated out of time, achieving iconic status as a seminal statement of America's abiding foreign policy principles. But at the time what Washington said was less important than the fact that he was saying it. Historians have noted that Washington was establishing the two-term precedent for American presidents, a precedent violated only once, by Franklin Roosevelt, and then enshrined as law in the Twenty-Second Amendment (1951). More basically, however, he was leaving office under his own power, not dying in office like a monarch, making the simple point in dramatic fashion that republican leaders, no matter how indispensable, were all disposable. It was the farewell rather than the address itself that struck most Americans, since the very idea of the United States without Washington was both unprecedented and unimaginable. The dominant reaction was that the father of the founding was saying goodbye to his children, who must now fend for themselves.[40]

Though a distinct minority, Washington's critics, still incredulous at losing the battle over the Jay Treaty, seized upon the Farewell Address to denounce him as a traitor. Bache reprinted the trumped-up charges of Washington's role as a British spy during the war. Thomas Paine entered the lists in the *Aurora*, celebrating Washington's departure, actually praying for his "imminent death," ending with the prediction that "the world will be puzzled to decide whether you are an apostate or an imposter, whether you have abandoned good principles, or whether you ever had any." Rebuttals to Paine's open letter were equally extravagant, describing him as "that noted sot and infidel" whose intemperate assaults on Washington's reputation resembled "the futile efforts of a reptile infusing its venom into the Atlantic or ejecting its filthy saliva towards the Sun."[41]

It was not mere coincidence that Washington devoted over half of the Farewell Address to a high-toned condemnation of such vituperations. For his memories of the highly partisan and deeply personal debate over the Jay Treaty were still raw, and he regarded them as ominous harbingers of a demagogic turn in domestic politics that rendered any coherent American foreign policy impossible and, not so incidentally, put the still fragile American republic at risk. Thus his injunction to put party labels aside and embrace a collective identity as Americans united under one government:

> This government, the offspring of our own choice uninfluenced and unawed, adopted upon full investigation & mature deliberation, completely free in its principles, in the distribution of its powers, uniting security with energy, and containing within itself a provision for its own amendment, has a just claim to your confidence and your support. . . . The very idea of the power and right of the People to establish Government presupposes the duty of every Individual to obey the established Government.[42]

For most of the twentieth century, both scholars and ordinary readers of the Farewell Address paid little attention to Washington's wisdom on this score, preferring to focus on his prescription for American foreign policy at the end of the address. There are, in fact, compelling reasons to regard his message about national unity as both obvious and platitudinous, and only a recovery of the political context allows for an appreciation of his meaning.

Put simply, Washington's words require the recognition that the United States had adopted a national government *before* it was a unified nation. The opening words of the Constitution—"We the people of the United States"—were more a wish than a reality in late-eighteenth-century America. As one historian so nicely put it, the Constitution was "a roof without walls," meaning a political structure designed to facilitate a national ethos that did not exist. Washington's plea for all citizens to regard themselves as Americans united under a single government can be comprehended only within that prenational context. His thinking at the time was more distinctive than it appears now, because he was arguing that America's revolutionary energies should be harnessed to the larger purposes of nation-building, while others, most prominently Jefferson, regarded that argument as a betrayal of the revolution itself.[43]

The early pages of the Farewell Address are time-bound reminders of the controversial character still surrounding any clear expression of federal sovereignty over the states in the 1790s. It also provides yet another glimpse of Washington's impeccable judgment, for he was urging his fellow Americans to align themselves in the direction that history was headed.

The final pages of the Farewell Address are the most famous, chiefly because they charted the course of American foreign policy for the next century and beyond. Here is the most salient passage:

> The great rule of conduct for us in regard to foreign nations is in extending our commercial relations, to have with them as little political connection as possible. . . . Europe has a set of primary interests which to us have none; or a very remote rela-

tion. . . . 'Tis our true policy to steer clear of permanent Alliances with any portion of the foreign world.[44]

Washington had made much the same point three years earlier in his Proclamation of Neutrality. There he had explained that his primary motive was to avoid war with France or Great Britain, mainly because the infant American republic required time to outgrow its infancy. In effect, he was thinking short term and was even explicit about the time frame he had in mind: "Twenty years peace with such an increase of population and resources as we have a right to expect, added to our remote situation from the jarring powers, will in all probability enable us in a just cause to bid defiance to any power on earth." His estimate of "twenty years," it turned out, came close to predicting the outbreak of the War of 1812, which became unavoidable because the theoretical distinction between commercial and diplomatic relations did not work in practice. This flaw remained embedded in American foreign policy until 1917, when it became the chief reason Woodrow Wilson ended American isolation by sending troops "over there" in World War I.[45]

Despite this fundamental flaw, any foreign policy prescription that lasts for over a century must be regarded an extraordinary success. To be sure, the controversy surrounding Washington's wisdom at the time of its utterance was shrill, even scatological. The editors at the *Aurora* described the Farewell Address as "the loathing's of a sick mind" and its author "a tyrannical monster." But in the course of the nineteenth century, the doctrine of American isolation levitated beyond the controversial context of its origins to become the foreign policy version of Jefferson's self-evident truths in the Declaration of Independence. Congress made a reading of the Farewell Address mandatory on Washington's birthday every year, and its most salient words became creedal convictions in the American catechism, to be memorized by all citizens, thereby enjoying the unique status of a classic so seminal that it defied disagreement or even discussion.[46]

Recovering the time-bound wisdom of any classic is always hard, because its endurance depends on its prophetic prowess, which always looks obvious in retrospect, after the prophecy has become history. In the case of Washington's vision in the Farewell Address, hindsight reveals a visionary understanding of how to align an emerging American nation with the geographic, demographic, and international currents destined to shape the contours of the Western world for the foreseeable future.

Geographically, Washington assumed that the location of the North American continent between the earth's two largest oceans provided splendid isolation from foreign enemies, what one historian has called "free security," meaning that distance made a large military establishment unnecessary. Demographically, he recognized that the vast American interior with its abundance of natural resources provided ample space for American expansion, and once connected by roads and canals—railroads were yet unforeseeable—would make the United States economically self-sufficient. Diplomatically, the long-term advantage of the Jay Treaty placed American commerce within the protective fold of the British fleet, which ruled the waves for the next century. There was no way that Washington could have known about Waterloo, or about the long era of European stability established at the Congress of Vienna (1815). So good fortune as well as foresight verified his vision, giving it the latter-day appearance of a providential proclamation.

❖

The very success of Washington's isolationist prescription has tended to deflect attention from a deeper message, not so much about the proper direction of American foreign policy as about the way in which it should be formulated. These words constitute the seminal statement of the realistic foreign policy tradition in American history: "There can be no greater error to expect, or calculate upon real favors from Nation to Nation. 'Tis an illusion which experience must cure, which a just pride ought to discard." Washington was insisting that the relationship between individuals, which could often be conducted on the basis of mutual trust, did not apply to nations. All nations, including the United States, could never depend upon trust but must behave solely on the basis of interest.[47]

In the context of his own time, this was a defense of the Jay Treaty, which repudiated the Franco-American alliance and aligned America's commercial interests with British markets as well as with the protection of the all-powerful British fleet. It was also a repudiation of Jefferson's love affair with the French Revolution as a sentimental attachment rooted in some combination of nostalgia and seductive ideals (i.e., Liberty, Equality, and Fraternity) that floated dreamily in Jefferson's fertile imagination. For Jefferson, such ideals *were* the supreme reality. Washington regarded them as dangerous illusions that deflected attention from the long-term interests of the American people.

In the much larger context of European history, the doctrine of realism enjoyed a distinguished intellectual lineage reaching back to ancient Greece and the Melian Dialogue by Thucydides, which depicts all moralistic ideals as meaningless postures of powerless victims (i.e., "The powerful exact what they can, and the weak grant what they must"). Looking forward, it is customary to view American diplomatic history as an ongoing conversation between idealists and realists, although attempts to apply these abstract categories in specific foreign policy crises have proven maddeningly difficult. The leading American realists of the twentieth century, for example, were George Kennan and Henry Kissinger, but they disagreed over how to define American "interests" throughout the Cold War. Nevertheless, if the overarching dialogue between realism and idealism is the centerpiece of American foreign policy, Washington's Farewell Address is the primal source of the realistic tradition.[48]

In part because of his rock-ribbed realism, Washington did not believe that the American experience, or the republican values and institutions created during the American Revolution, were transferable to other countries lacking the distinctive political, demographic, and geographic advantages of the United States. America was the historical exception, not the rule, and any attempt to transplant its revolutionary values in French or European soil would most likely fail spectacularly. He sounded a cautionary note for all subsequent American statesmen of the Jeffersonian persuasion who sought to bring democratic principles to faraway places in Asia and the Middle East. It is a rich irony that precisely because Washington regarded the origins of the United States as exceptional, he could not endorse the modern version of American exceptionalism.

——— ◆ ———

Realism for Washington was not a philosophical doctrine he acquired by reading so much as a state of mind he internalized from experience. During the French and Indian War, he had watched fellow soldiers go down around him in heaps of blood and gore because they were standing at the wrong place at the wrong time. As master of Mount Vernon, he had learned to mistrust his consignment agent in London, Robert Cary, who he believed was swindling him into bankruptcy, and also his field slaves, who worked only when watched. As commander of the Continental Army, he concluded that patriotism was a wholly inadequate source of motivation for regular troops, and that militia could be counted on to run away in battle. As president, he was disappointed but not surprised to discover that erstwhile friends— Jefferson was the chief culprit—were slandering him behind his back, and that his Republican critics were prepared to play politics with American foreign policy, thereby putting the very survival of the American republic at risk for their own partisan interests.

At a more personal level, he created space around himself that only a few intimate friends were permitted to enter—Lafayette, Knox, Hamilton, and of course Martha. But otherwise his distancing mechanisms were legion, and woe to anyone who crossed the line uninvited. He ordered Martha to destroy all their correspondence upon his death, in part because he did not believe his innermost thoughts were anyone's business, in part because he did not trust posterity to judge his personality.

His realistic approach to foreign policy, then, was only a piece of his larger perspective on life itself: the fates were fickle, and one could trust only what one could control; human nature seldom rose to its highest aspirations; all utopian expectations for paradise on earth were delusional dreams destined to end at the guillotine or firing squad wall. His one attempt to act on a moral principle—the effort to rescue Native Americans from genocide—had ended in abject failure for all the realistic reasons that he had done his best to subvert.

Therefore, it was perfectly in character for Washington to leave instructions in his will not to bury his body until three days after he died, believing as he did that Jesus could not possibly have risen from the dead and so was probably buried alive. There were no ministers or priests in the room during his final hours, only well-intentioned doctors whose barbaric bleedings and purgings made his passing an agony. Artists quickly produced paintings and prints depicting his ascension to heaven alongside admiring angels. For Washington, however, there was no such thing as heaven, either on this earth or elsewhere. A realist to the end, he believed he was going, as he put it, "to the dreary mansion of my ancestors," which meant into the ground.[49]

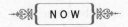

At Peace with War

It is in the nature of democracies to have, for the most part, the most confused or erroneous ideas on external affairs, and to decide questions of foreign policy on purely domestic considerations.

Alexis de Tocqueville, Democracy in America *(1835)*

. . .

The American narrative is morally unresolvable because the society that saved humanity in the great conflicts of the twentieth century was also a society built on enormous crimes—slavery and the extinction of the native inhabitants.

Robert D. Kaplan, Earning the Rockies *(2017)*

The Berlin Wall fell in 1989, exactly two centuries after George Washington assumed the presidency of the first large-scale republic in modern history. The collapse of the Soviet Union two years later marked a truly historic moment, which was not merely the end of the Cold War but also the triumph of the republican framework that Washington had led into a deeply skeptical world.

What came to be called the liberal tradition—representative government, popular sovereignty, a market economy, the rule of law—proceeded to vanquish the European monarchies in the nineteenth century, then the totalitarian dictatorships led by Germany, Japan, and the Soviet Union in the twentieth. The implosion of the Soviet Union could plausibly be described as the final chapter in a long story, in which the American model for the nation-state defeated communism, the only remaining autocratic alternative to democracy, thereby clinching victory for the vision Washington had glimpsed so long ago. In this triumphant spirit, Francis Fukuyama proclaimed that "liberal democracy may constitute the end point of man's ideological evolution," even "the end of history," a phrase almost designed to provoke the gods.

More specifically, the end of the Cold War left the United States as the undisputed superpower. This claim was not a rhetorical exaggeration. In 1991 the United States generated 26 percent of global GDP with less than 3 percent of the population. The dollar was the global currency; English was the global language. Militarily, America spent more on defense than the next twenty nations combined, projecting its power abroad with over 600,000 combat troops and support garrisons in more than forty countries. No imperial power in recorded history, neither the Roman empire nor the British empire at its zenith, enjoyed such supremacy.

The first occasion for the United States to display its new superpower status came with the Gulf War (1991), which became a poster child for America's hegemonic role in the post–Cold War era. Under a United Nations mandate to remove Iraqi forces from Kuwait, the United States deployed an overwhelming force of half a million troops that also enjoyed the support of a thirty-nation coalition. The military campaign was swift and successful, American casualties were low, and the costs were shared by the coalition countries, all of whom welcomed American leadership in securing the flow of oil through the Persian Gulf. President George H. W. Bush resisted the advice to pursue the Iraqi army back to Baghdad, calling it an unnecessary expansion of America's main mission. All in all, the new American leadership model was multilateral rather than unilateral, limited rather than unlimited, and decisive rather than protracted.

But hindsight, the historian's crystal ball, exposes four ominous features in the Gulf War story that would haunt America's superpower status in the ensuing decades. First, in his speech to the American people justifying the robust military commitment, President Bush coined the term *new world order*, implying that the collapse of the Soviet Union had created the unique opportunity to remake the world in America's image. Second, in the debate leading up to the war, Bush claimed the sole authority to commit American troops as commander in chief, a continuation of expanded executive power during the Cold War, in open defiance of language in the Constitution vesting that responsibility and role in Congress. Third, the insertion of American combat troops into the Middle East established a modern precedent for Western intrusion into the Muslim world that was eerily reminiscent of the ill-fated European Crusades so long ago. And fourth, the Gulf War short-circuited the debate over what was called the "peace dividend," meaning a reduction in defense spending that should occur now that the demise of the Soviet Union had removed the major rationale for the massive military establishment created during the Cold War.

The fourth feature is most mystifying because it was a nonevent. But the failure to develop a comprehensive strategy for American foreign policy once the Cold War ended proved to be the most consequential event of all. It can be explained in part by the fact that the sudden collapse of the Soviet Union took most American intelligence officials by surprise, itself a failure rooted in exaggerated estimates of the military and economic prowess of our designated Evil Empire. And then the Gulf War generated an immediate crisis that crowded out any strategic deliberation. As a result, deciding the direction of American foreign policy soon became an inherently improvisational process that developed on a case-by-case basis in response to crises that popped up like blips on the global radar screen.

One might envision the United States as a sailor venturing into vast and turbulent seas without a compass but with two heartfelt articles of faith to guide him: first, that the liberal model embodied in the American ship of state was sailing with the winds of history at its back, so that it was now, at long last, possible to act decisively on the Wilsonian promise to make the world safe for democracy; second, that the overwhelming military superiority of the American juggernaut meant that victory was inevitable, not only because the cause was just but also because the firepower at its disposal was invincible. Given these priceless assets, what could possibly go wrong?

⋯ ⋙✦⋘ ⋯

The most jolting answer to that question was first sighted in the skies over New York and Washington on September 11, 2001. The attack by Islamic terrorists on 9/11 represented the end of America's "splendid isolation," the first assault on the mainland of the United States since the British invasion during the War of 1812. (American national security had been vulnerable to foreign penetration since the mid-1960s, when the Soviet Union installed intercontinental ballistic missiles.) In what might be called the diplomacy of catharsis, the administration of President George W. Bush channeled this anxiety into support for an invasion of Iraq by postulating a link between 9/11 and the regime of Saddam Hussein. As America's top counterterrorist expert Richard Clarke described the decision, it was as if, in response to the Japanese attack at Pearl Harbor, the United States had invaded Mexico.

More ominously, the American government had inadvertently discovered a worthy successor to the Soviet Union as the new Evil Empire. The prevailing belief that Islamic terrorism represented an existential threat to national security comparable to a nuclear exchange during the Cold War was rationally ridiculous but, in the immediate aftermath of 9/11, emotionally compelling. Defense spending grew exponentially as a vast new Homeland Security and intelligence bureaucracy materialized almost overnight. All plans for reductions in the defense budget after the Cold War evaporated. The national debt soared past $12 trillion and kept climbing after the Great Recession of 2008.

Meanwhile, events in the Middle East made a mockery of any global version of Manifest Destiny. The overthrow of Saddam Hussein provoked a civil war between Sunni and Shia factions that exposed the awkward fact that no such entity as the "Iraqi people" existed. Loyalties were resolutely sectarian and tribal, which effectively meant that the Shia majority, once elected under a new American-sponsored constitution, proceeded to persecute and alienate the Sunni minority, many of whom went over to the emerging coalition of radical Islamists after most American troops departed in 2009. In neighboring Afghanistan, where the physical terrain was even more treacherous and the sectarian culture more splintered, the United States spent more on nation-building than it had spent on the Marshall Plan for all of Europe, with little to show for it.

If we step aside to scan the historical landscape during the quarter century after the Cold War, the most distinctive feature is nearly perpetual war, and the most distressing fact is that the overwhelming military superiority of the United States did not produce successful outcomes. Quite the opposite. In the most significant theater of American intervention, the Middle East, the strategic consequences have proven worse than disappointing, indeed counterproductive, by driving Iraq into the orbit of Iran and radicalizing Iraq's Sunni population, which became the nucleus for ISIS. Beyond the Middle East—in Somalia, Kosovo, and Libya—developments have also failed to follow the script that liberal prophets predicted. The American political recipe for success has proven unpalatable for people and places with different histories, religions, and political traditions.

There was no "peace dividend" because there was no peace, and there was no peace in part because the United States made going to war easy. It was supposed to be hard, what Washington had called "the dernier resort," requiring a declaration of war by the full Congress. The last time the United States went to war as the Constitution stipulated was December 8, 1941. The common practice was for the Senate to delegate the authority to the president, who then made the decision as commander in chief.

Nor was any public sacrifice required. Since President Richard

Nixon ended the draft in 1973, the burden of military service has fallen on a small minority of working-class men and women. Nothing like the mass protests against the Vietnam War occurred in the post–Cold War era, for the simple reason that two generations of middle-class, college-age citizens have never had to factor military service into their personal agendas. A serious but unspoken moral dilemma lurks beneath this convenient arrangement, when the chief beneficiaries of America's status as the dominant world power are immunized from obligations that come with those benefits.

An analogous disconnect has also been institutionalized by concealing the costs of war. The budget for the military campaigns in Iraq and Afghanistan, for example, was kept on a separate ledger, as if on a credit card. Instead of a tax increase to cover a portion of the costs, President Bush pushed through a major *reduction* in taxes, thereby passing the bill (or buck) to posterity. Such financial and accounting chicanery reinforced the larger pattern of deception in the post–Cold War era, making war almost painless: it is not declared, few have to fight, and no one has to pay. Only a small group of veterans, who are currently committing suicide in record numbers, experience firsthand that the United States is engaged in a perpetual war.

⟶ ⟻⟶⟼ ⟶

It is difficult to focus critically on the strategic failure of American foreign policy in the post–Cold War years when the central problem is the absence of any comprehensive strategy at all. It does seem clear that the Middle East has become a disproving ground for assumptions about the inevitable triumph of the liberal order. And that painful realization raises larger questions about the wisdom of military interventions that require the transformation of entire societies, usually a long-term, expensive, and thankless task for which the short attention span of the American public is unprepared. Moreover, in the absence of any explicit articulation of America's strategic priorities, control over the direction of foreign policy has effectively shifted to the Pentagon in what became a global version of "mission creep." The creation of five military regions covering the entire world, each under a senior general or admiral who functions as a kind of proconsul in the mode of the Roman Empire, represents an unspoken but de facto commitment to defend ill-defined American interests anywhere and everywhere. This defense-driven expansion of America's global obligations is also reflected in the 16-to-1 ratio of military to diplomatic spending throughout the post–Cold War era.

The combination of limitless goals and a fully militarized foreign policy has troubling implications because it mirrors the fateful pattern of rise and fall that has caught almost all preceding world powers in its web. The authoritative account of this imperial syndrome is *The Rise and Fall of the Great Powers* (1987) by Paul Kennedy, which identified the fatal flaw as "imperial overstretch," meaning the excessive growth of military costs required to manage far-flung obligations, which then saps the economic strength responsible for the earlier ascendance. (Several members of the founding generation, Adams most prominently, were thoroughly familiar with the classical version of this cyclical pattern from the works of Tacitus on the Roman Empire and viewed the misguided policies of the British Empire as the modern version of the same imperial story.) Lurking in the decline-and-fall syndrome is the implication that all empires, like all mortals, must come and go, and that the chief reason for their demise is that the world is an inherently unmanageable place that eventually devours the strength of any and all superpowers that history selects for what is, in effect, an impossible mission. Based on the first quarter century of its reign as the sole superpower, the United States, which tends to regard itself as the "exceptional nation," is not proving an exception to one of history's most enduring narratives.

⟶ ⟶ ⟵ ⟵

If we are seeking guidance from the past on how to make foreign policy decisions in a deliberative rather than improvisational fashion, preferably like past decisions that we now know proved prescient, George Kennan deserves special notice. Kennan was the chief architect of the doctrinal framework for American strategy in the Cold War that came to be called "containment." His central insight, made public in his "Sources of Soviet Conduct" (1947), was to turn the ideological prophecy of Marxism-Leninism on its head, for he argued that communism, not capitalism, was sown with the seeds of its own destruction, thereby making any direct military conflict with the Soviet Union unnecessary. If the United States and its allies blocked Soviet expansion into Western Europe and confined its sphere of influence to the Eurasian continent, the inherent contradictions within Soviet-style communism would, over time, make both economic growth and political control unsustainable. Kennan opposed the Vietnam War as an unnecessary and misguided waste of American resources, then lived long enough to celebrate the vindication of his vision with the implosion of the Soviet Union in 1991.

How can we explain the analytical prowess of Kennan's strategic thought process? He was stationed at the American embassy in Moscow, observed firsthand the brutality of Stalin's regime as a witness to the Moscow Trials during the late 1930s, and realized earlier than most that our Soviet ally in World War II would become an implacable enemy once the war was won. He was fluent in Russian and deeply read in Russian history and literature as well as in the political treatises of Marx, Engels, and Lenin. He was an unabashed realist who thought historically, meaning that he had little patience with theoretical models or moralistic assumptions with utopian expectations; indeed, those were the very flaws that made communism an inherently delusional ideology. More pragmatically, he realized that no nation, not even the United States, possessed unlimited resources, so any realistic strategy needed to prioritize its commitments, to identify what must be done and what must *not* be done. On that score, there was no need to wage a costly war against the Soviet Union once you truly believed that, left to its own devices, it was doomed to dissolution.

There is another voice from further back that merits our attention, though not for the obvious reasons. George Washington's prescription for an isolationist foreign policy enjoyed a lengthy life-span but became anachronistic by the end of the nineteenth century, when the frontier era ended and the United States surpassed Great Britain as the world's dominant economy. The irrelevance of isolationism was not fully exposed until the interwar years (1920–40), when the global order collapsed in the absence of an American international presence, leading to the ascendance of totalitarian regimes in Germany, Japan, and the Soviet Union. Ever afterward isolation ceased to exist as a viable American option. The question was not whether the United States should play its role as a world power but how to do so.

Washington's enduringly relevant message in the Farewell Address can be found in the realistic reasoning that shaped his isolationist vision, which emphasized the unique geographic and demographic conditions the United States enjoyed. Unlike Jefferson, who believed that the liberal values the founding generation had discovered were universal principles destined to spread throughout the world, Washington believed they were products of a highly distinctive set of historical circumstances unlikely to be duplicated elsewhere. Adams tended to concur with Washington and engaged in a friendly debate with Jefferson during their twilight years, arguing that America's political values would never take root in Latin America because Spanish and Catholic traditions predisposed that region to hierarchical political systems. Adams's son, John Quincy Adams, the most prominent and influential foreign policy thinker of the antebellum era, also agreed that the United States could serve as a role model for republican institutions but must never attempt to become a messianic missionary or, even worse, an imperious intruder in the British mode. As he put it in a Fourth of July speech (1821) that George Kennan loved to quote, "America goes not abroad in search of monsters to destroy."

Beyond the legacy of isolationism, then, Washington and his generation left a legacy of American exceptionalism that meant exactly the opposite of what that term came to mean in the twentieth century. In effect, precisely because the conditions shaping the American founding were unique, it was highly problematic to presume that the American model was transportable beyond the borders of the United

States. As for Jefferson, whose formulation of the founding legacy foresaw its global triumph (i.e., "May it be to the world, what I believe it will be, in some parts sooner, to others later, but finally to all"), even he assumed that liberal principles, by definition, could never be imposed by force but only discovered by distant peoples in their own time and in their own ways.

The phrase that has come to capture this neoisolationist tradition is "city on a hill," which also, like "American exceptionalism," abounds in ironies. It was coined by John Winthrop in 1630 to describe a Puritan paradise where each person had a predestined place in a fixed social hierarchy; it was a medieval rather than a democratic vision. President Ronald Reagan frequently used the phrase "shining city on a hill" without seeming to fully realize that it described a United States that remained a distant beacon to the world and focused its fullest energies on improving itself rather than on overseeing the global order.

These voices from the past speak from different contexts with distinctive political accents, but they constitute a chorus in sounding three clear notes. First, the United States has committed the predictable mistakes of a novice superpower most rooted in overconfidence bordering on arrogance; second, wars have become routinized because foreign policy has become militarized at the same time as the middle class has been immunized from military service; and third, the creedal conviction that American values are transplantable to all regions of the world is highly suspect and likely to draw the United States into nation-building projects beyond its will or capacity to complete. If we ever have a sustained conversation about America's role in the world, in effect the conversation we did not have at the end of the Cold War, these three lessons learned over the last quarter century should be placed on the table at the start.

＊＊＊

The conversation has already begun within scholarly circles and the foreign policy establishment. There is a discernibly chastened tone to the dialogue, a shared sense that the world has not followed the liberal script that so many expected in the immediate aftermath of the Cold War. Hindsight now makes clear that the Cold War imposed a coherent framework on the international world (i.e., West versus East, democracy versus communism) that provided a measure of strategic, even moral certainty for the designated champion of the West. Specific diplomatic decisions fit within a larger strategic scheme that framed choices in unambiguous, nonnegotiable terms. And these terms conveniently coincided with the Jeffersonian side of the American Dialogue (i.e., freedom versus tyranny), which required no explanation to an American audience.

That era has ended. The Cold War has proved to be a temporary interlude that gave a false sense of credibility to the term *world order*. The global landscape has recovered its baffling, multilayered complexity and no longer fits within a bimodal frame. It's as if the gods replaced their binoculars with a kaleidoscope. Whether the United States is historically equipped to lead in the new global context remains an open question.

The improbable election of Donald Trump has placed an exclamation point after that question. His presidential campaign featured the promise to "Make America Great Again" with "Again" deliberately vague. For his white supremacist supporters, it meant before the civil rights movement. For voters in Appalachia and the Rust Belt, it meant before globalization took away their jobs. His other promise to "Make America First" echoed the slogan of those who opposed American entry into World War II, suggesting a return to the isolationist America of the interwar years (1920–40). And by renouncing American commitment to the Paris Accords that set limits on carbon emissions, endorsing the British exit from the European Union, questioning the viability of NATO, and threatening to withdraw from the North American Free Trade Agreement, Trump effectively announced that the United States was relinquishing its role as the designated superpower.

It is clear that Trump's controversial presidency is an American version of Brexit, a "back to the future" retreat to fortress America in reaction to the disorienting and destructive forces of the global marketplace. It is also clear that Trump embodies, in almost archetypical form, the demagogic downside of democracy. In the ancient world, for example, Thucydides warned about the vulnerability of the Athenian citizenry to the jingoistic rhetoric of Cleon. Cicero delivered a similar warning about the conspiratorial tactics of Catiline, which threatened the survival of the Roman Republic. Washington echoed the same message in his Farewell Address, lamenting the manipulation of popular opinion by the Republican opposition to the Jay Treaty and the intrusion of inflammatory domestic disputes into foreign policy.

Throughout history, then, the fate of nations with political frameworks based on public opinion has always been haunted by the specter of charismatic charlatans with a knack for exploiting popular fears. In that sense, the Trump presidency, while wholly unexpected, was eminently predictable, almost overdue. (Historians are the undisputed champions at after-the-fact wisdom that reveals why unexpected outcomes were always inevitable.) Much like meteors streaking across the horizon, demagogues tend to enjoy only limited life-spans, so the Trump presidency is likely to resemble the proverbial blip on the historical radar screen.

But whatever his duration, Trump has exposed the deep pools of isolationist sentiment that always lurked beneath the surface in the rural regions of the American heartland, now raised to relief by residents who see themselves as victims rather than beneficiaries of the globalized marketplace America is defending. Moreover, the very fact that a person with Trump's obvious mental, emotional, and moral limitations could be chosen to lead the free world casts a dark shadow of doubt over the credibility and reliability of the United States as the first democratic superpower.

In addition to being the first democracy, the United States also carries two burdens that no previous world power had to bear: it is the first superpower with anti-imperial origins, and it is the first superpower to assume that role in the postimperial era. These unique legacies, with morally admirable implications that flow from the founding, pose political and strategic problems that limit America's conduct in its role as the dominant power.

The British historian Niall Ferguson provides the fullest treatment of America's anti-imperial problem in *Colossus: The Price of America's Empire* (2004). He poses the problem with a distinctive British accent, asking whether the United States is up to the task of replacing Great Britain as the guarantor of global order. Ferguson describes America on the basis of its sheer size and resources as even more economically and militarily equipped than his British ancestors to play the leadership role. But he concludes that the United States is "an empire in denial" that lacks the will to stay the course in Iraq and Afghanistan in the same reliable fashion Great Britain displayed in its sustained occupations of India, Egypt, and South Africa.

One can only imagine George Washington rolling over in his grave. For the very suggestion that the British Empire should serve as the role model for American leadership in the world defies the core values of the American founding. A republic, by definition, cannot be an empire. This is a principled conviction deeply embedded in America's DNA. It is the chief reason why protracted wars have seldom enjoyed popular support in American history, and the underlying reason why nation-building projects in faraway places invariably become politically unpalatable. For they closely resemble, and often are, imperial projects.

It is useless to accuse the United States of lacking "the will to power," as Ferguson does, since that purported deficiency is rooted in what Lincoln called "the mystic chords of memory" that enshrined the successful war against British imperialism as the primal source of American patriotism. There are exceptions to the larger pattern—the occupation of the Philippines, for example. But as a general rule there is a clock running on all American military occupations of foreign countries that our British, Spanish, Ottoman, and Roman predecessors did not need to contemplate.

Also unprecedented is the problem the United States faces as the first superpower of the postimperial era. All previous world powers were empires whose global ascendance to that status was a collateral consequence of the power acquired by extracting wealth from the colonies they controlled. Great Britain did not occupy South Africa and fight the Boer War primarily to shoulder "the white man's burden" in some Kiplingesque commitment to racial justice. It did so in order to ensure British control of the lucrative diamond market.

In the postimperial age, no analogous economic incentive exists for the United States. When Donald Trump, speaking as a presidential candidate, proposed that the United States should have "taken the oil" before exiting Iraq in 2009, the very suggestion produced incredulous criticism from all sides, and he quickly dropped the idea. As a former colony in an anti-imperial age, the United States cannot do colonization.

As a result, the role of superpower in the twenty-first century is unlikely to prove cost-effective. When the ledger is closed on the military budget for Iraq and Afghanistan, the cost will approach $4 trillion. Such a sum, if spent on domestic priorities, could have shored up Medicare for a generation and paid for the restoration of America's aging infrastructure. These are difficult trade-offs to justify in a democracy. Moreover, as already noted, a sizable minority of America's working class are victims of the very global order the United States is spending so much to sustain, the very constituency that made Trump's presidency possible.

There are, then, some compelling questions surrounding America's future as a superpower based on long-standing legacies. Do our origins as a republic based on popular consent impose limitations that make American reliability as a world leader problematic? Is the neo-isolationist message of the Trump presidency a harbinger of the future or a temporary aberration? Is America's seventy-year reign at the top ending? Are there any voices from the founding still sufficiently resonant to point in a different direction?

One prominent student of American foreign policy, Robert D. Kaplan, has addressed this cluster of questions in a distinctive format. His intriguingly titled *Earning the Rockies* (2017) is a memoir of his coast-to-coast trek in 2015 that quickly became a meditation on America's role in the world, prompted by his conviction that "the answers to our dilemmas overseas lie within the continent itself." Kaplan is self-consciously echoing and updating Washington's earlier version of American continental empire as a geographic asset destined to dictate the future direction of American history.

What Washington viewed as a providential gift that permitted the infant republic to flourish as a secure, self-sufficient nation, Kaplan describes as a providential platform from which the mature American republic can project its unmatched economic and military prowess abroad. Due to technology, distance has now disappeared from the strategic equation, thereby rendering isolation impossible. Now the Atlantic and Pacific are no longer protective shields but unique access points to both Europe and Asia. Kaplan adopts Washington's realistic approach to foreign policy, still driven by geography, but now revised to fit a wholly globalized world.

His analysis of the forces propelling the United States outward is almost gravitational. It is not a matter of *choosing* a direction. America's fate is built into its location, natural resources, and the coastal contours of the continent. For Kaplan, America's destiny as a super-power is just as manifest as its earlier expansion across the Rockies. Any attempt to resist that destiny will prove as futile as the effort to rescue the victims of globalization in the American heartland from their sad but inevitable fate. There are two Americas out there, one connected to the global economy, the other marooned in interior islands of joblessness, despair, and addiction. There is no question which one owns the future.

Kaplan also goes back to the founding for his forecast of America's conduct in its fated role as unrivaled world power, which once again channels Washington's experience. We should expect great triumphs and great tragedies during America's continued reign at the top, he argues, because the oscillation between these two sides of our domestic history is likely to persist in our future foreign policy. "The American narrative is morally unresolvable," he observes, "because the society that saved humanity in the great conflicts of the twentieth century was also a society built on enormous crimes—slavery and the extinction of the native inhabitants." If our role in the world is clear, how we play that role will probably defy any semblance of coherence or moral clarity. We are both fated to lead and fated to do so erratically and impulsively. Alexis de Tocqueville's words at the end of *Democracy in America* come to mind: "I am full of apprehension and hope." Our ongoing dialogue should pay respect to both sides of that thought.

Leadership

Public affairs go on pretty much as usual, perpetual chicanery and rather more personal abuse than there used to be.
Our American Chivalry is the worst in the World. It has no
laws, no bounds, no definitions; it seems to be all a caprice.

John Adams to Thomas Jefferson, April 17, 1826

The British philosopher Alfred North Whitehead once observed
that there were only two occasions in the history of Western civilization when the political leadership of an emerging nation behaved
as well as anyone could reasonably expect. The first was Rome under
Caesar Augustus; the second was the United States under that collection of characters called the founders. The clear consensus among
scholars is that the political leadership that emerged in the last quarter of the eighteenth century displayed more creative talent than any
subsequent generation of American statesmen. Polls of historians and
political scientists routinely rank Abraham Lincoln and Franklin Roosevelt ahead of George Washington on the list of great American presidents, but the range of political creativity surrounding Washington,
chiefly Adams, Jefferson, Franklin, Madison, and Hamilton, has no
serious competitor as a gallery of greats.*

---

*I will forgo any attempt at defining political leadership on the assumption that it is
best understood when we see it in action. For those disposed toward a more theoretical

How to account for this unexpected explosion of political talent in an emerging nation on the fringe of the Atlantic world is a question that has attracted multiple explanations, both at the time and ever since. Over fifty years ago the historian Douglass Adair put the question most mischievously. The white population of Virginia in 1790 totaled about 400,000 souls, Adair noted, which was slightly smaller than the current population of Wilkes-Barre, Pennsylvania. If we conducted a rigorous survey of the residents of Wilkes-Barre, could we expect to find the likes of George Washington, Thomas Jefferson, James Madison, Patrick Henry, George Mason, and John Marshall?

Obviously not. And an updated version of Adair's question would solicit the same answer. The population of the United States according to the first census in 1790 was just shy of 4 million, and the two leading candidates for president the previous year were George Washington and John Adams. The population in 2016 was 315 million, and two candidates for president were Hillary Clinton and Donald Trump.

Such juxtapositions, the historical equivalent of shooting fish in a barrel, should be avoided at the start, since it ends the conversation about leadership before it can begin. Similarly, one explanation for the singular status of the founding generation needs to be ruled inadmissible: there can be no reference to divine intervention. Soon after their departure, a thick cloud of incense formed around the founders that required over a century to dissipate. But it is still fashionable for some wholly secular historians to use words like *miracle, sacred,* and *godlike* to describe the achievement of the revolutionary generation. Such lingering vestiges of religiosity corrupt any serious inquiry into the sources of their creativity. The founders desperately wanted to be remembered. But they must not be canonized.

What, then, did these fully flawed patriarchs achieve? With the advantages of hindsight, we can say they made three major contribu-

---

discussion, the work of James MacGregor Burns is the best place to start, specifically *Leadership* (1978) and *Transforming Leadership* (2003).

tions to modern political thought of enduring significance. They also failed to resolve two deep-rooted problems that, in the end, must be listed as tragedies.

⊷ ⚏ ↢

On the triumph side of the ledger, they created the first nation-size republic. It was previously presumed that republican governments based on popular consent could function only in small areas like Swiss cantons or Greek city-states, because republics were supposedly incapable of imposing authority over a large and far-flung population. This is what Lincoln meant during the Civil War when he described the conflict as the acid test of whether "any government so conceived and so dedicated can long endure." Over two centuries since its founding, the American republic has endured, in the process becoming the model for the liberal state in the modern era. There were, in effect, two foundings: winning a war for independence and creating a large-scale republic. The two achievements taken together are what make the American Revolution a revolution.

Second, they created the first wholly secular state. Before the American founding, it was assumed that state support for an established religion was a mandatory feature of all viable governments, because it enforced a consensus on the common values that made a collective sense of purpose possible. While many of the states retained various Protestant establishments well into the nineteenth century, the founders insisted on a complete separation of church and state at the national level, thereby overturning the long-standing presumption that only shared religious convictions could hold a nation together.

Third, they rejected the conventional wisdom, agreed upon since Aristotle, that political sovereignty was by definition singular and indivisible and must reside in one agreed-upon location. The Constitution defied this assumption by creating multiple and overlapping sources of authority in which the blurring of jurisdiction between federal and state levels, as well as between and among branches of government, became an asset rather than a liability. The very idea of sovereignty became problematic, and its rhetorical depository, "the people," an inherently elusive location.

The two conspicuous failures of the revolutionary generation involved Native Americans and African Americans, more specifically the inability to avoid Indian removal, a covert form of genocide, and the failure to put slavery on the road to extinction before it necessitated the bloodiest war in American history to end it. The fact that these failures were tragedies is beyond debate. The more difficult question is whether they are best understood as Greek or Shakespearean tragedies, meaning inherently unsolvable for reasons beyond human control or susceptible to solution with the right kind of political leadership.

By my lights, the Native American dilemma was a Greek tragedy, in the sense that the problem became intractable and unsolvable once the demographic wave of white settlers began flowing across the Alleghenies after the United States acquired the eastern third of the North American continent in the Treaty of Paris (1783). Washington devoted his fullest energies to the creation of a series of Native American homelands east of the Mississippi, which would have avoided Indian removal and provided a framework for the just resolution of what was clearly a moral problem in the fullest meaning of that term. But the combination of demography and democracy overwhelmed Washington's most focused and strenuous leadership, suggesting that once the torrent of white settlers began pouring into Indian country, nothing could have altered the outcome.

As already noted, slavery is the original sin of American history, and if it is made the ultimate test of leadership for the revolutionary generation, then the founders failed the test. This is not just a tragedy but America's defining tragedy. And the only question is whether it belongs in the Greek or Shakespearean category. Was there any way to end slavery short of war?

In framing that debate, the following facts must be faced squarely. All the prominent founders, including southern slave owners, recognized that slavery contradicted the core values of the American Revolution. Most of the founders thought that the window of opportunity to end slavery was opening—that it would die a natural death if isolated in the Deep South, because slave labor could not compete with free labor, a misreading of history rooted in a failure to foresee the emergence of the Cotton Kingdom. Any effort to put slavery on the road to extinction during the Constitutional Convention would have rendered the ratification of the Constitution impossible, leaving the southern states free to extend the slave trade indefinitely and silence all criticism of slavery itself. And last and most worrisome, although the founders were capable of imagining a nation-size republic and a secular state, they were incapable of imagining a biracial society, which meant that any emancipation scheme bore the enormous burden of transporting the free black population to some distant location outside the nation's borders.

The problem became intractable after 1820, when the Missouri Compromise allowed for slavery's expansion and cotton production became the mainstay of the southern economy. At that point slavery became a Greek tragedy. Before that date, however, the window of opportunity to end slavery was still open. (Washington thought a full-scale debate should begin after the slave trade ended in 1808.) But no one stepped forward at the national level to provide the kind of leadership on slavery that Washington had attempted to provide on the Native American question. In the wake of the Louisiana Purchase, Jefferson was perfectly positioned to play that role; and all the political and economic ingredients were present to enact a gradual emancipation plan that included removal of the emancipated slaves to the newly acquired western territories. This must be judged a failure of leadership in the Shakespearean mode, with racism the fatal flaw.

Slavery will forever remain the signature sin of the founding. Any historical interpretation that ignores or obscures that indisputable fact is unworthy of serious consideration. Facing it, however, must not be allowed to end the argument about the leadership legacy of the founders. The whole point about the founding, which defies any wholly moralistic agenda, is that the triumphs and tragedies coexisted, indeed were mutually dependent. The moral imperative to end slavery had to compete with the political imperative to win the war against Great Britain and then create a national government, both goals that required the inclusion of slaveholding states. Within the constraints imposed by that intractable reality, the founders managed to maximize the creative possibilities of their time more fully than any subsequent generation of political leaders in American history. The salient question is how they did it.

One answer, which came from the revolutionary generation itself, is sprinkled throughout the letters of several founders. The clearest articulation of this "crisis" explanation appeared in David Ramsay's *History of the American Revolution* (1789): "The Revolution called forth many virtues and gave occasion for the display of abilities which, but for that event, would have been lost to the world. In the years 1775 and 1776, the country being suddenly thrown into a situation that *needed* the ability of all its sons, a vast expansion of the human mind speedily followed. It seemed that the war not only required but *created* talents." Washington made the same argument to explain the improbable passage and ratification of the Constitution. The very hopelessness of the task, and the strength of the opposition, he observed, "had called forth abilities which would otherwise not perhaps been exerted that have thrown new lights on the science of Government [i.e., the Federalist Papers], that have given the rights of man a full and fair discussion."

This explanation anticipated the argument of Arnold Toynbee in *A Study of History* (abridged edition, 1954) that leadership appears only in societies undergoing great crises. Although historians of the Civil War might contest the claim, the American Revolution is arguably the greatest political crisis in American history. If it had failed, Washington would have remained an inconsequential Virginia squire, Adams an obscure country lawyer. This crisis explanation also reminds us that Jefferson's felicitous words in the Declaration, "our lives, our fortune, and our sacred honor," were an accurate description of the all-or-nothing risk the leaders of the movement for independence were required to run. Once committed to "The Cause," leadership became the only option forward; there was no turning back.

Another explanation that amplifies the crisis argument comes from Douglass Adair in an essay entitled "Fame and the Founding Fathers" (1966). As the title suggests, all the prominent founders were obsessed with living on in the memory of subsequent generations. Adams is most articulate about this quest for secular immortality, which he acknowledged was an irrational impulse, but the collected writings of all the founders are so voluminous in large part because they preserved their letters for our subsequent scrutiny. Similarly, those iconic portraits by John Trumbull and Gilbert Stuart show us men who were posing for posterity.

Adair called attention to the fact that the revolutionary generation came of age at a moment in Western history when the prospect of everlasting life in a Christian version of the hereafter was becoming problematic, so that living on in the memory of succeeding generations became the only assured afterlife. The election that counted most for the founders was posterity's judgment, and they chose to win that vote by conducting themselves according to a classical code that linked their personal ambitions to the larger agenda of nation-making. They were, in effect, on their best behavior because they knew we would be watching. (Washington's decision to free his slaves in his will, for example, was motivated by his realization that failure to do so would forever stain his reputation.) The crisis explanation helps us understand why a political elite emerged when it did. Adair's focus on fame helps explain the distinctively classical character of leadership the founders consciously strove to imitate.

Gordon Wood provides another angle from which to view the leadership question. He describes the revolutionary era as a truly special moment that afforded opportunities for political leadership and creativity never possible before and never achievable since. It was,

Wood argues, simultaneously a postaristocratic and predemocratic age. On the one hand, this meant that politics was open to a whole class of talented men (women were still unimaginable as leaders outside the family) who would have languished in obscurity in Europe or Great Britain because they lacked the proper bloodlines. There was still a discernible social hierarchy in America, but compared to all other advanced societies at that time, the United States afforded an unprecedented opportunity for movement from bottom to top. As a result, when the revolutionary crisis arrived, it could draw upon the latent talent from a segment of the population never before allowed access.

On the other hand, the founders were a self-conscious elite, what Jefferson called a "natural aristocracy" based on merit rather than blood. They were therefore immune to democratic mythology about the innate wisdom of the common man, completely comfortable with their own superiority. All of the first five presidents regarded the act of campaigning for office as a confession that they were not statesmen but demagogues. While popular opinion was hardly irrelevant, it was regarded as flighty, shortsighted, and easily manipulated. The ultimate allegiance of the founders was not to "the people" but to "the public," which was the long-term interest of the citizenry that they, the founders, were obligated to serve regardless of the short-term political consequences. During his retirement, for example, Adams boasted that his greatest achievement as president was to lose the election of 1800, because his defeat was a direct consequence of his unpopular but historically correct decision to avoid war with France.

By straddling these two worlds, without belonging completely to either one, the founders maximized the leadership potential of both. The founders were America's first Lost Generation, for the moment they occupied can never come again. As Wood is at pains to show, all of the founders who lived long enough to witness the emergence of a full-blooded democratic political culture in the 1820s regarded it as an alien presence and not at all what they had in mind when they launched the American experiment in 1776. While there is much to admire in the founders, the distinctive brand of leadership they provided is impossible to duplicate because—and this is deeply ironic—we inhabit a democratic America that they made possible but that then made them impossible.

A slightly different interpretive angle on the special character of the revolutionary generation comes from Bernard Bailyn, who focuses on the distinctive geographic location of the founders. As already noted, Washington identified the isolation of the North American continent and the enormous trust fund provided by the acquisition of a western empire east of the Mississippi as priceless assets that afforded the founders leadership opportunities denied to previous nation-builders. Bailyn is more interested in the location of the founders on the periphery of the British Empire, perhaps the last place one should expect to find an explosion of political creativity that changed forever the way we think about government. Bailyn poses the question for dramatic effect: How could this backwoods population of 3 to 5 million farmers, mechanics, and minor gentry, far removed from the epicenters of learning in London and Paris, somehow produce thinkers and ideas that fundamentally transformed the landscape of modern politics?

Bailyn's answer is counterintuitive, that less was more. His earlier work on the Scottish Enlightenment prepared him to notice that being on the periphery in Edinburgh rather than the cosmopolitan center of London allowed Scottish thinkers like David Hume and Adam Smith to range more widely because their imaginations were not constrained by encrusted traditions, embedded institutions, and socially sanctioned inhibitions. Likewise for American thinkers like Adams, Madison, and Jefferson, the cultural stigma of being mere provincials turned out to be more of an asset than a liability, since they were free to question the old self-evident truths and invent their own without fear of offending established sources of authority because, in fact, there were none.

For instance, certain radical ideas, like divided sovereignty and separation of church and state, which were consigned to the fringes of British political thought, could and did enter the mainstream in the American context, where they were then sanctioned as cherished revolutionary principles. Like Wood, Bailyn emphasizes the distinctive historical conditions that shaped the achievement of the founding era, which makes it forever alluring and forever gone.

Finally, I have argued that the political achievement of the revolutionary generation was partially a function of its ideological and even temperamental diversity. We speak of the founders in the plural because the American founding was a collective enterprise. Yet the founders harbored different beliefs about what the American Revolution meant, as the Adams-Jefferson correspondence most fully exposes. This political and psychological diversity enhanced creativity by generating a dynamic chemistry that surfaced in the arguments that ensued whenever a major crisis materialized. Diversity made dialogue unavoidable.

If left alone, Jefferson would have carried the infant nation perilously close to anarchy. Hamilton would have erred on the side of autocracy. The collision of convictions not only enriched the intellectual ferment, it also replicated the checks and balances embedded in the Constitution with a human version of the same balancing principle. Because the face of the American founding was, and still is, a group portrait, our depiction of the revolutionary generation has never developed into a one-man despotism in the Napoleonic mode, and the political legacy it bequeathed to posterity defied any one-dimensional definition.

As a result, the founders will forever resist exclusive ownership by any political party or ideological camp. To paraphrase Walt Whitman, the founders contained multitudes. The American Dialogue they framed is a never-ending argument that neither side can win conclusively. It is the argument itself, not the answer either liberals or conservatives provide, that is the abiding legacy.

+ · ⊫◈⊨ · +

Whether that legacy still speaks to us depends almost entirely on whether we are listening and willing to engage in argument. In that spirit, consider the following three stories, all true, and all singular examples of leadership that had significant historical consequences. What qualities of mind and heart did these three founders bring to the task at hand that shaped their behavior? If leadership requires knowing where history is headed, how did they grasp the answer to that question so assuredly? Would any foreseeable crisis in our time be capable of generating equivalently decisive responses?

MOUNT VERNON, MAY 1775

The battles at Lexington and Concord had just happened, amplifying the urgency to gather the delegates to the Continental Congress in Philadelphia. Accompanied by his trusted manservant, Billy Lee, George Washington was preparing to mount up for the ride to Philadelphia. He was wearing his old military uniform from French and Indian War days, a sartorial statement of considerable significance. For while most of the delegates traveling to Philadelphia were presuming that their pressing task was to defuse the crisis and find a way to avoid war with Great Britain, Washington had come to believe that there was no longer any middle course, indeed that the war had already begun.

This was the defining moment in Washington's public life. Many years later, at his funeral in 1799, his old cavalry commander Henry Lee uttered the eulogy that has echoed through the ages, proclaiming Washington as "first in war, first in peace, and first in the hearts of his countrymen." The first of these firsts, which then led to the others, took shape in Washington's mind on the front lawn of Mount Vernon in mid-May 1775.

We know what was on his mind because of the instructions he gave to Lund Washington, a cousin and manager of his Mount Vernon estate. He ordered Lund to remove his books and Martha—presumably not in that order—if and when the British navy sent ships up the Potomac to destroy Mount Vernon. Washington was fully aware that he was about to commit treason against the British Empire, and the loss of his beloved Mount Vernon was a price he should expect to pay for his insubordination. While most of his fellow delegates to the Continental Congress were hedging their bets, Washington was all in, and once committed, he never looked back.

A revealing postscript to this story occurred six years later. Although Washington's name headed the list of prominent American rebels scheduled for hanging if and when the British won the war, they never saw fit to target Mount Vernon, probably because Virginia did not become a theater of action until 1781, when General Cornwallis moved the British army up from South Carolina. Shortly thereafter a British frigate sailed up the Potomac and anchored off Mount Vernon. Lund Washington went out to confer with the British captain, who explained that he was fishing for herring. Taking no chances, Lund sent a small skiff out to the British ship loaded with "sheep, hogs, and an abundant supply of other articles as a present," then reported this successful act of appeasement to Washington, who immediately let it be known that he was not at all pleased with the news.

"You ought to have considered yourself as my representative," he scolded Lund, "and should have reflected on the bad example of communicating with the Enemy, and making a voluntary offer of refreshments to them with a view to prevent a conflagration." As Washington saw it, Lund had stained his honor by compromising his character in order to preserve his property. "It would have been a less painful circumstance to me," Washington angrily concluded, "to have heard that in consequence of your non-compliance with their request, they had burnt my House, and laid the Plantation to ruins." His commitment to what he called "The Cause" had become synonymous with who he was.

VERSAILLES, AUGUST 1782

It was pure chance that left John Jay the sole American diplomat in Paris available to launch the negotiations for ending the American war for independence. Thomas Jefferson had declined the offer to serve on the negotiating committee, citing the recent death of his wife. His replacement, Henry Laurens of South Carolina, had been captured at sea by the British and thrown into the Tower of London as a prisoner of war. John Adams was fully engaged in Amsterdam and Leyden, trying to arrange a loan with the notoriously tightfisted Dutch bankers that would pay off America's huge war debt. Benjamin Franklin was incapacitated with a flare-up of gout, though nearby at his quarters outside Paris. So Jay was left by himself to launch preliminary discussions, what he described as "the skirmishing business," with the Spanish minister to France, Count Aranda. They met in the cavernous royal library at Versailles. It was August 3, 1782.

The meeting with Aranda was necessary because the American negotiations were under strict orders "to undertake nothing without the knowledge and concurrence of France" and since the French were bound by treaty to consult with Spain, Jay was obligated to meet with the Spanish minister to appease the French. As convoluted as this might seem, solidarity with France made diplomatic sense, because French financial and military assistance had proven crucial in turning the tide of war, then achieving the final victory at Yorktown that broke the British will to continue the conflict. So there were complicated but compelling reasons why the American and Spaniard were hunched over a table, looking down at a map of North America.

Jay made no comment as Aranda put his finger on what is now Lake Erie, moved it down through mid-Ohio, then farther south to the Florida Panhandle near modern-day Tallahassee. Everything east of that line, Aranda declared, belonged to the United States, everything west to Spain. He was essentially carving up the British Empire in North America and claiming a share of the spoils for Spain.

Jay hesitated for only a few seconds, then announced that he had no need to draw a line. He pointed to the Mississippi River as the new western border of the United States. He had received no guidance from his superiors in the Confederation Congress on the territorial question. On his own, since distance made consultation impossible, Jay decided to claim all of Britain's empire in North America south of Canada. And he declared that claim to be nonnegotiable.

He went directly from Versailles to Franklin's quarters to tell America's senior statesman what he had done. Pacing back and forth while puffing away on his clay pipe as Franklin lay on the sofa listening, Jay explained that it was now abundantly clear that America's long-term interests demanded that the negotiating team disregard their orders to consult with the French, then tossed his clay pipe into the fireplace for emphasis. For if they obeyed their instructions, American interests would be held hostage to predatory French and Spanish claims on North America, thereby replacing the British with another pair of European imperialists. The only way to avoid that outcome was to violate their instructions and make a separate peace with the British. Franklin, whose loyalties to the French ran deep, needed several days to digest Jay's radical proposal but eventually concurred. When Adams came down from Holland, his reaction was more immediate. Jay's decision to bypass the French struck him as a wonderful idea. "It is glorious to have broken such orders," Adams pronounced, "and so it will appear to all posterity."

Although the delegates to the Confederation Congress were initially outraged by what they described as an act of insubordination verging on treason, events proved Adams's prediction correct. When the terms of the Treaty of Paris were published in the newspapers, the American triumph was so lopsided that all accusations of treason ceased. For not only had the United States won world recognition of its independence, it had also acquired a landmass larger than England, France, and Spain put together. The British negotiators, in fact, were so embarrassed at the outcome that they refused to show up for the commissioned portrait done by Benjamin West, who left their place on the canvas blank.

Humility was not a natural act for Adams, but he went to his grave praising Jay for his leadership in Paris, insisting that "Jay was more important than any of the rest of us, indeed had almost as much weight as all the rest of us together." As far as Adams was concerned, Jay was second only to Washington in the American pantheon when it came to clarity of judgment and independence of mind. And when Washington reluctantly accepted the presidency, the first person he asked to join his cabinet was Jay, who could have any post he preferred. (Jay preferred to be the first chief justice of the Supreme Court.) While Jay is not quite a forgotten founder—he has a college of criminal justice named after him—he was more highly regarded by his peers than he has been by posterity.

PHILADELPHIA, SEPTEMBER 1787

The central disagreement dividing the delegates to the Constitutional Convention throughout the summer of 1787 was whether they were revising the Articles of Confederation or replacing them. If the former, the United States was still a confederation; if the latter, a new nation. There were two ghosts at the banquet: monarchy, which they could not stop talking about whenever executive power was on the table; and slavery, which was too threatening to mention by name. But the central debate, which could be resolved only by a combination of compromise and intentional ambiguity, was how to share sovereignty between state and federal levels of government.

At least at the verbal level, the matter was resolved in the first seven words of the Constitution: "We the people of the United States." Down in Virginia, where Patrick Henry was preparing to fire his most passionate rhetorical salvos at the proposed Constitution, his chief target was those seven words. "Have they said, 'we the states,' this would be a confederation,'" he insisted. "The question thus turns on that poor little thing, the expression 'We the people' instead of the States of America."

What Henry did not know was that the first draft of the Constitution said almost precisely what he wanted it to say. It read: "We the people of New Hampshire, Massachusetts, Connecticut," then state by state down the Atlantic coast. But the Committee on Style and Arrangement changed the wording of the preface, indeed revised the language of the entire document, compressing twenty-three articles in the first draft into seven, simplifying, shortening, and clarifying the language into the format and style we now recognize as the Constitution.

Although both Madison and Hamilton served on this committee, the editorial task was delegated to a representative from Pennsylvania named Gouverneur Morris, who single-handedly made the revisions over a four-day period in mid-September. "The finish given to the style and arrangement of the Constitution fairly belongs to his pen," Madison later observed, "and a better choice could not have been made, as the performance of the task proved." While most Americans know that Thomas Jefferson wrote the Declaration of Independence, few know who wrote the Constitution. And if told it was Gouverneur Morris, even fewer would know who he was.

He was, in fact, a tall, peg-legged, colorful native of New York, famous for his edgy wit and his questionable behavior toward other men's wives. Although there are no major monuments to Morris to prompt our memories of his prowess, if you visit the Virginia capital in Richmond, you can catch a glimpse of him, or part of him, for there is a majestic Houdon statue of Washington at the front of the building, and Washington's sculptured torso is actually a rendering of Morris, who was approximately the same height and size as Washington. Houdon for that reason asked Morris to pose as a model for his Washington sculpture while he was serving as American minister to France in the early 1790s.

During that same time, Morris's letters back to Washington provide an extended example of his distinctive style, as well as his critical response to the French Revolution, which he depicted as a utopian experiment gone awry in ways the American Revolution had sensibly avoided. When asked in later years to wax eloquent on his role in the Constitutional Convention, he preferred to downplay his contribution and undermine all mythical renderings of the document itself. "In adopting a republican form of government," he joked, "I not only took it as a man does a wife, for better or for worse, but what few men do with their wives, I took it knowing all its bad qualities." He was most troubled by the failure to face squarely the problem of slavery.

Although Madison is usually described as the "Father of the Constitution," a plausible case can be made that Morris is more deserving of the title. Madison's major contributions were made before the convention, in setting the agenda, then after, in orchestrating the ratification process as Publius alongside Hamilton in the Federalist Papers. During the convention, Morris rose to speak more often than any other delegate, offered some of the sharpest criticisms of slavery as a cancer that must be removed before it spread, and garnered more favorable commentary from fellow delegates for his oratorical prowess. (The same delegates frequently reported that Madison spoke so softly they could not hear what he said.) Most persuasively, Morris actually wrote the version of the Constitution in the iconic form that has come down to us now.

The most important words, of course, came at the very beginning and constitute what might well be the most consequential editorial act in American history. Jefferson's famous words in the Declaration also come near the beginning, and enshrine individual rights in a semi-sacred creed that has echoed across the centuries. Morris's words "We the people" provide an answering echo on the other side of the American Dialogue, sounding the parallel truth that our rights and responsibilities coexist in a collective whole that is greater than the sum of its parts. Although Jefferson's words are forever, Morris's words enjoy a special relevance in our own troubled time, since they remind us that we rise or fall together, as a single people.

ACKNOWLEDGMENTS

Four friends read the entire manuscript at various stages of its evolution: Susan Dunn, Mark Kimble, Robert Moore, and Douglas Wilson. Taken together, they represented a team of veteran scholars, writers, and truth-tellers that could be counted on to rein me in or urge me on as they saw fit. Robert merits a special salute for assiduous attention to detail that defies most meanings of diligence.

Specific chapters were read by Mary Sarah Bilder, Robert Dalzell, Vincent Ferraro, Gay Gaines, Fred Mosley, and Michael Ponsor. Special thanks are due to Douglas Ginsberg for engaging me in an ongoing debate about originalism.

My editor at Knopf, Dan Frank, refuted the widespread impression that editors at major publishing houses no longer edit. At a crucial stage, Dan stepped in with a heavy hand and sharp pencil to rescue the manuscript from the looming abyss.

Linda Fernandes, my longtime assistant, deciphered my scrawl—I still write longhand—and continued to obscure the extent of my technological incompetence. I have no research assistants, but Linda assists in everything else.

My wife, Ellen Wilkins Ellis, told me to walk the dogs whenever I couldn't find the right word and chastised me for not listening when my mind was back there in the eighteenth century.

Nearly fifty years ago, when I was a graduate student at Yale, Elting Morison invited me to co-teach a seminar with him on biography (i.e., "Joe, I think we should begin with Jesus and the New Testament, don't you?"). Through my own teaching career, mostly at Mount Holyoke, the Morison style served as my standard, though it required a depth of knowledge I could only recognize but never reach. If this book has a voice, it comes from countless conversations in the classroom, where Morison first showed me how a genuine dialogue looks and sounds.

Joseph J. Ellis
AMHERST, MASSACHUSETTS

NOTES

The following endnotes represent my attempt to do two things: first, cite the primary and secondary sources that most influenced my interpretations of Thomas Jefferson, John Adams, James Madison, and George Washington in the "Then" sections of each chapter; and second, provide a selective bibliography of those books and articles that informed my efforts to glimpse the historical patterns shaping our current political and policy debates in the "Now" sections. My goal in both venues is to steer a sensible course between academic overkill and benign neglect, which is to say between too much and too little.

ABBREVIATIONS

Titles

AFC   Lyman H. Butterfield et al., eds., *Adams Family Correspondence*, 10 vols. to date (Cambridge, Mass., 1963–)

AJL   Lester B. Cappon, ed., *The Adams-Jefferson Letters: The Complete Correspondence Between Thomas Jefferson and Abigail and John Adams*, 2 vols. (Chapel Hill, 1959)

AP   Robert J. Taylor et al., eds., *The Papers of John Adams*, 13 vols. to date (Cambridge, Mass., 1983–)

DA   Lyman H. Butterfield et al., eds., *The Diary and Autobiography of John Adams* (Cambridge, Mass., 1966)

DHRC   Merrill Jensen, John Kaminski, and Gaspar Saladino, eds., *Documentary History of the Ratification of the Constitution*, 26 vols. to date (Madison, Wis., 1976–)

HP	Harold C. Syrett and Jacob E. Cooke, eds., *The Papers of Alexander Hamilton*, 26 vols. (New York, 1961–79)
JP	Julian Boyd et al., eds., *The Papers of Thomas Jefferson*, 32 vols. to date (Princeton, N.J., 1950–)
LDC	Paul H. Smith et al., eds., *Letters of Delegates to Congress, 1774–1789*, 29 vols. (Washington, D.C., 2000)
MAP	*The Microfilm Edition of the Adams Papers*, 608 reels (Boston, 1954–59)
MP	William T. Hutchinson et al., eds., *The Papers of James Madison*, 21 vols. to date (Chicago and Charlottesville, Va., 1962–)
Portable	Merrill D. Peterson, ed., *The Portable Thomas Jefferson* (New York, 1975)
PWCS	W. W. Abbot and Dorothy Twohig, eds., *The Papers of George Washington: Confederation Series*, 16 vols. (Charlottesville, Va., 1992–97)
PWPS	W. W. Abbot and Dorothy Twohig, eds., *The Papers of George Washington: Presidential Series*, 12 vols. to date (Charlottesville, Va., 1987–)
RL	James Morton Smith, ed., *The Republic of Letters: The Correspondence Between Thomas Jefferson and James Madison, 1776–1826*, 3 vols. (New York, 1995)
WMQ	*William and Mary Quarterly*, 3rd series
Works	Charles Francis Adams, ed., *The Works of John Adams*, 10 vols. (Boston, 1850–60)
WTJ	Paul Leicester Ford, ed., *The Writings of Thomas Jefferson*, 10 vols. (New York, 1892–99)
WW	James C. Fitzpatrick, ed., *Writings of George Washington*, 39 vols. (Washington, D.C., 1931–39)

Persons

AA	Abigail Adams
AH	Alexander Hamilton
JA	John Adams
JM	James Madison
TJ	Thomas Jefferson
GW	George Washington

CHAPTER 1: RACE

Then: Thomas Jefferson

1. Henry S. Randall, *The Life of Thomas Jefferson*, 3 vols. (New York, 1958), 1:11; Edwin Morris Betts, ed., *Thomas Jefferson's Farm Book* (Princeton, 1953), 18; Roger Wilkins, *Jefferson's Pillow: The Founding Fathers and the Dilemma of Black Patriotism* (Boston, 2001).

2. *JP* 1:169; Joseph J. Ellis, *American Sphinx: The Character of Thomas Jefferson* (New York, 1997), 24.

3. *WTJ* 1:68.

4. Merrill D. Peterson, *The Jefferson Image in the American Mind* (New York, 1960), 234, for the Parton quotation.

5. Douglas A. Wilson, "Thomas Jefferson's Early Notebooks," *WMQ* 42 (1985): 433–52.

6. Merrill D. Peterson, ed., *Visitors to Monticello* (Charlottesville, Va., 1989), 13.

7. John Chester Miller, *The Wolf by the Ears: Thomas Jefferson and Slavery* (New York, 1977), 4–5.

8. Ibid., 5–6; David Brion Davis, *Was Jefferson an Authentic Enemy of Slavery?* (Oxford, 1972), 21.

9. The quotation from *Summary View* is most conveniently available in *Portable*, 14–15.

10. The Adams quotation is from *JP* 1:675–76.

11. Julian Boyd, *The Declaration of Independence: The Evolution of the Text* (Princeton, 1945); Pauline Maier, *Sacred Scripture: Making the Declaration of Independence* (New York, 1997).

12. *Portable*, 238–39.

13. Jefferson's notes on the editorial changes made in his draft of the Declaration are in *JP* 1:314–15.

14. Gunnar Myrdal, *An American Dilemma: The Negro Problem and Modern Democracy* (New York, 1944), 8–9.

15. Maier, *American Scripture*, 123–25, is the best succinct summary, though Garry Wills, *Inventing America: Jefferson's Declaration of Independence* (New York, 1978), 240–41, is more compelling on the implications of the phrase "pursuit of happiness."

16. Dumas Malone, *Jefferson the Virginian* (Boston, 1948), 261–85; Kevin

Gutzman, *Virginia's Revolution: From Dominion to Republic, 1776–1840* (Lanham, Md., 2007), 7–43.

17. Miller, *Wolf by the Ears,* 19–23.

18. Deed of the Virginia Cession, 1 March 1784, *JP* 5:578; Plan for the Government of the Western Territory, 3 February–23 April 1784, ibid., 580–616; TJ to Jean Nicholas Demeunier, June 1786, *JP* 10:63.

19. TJ to JM, 11 May 1785, *JP* 8:147–48; JM to TJ, 15 November 1785, *JP* 9:38–39.

20. *Portable,* 214–15.

21. Ibid., 186–93.

22. David Ramsay to TJ, 3 May 1786, *JP* 9:441.

23. George M. Fredrickson, *The Black Image in the White Mind: The Debate on Afro-American Character and Destiny, 1817–1914* (Middletown, Conn., 1987), chap. 8; Winthrop D. Jordan, *White over Black: American Attitudes Toward the Negro, 1550–1812* (Chapel Hill, N.C., 1968), 482–512; Benjamin Rush to Pennsylvania Abolition Society, 14 January 1795, in L. H. Butterfield, ed., *Letters of Benjamin Rush* (Princeton, 1951), 2:758.

24. *Portable,* 93–103, for Jefferson's defense of Native Americans as the biological equal of white Europeans.

25. TJ to Marquis de Chastellux, 7 June 1785, *JP* 8:186; TJ to Richard Price, 7 August 1785, ibid., 356–57; TJ to Edward Rutledge, 14 July 1787, *JP* 11:589; TJ to Brissot Le Warvillle, 11 February 1785, *JP* 12:577–78.

26. TJ to Edward Bancroft, 26 January 1789, *JP* 14:492.

27. James A. Bear, ed., *Jefferson at Monticello* (Charlottesville, Va., 1967), for the description of Sally Hemings from the testimony of an older slave, Isaac Jefferson.

28. Annette Gordon-Reed, *The Hemingses of Monticello: An American Family* (New York, 2005), has become the authoritative account. The seminal source on slave life at Monticello on which all subsequent accounts depend is Lucia Stanton, "Those Who Labor for My Happiness: Thomas Jefferson and His Slaves," in Peter Onuf, ed., *Jeffersonian Legacies* (Charlottesville, Va., 1993), 147–80, which was based on the massive research program that Stanton directed at Monticello.

29. E. A. Foster et al., "Jefferson Fathered Slave's Last Child," *Nature,* 5 November 1998, 27–28. See also Eric S. Lander and Joseph J. Ellis, "DNA Analysis: Founding Father," ibid., 13. My own summary of the circumstantial evidence in the pre-DNA days, which led me to doubt

Jefferson's paternity, is in *American Sphinx*, 303–7. The earliest scholarly advocate for the Jefferson-Hemings liaison was Fawn Brodie, *Thomas Jefferson: An Intimate History* (New York, 1974).

30. William Short to TJ, February 27, 1798, quoted in Nicholas Guyatt, *Bind Us Apart: How Enlightened Americans Invented Racial Segregation* (New York, 2016), 115–17.

31. Translated and quoted in Stanton, *Jeffersonian Legacies*, 174.

32. The story of the Quaker petition and the debate in the House in spring of 1790 is told in Joseph J. Ellis, *Founding Brothers: The Revolutionary Generation* (New York, 2000), 81–119.

33. Ibid., 48–80, 162–205. See also Lance Banning, *The Jeffersonian Persuasion: Evolution of a Party Ideology* (Ithaca, N.Y., 1978); Richard Buel, Jr., *Securing the Revolution: Ideology in American Politics* (Ithaca, N.Y., 1972); and most magisterial, Stanley Elkins and Eric McKitrick, *The Age of Federalism: The Early American Republic, 1788–1800* (New York, 1993).

34. My conclusion that Jefferson's repudiation of federal authority over domestic policy was authentic, and not a constitutional device primarily designed to protect slavery, is based on a close reading of the Jefferson-Madison letters, conveniently available in James Morton Smith, ed., *The Republic of Letters: The Correspondence Between Thomas Jefferson and James Madison, 1776–1826*, 3 vols. (New York, 1995). From a constitutional perspective, Jefferson consistently maintained that the United States was still a confederated union, not a sovereign nation-state.

35. TJ to George Logan, 11 May 1805, *WTJ* 8:141.

36. My longer version of this important episode is available in "The Purchase," a chapter in *American Creation: Triumphs and Tragedies at the Founding of the Republic* (New York, 2007), 204–40.

37. Ibid., 231; TJ to James Monroe, 24 November 1801, *WTJ* 8:141.

38. TJ to James Monroe, 24 November 1801, *WTJ* 8:106. See also TJ to James Monroe, 2 June 1802, ibid., 152–54; TJ to Rufus King, 13 July 1802, ibid., 162–63.

39. TJ to Eli Whitney, 13 November 1793, *WTJ* 6:448.

40. TJ to Jared Sparks, 4 February 1824, *WTJ* 10:289–93.

41. TJ to Edward Coles, 25 August 1814, *Portable*, 545–47. On Coles, see Kurt E. Leichtle and Bruce G. Carveth, *Crusade Against Slavery: Edward Coles, Pioneer of Freedom* (Carbondale, Ill., 2011).

42. TJ to John Holmes, 22 April 1820, *WTJ* 10:157.

43. TJ to Albert Gallatin, 26 December 1820, ibid., 177–78.

44. TJ to John Holmes, 22 April 1820, ibid., 158.

45. TJ to Hugh Nelson, 7 February 1820, ibid., 156. On the diffusion theme, see Ellis, *American Sphinx*, 264–69.

46. JM to TJ, 27 June 1823, TJ to JM, 24 December 1825, *RL*, 1868–70, 1943–46.

47. Lafayette to TJ, 1 June 1822, Gilbert Chinard, ed., *Letters of Lafayette and Jefferson* (Baltimore, 1929), 409.

48. TJ to Fanny Wright, 7 August 1825, *WTJ* 10:343–45.

49. TJ to William Short, 18 January 1826, ibid., 361–62.

50. Betts, *Farm Book*, preface; Gordon-Reed, *Hemingses of Monticello*, 504–40; Jan Lewis, "The Blessings of Domestic Society: Thomas Jefferson's Family and the Transformation of American Politics," in *Jeffersonian Legacies*, 109–46; Stanton in *Jeffersonian Legacies*, 151–59; the quotation from La Rochefoucauld-Liancourt is in Peterson, *Visitors to Monticello*, 30.

51. Robert Fogel and Stanley Engerman, *Time on the Cross: The Economics of American Negro Slavery* (Boston, 1974); Herbert Gutman and Richard Sutch, "Victorians All: The Sexual Mores and Conduct of Slaves and Their Masters," in Herbert Gutman, ed., *Reckoning with Slavery: A Critical Study in the Quantitative History of Negro Slavery* (New York, 1976); Joel Williamson, *New People: Miscegenation and Mulattos in the United States* (New York, 1980); Martha Hodes, *White Women, Black Men: Illicit Sex in the Nineteenth-Century South* (New Haven, Conn., 1997); Joshua D. Rothman, *Notorious in the Neighborhood: Sex and Families Across the Color Line in Virginia, 1787–1861* (Chapel Hill, N.C., 2003).

52. TJ to Francis C. Gray, 4 March 1815, *WTJ* 9:273; Betts, *Farm Book*, 38. While color was Jefferson's primary criterion for emancipating his slaves, age and loyalty mattered as well, as did the Hemings connection. Burwell Hemings, John Hemings, and Joe Fossel were all three-quarters white and freed in his will. Jefferson's Will, March 1826, *WTJ* 10:392–96.

53. These samples of what we might call Jefferson's heartfelt duplicities come from his career in the 1790s. A fuller version can be found in Ellis, *American Sphinx*, 152–68.

54. TJ to JM, 17 February 1826, in Smith, *RL*, 1966; TJ to Roger C.

Weightman, 24 June 1826, *WTJ* 10:392–96. The authoritative work on Jefferson's debt is Herbert E. Sloan, *Principle and Interest: Thomas Jefferson and the Problem of Debt* (New York, 1995). Looking back from the edge of the grave, Jefferson expressed "my wonder that I should have been so long as 60 years in reaching the result to which I am now reduced." See TJ to James Monroe, 8 March 1826, *WTJ* 10:383.

55. The auction scene is described most fully in Stanton, "Those Who Labor," 147–48. See also Sarah N. Randolph, *The Domestic Life of Thomas Jefferson* (Charlottesville, Va., 1978), 425–27.

56. Susan Dunn, *Dominion of Memories: Jefferson, Madison and the Decline of Virginia* (New York, 2007).

57. Guyatt, *Bind Us Apart*, 5; Jordan, *White over Black*, 569, which described colonization as a "compelling fantasy."

58. Guyatt, *Bind Us Apart*, 2–13 and passim.

59. Peterson, *Jefferson's Image*, 432–39; James E. Young, *The Texture of Memory: Holocaust Memorials and Meaning* (New Haven, Conn., 1993), for the difference between memorializing and remembering the past.

Now: Abiding Backlash

Alexander, Michelle. *The New Jim Crow: Mass Incarceration in the Age of Colorblindness*. New York, 2010.

Anderson, Carol. *White Rage: The Unspoken Truth of Our Racial Divide*. New York, 2016.

Berlin, Ira. *The Long Emancipation: The Demise of Slavery in the United States*. Cambridge, Mass., 2015.

Blackmon, Douglas. *Slavery by Another Name: The Re-Enslavement of Black Americans from the Civil War to World War II*. New York, 2008.

Clark, Kenneth. *Dark Ghetto: Dilemmas of Social Power*. New York, 1965.

Coates, Ta-Nehisi. *Between the World and Me*. New York, 2015.

Daniels, Cora. *Ghettonation: A Journey into the Land of Bling and Home of the Shameless*. New York, 2007.

Drake, St. Clair, and Horace R. Cayton. *Black Metropolis: A Study of Negro Life in a Northern City*. Chicago, 1945.

Du Bois, W. E. B. *The Souls of Black Folk*. Atlanta, 1903.

Duneier, Mitchell. *Ghetto: The Invention of a Place, the History of an Idea*. New York, 2016.

Edsall, Thomas B., and Mary D. Edsall. *Chain Reaction: The Impact of Race, Rights, and Taxes on American Politics*. New York, 1992.

Foner, Eric. *Reconstruction: America's Unfinished Revolution, 1863–1877.* New York, 1990.

Garvey, Amy Jacques. *Garvey and Garveyism.* London, 1968.

Glaude, Eddie S., Jr. *Democracy in Black: How Race Still Enslaves the American Soul.* New York, 2016.

Gottschalk, Maria. *Caught: The Prison State and the Lockdown of American Politics.* Princeton, 2015.

Guyatt, Nicholas. *Bind Us Apart: How Enlightened Americans Invented Racial Segregation.* New York, 2016.

Hacker, Andrew. *Two Nations: Black and White, Separate, Hostile, Unequal.* New York 1995.

Harlan, Louis R. *Booker T. Washington: The Making of a Black Leader, 1856–1901.* New York, 1972.

Jefferson, Margo. *Negroland: A Memoir.* New York, 2015.

Jordan, Winthrop. *White over Black: American Attitudes Toward the Negro, 1500–1812.* Chapel Hill, N.C., 1968.

King, Martin Luther, Jr. *Why We Can't Wait.* New York, 1964.

Lemann, Nicholas. *The Promised Land: The Great Black Migration and How It Changed America.* New York, 1992.

Lester, Julius, ed. *The Seventh Son: The Thought and Writings of W. E. B. Du Bois.* 2 vols. New York, 1971.

Massey, Douglas S., and Nancy A. Denton. *American Apartheid: Segregation and the Making of the Underclass.* Cambridge, Mass., 1993.

Masur, Louis P. *The Civil War: A Concise History.* New York, 2011.

Morrison, Toni, ed. *James Baldwin: Collected Essays.* New York, 2013.

———. *James Baldwin: Early Novels and Stories.* New York, 2012.

Moynihan, Daniel Patrick. *The Negro Family: The Case for National Action.* Washington, D.C., 1965.

Murray, Charles. *Losing Ground: American Social Policy, 1950–1980.* New York, 1984.

Osofsky, Gilbert. *Harlem: The Making of a Ghetto, 1890–1930.* New York, 1971.

Phillips, Kevin. *The Emerging Republican Majority.* New Rochelle, N.Y., 1969.

Pinckney, Darryl, ed. *James Baldwin: Later Novels.* New York, 2014.

Rich, Nathaniel. "James Baldwin and the Fear of a Nation." *New York Review of Books,* 12 May 2016, 36–43.

Sampson, Robert J. *Great American City: Chicago and the Enduring Neighborhood Effect.* New York, 2012.

Trillin, Calvin. *Jackson, 1964: And Other Dispatches from Fifty Years of Reporting on Race in America.* New York, 2016.

Wilkerson, Isabel. *The Warmth of Other Suns: The Epic Story of America's Great Migration.* New York, 2013.

Wilson, William Julius. *The Declining Significance of Race: Blacks and Changing American Institutions.* Chicago, 1978.

———. *The Truly Disadvantaged: The Inner City, the Underclass, and Public Policy.* Chicago, 1987.

———. *When Work Disappears: The World of the New Urban Poor.* New York, 1997.

Woodward, C. Vann. *The Strange Career of Jim Crow.* New York, 1955.

CHAPTER 2: EQUALITY

Then: John Adams

1. I have grappled with the Adams story in two books: *Passionate Sage: The Character and Legacy of John Adams* (New York, 1993), and *First Family: Abigail and John Adams* (New York, 2010).

2. JA to Benjamin Rush, 27 December 1812, *MAP*, Reel 19, 432; JA to Francis Vanderkamp, 27 December 1816, *Works* 10:235.

3. *DA* 1:x–xii.

4. *Passionate Sage*, 242; JA to Benjamin Rush, 25 July 1808, *MAP*, Reel 118.

5. Gordon S. Wood, *The Creation of the American Republic, 1776–1787* (Chapel Hill, N.C., 1969), 592.

6. JA to TJ, 15 July 1813, *AJL* 2:358.

7. Benjamin Rush to JA, 17 February 1812, *MAP*, Reel 119.

8. JA to TJ, 13 July 1813, and 16 December 1816, *AJL* 2:355–56, 500–1.

9. JA to TJ, 14 June 1813, 14 June 1813, 30 June 1814, 2 February 1819, *AJL* 2:330, 346–47, 461.

10. JA to TJ, 13 November 1815, ibid., 456.

11. TJ to JA, 8 April 1816, ibid., 467; JA to TJ, 6 May 1816, ibid., 472–73.

12. TJ to JA, 1 August 1816, ibid., 483; JA to TJ, 3 September 1816, ibid., 472–88.

13. TJ to Maria Cosway, 12 October 1786, *JP* 10:443–55.

14. TJ to JA, 27 June 1813, *AJL* 2:335–37.

15. JA to TJ, 9 July 1813, 13 November 1813, 19 December 1813, ibid., 351, 365, 456.

16. JA to TJ, 9 July 1813, ibid., 351–52.

17. TJ to JA, 28 October 1813, ibid., 387–92.

18. JA to TJ, 2 September 1813, 15 September 1813, ibid., 371, 376.

19. JA to TJ, 15 November 1813, ibid., 398.

20. JA to Joseph Mulligan, 20 November 1818, *MAP*, Reel 123.

21. TJ to JA, 11 January 1816, *AJL* 2:458–59; JA to TJ, 3 February 1816, ibid., 460–61.

22. JA to TJ, 12 November 1813, ibid., 394.

23. *Works* 4:219, 287–92. See also C. Bradley Thompson, *John Adams and the Spirit of Liberty* (Lawrence, Kan., 1998), for the fullest exegesis of *Defence* as a major contribution to American political thought.

24. JA to TJ, 15 August 1823, *AJL* 2:595–96.

25. *Works* 4:380–81; JA to TJ, 6 December 1787, *AJP* 1:213. See also the recent book by Luke B. Mayville, *John Adams and the Fear of American Oligarchy* (Princeton, 2016), which Mayville graciously allowed me to read prior to publication.

26. *Works* 4:585.

27. Ibid., 380–81.

28. Ibid., 453–54.

29. Ibid., 461–62.

30. John Taylor, *An Inquiry into the Principles and Policy of the Government of the United States* (New Haven, Conn., 1950; first published in 1814), 41, 244–45.

31. JA to Benjamin Rush, 28 August 1811, 3 July 1812, in John A. Schutz and Douglass Adair, eds., *The Spur of Fame: Dialogue of John Adams and Benjamin Rush, 1805–1813* (San Marino, Calif., 1966), 193, 228.

32. JA to Benjamin Rush, 15 September 1810, ibid., 121.

33. JA to John Pope, 4 April 1818, *MAP*, Reel 118; JA to John Taylor, 12 March 1819, *Works* 10:375; JA to Benjamin Rush, 28 August 1811, *Spur of Fame*, 193.

34. Mayville, *John Adams and Fear of American Oligarchy*, makes this recovery of Adams's relevance its central argument. See also Judith N. Shklar, *Redeeming American Political Thought* (Chicago, 1998), 146–58, which also calls for a new appreciation of Adams's critical posture toward the

idea of American exceptionalism. Thompson, *John Adams and the Spirit of Liberty,* argues along the same lines in his reassessment of *Defence.* Another earlier traveler on this path was John Patrick Diggins, *The Lost Soul of American Politics: Virtue, Self-Interest, and the Foundations of Liberalism* (Chicago, 1984).

35. JA to Richard Rush, 2 May 1814, *MAP,* Reel 95.

36. The significance of the marginalia in Adams's books was first noticed in Zoltán Haraszti, *John Adams and the Prophets of Progress* (Cambridge, Mass., 1952).

37. Ibid., 54–79, 116–38, 181–84, 187.

38. *DA* 1:33, for the quotation from the Adams diary. *Davila* takes up most of the pages in *Works 6.*

39. *Works* 6:239.

40. Ibid., 232–34.

41. Ibid., 237.

42. Linda Grant DePauw et al., eds., *Documentary History of the First Federal Congress,* 15 vols. (Baltimore, 1972–84), 9:3–13.

43. JA to J. A. Smith, 7 January 1817, *MAP,* Reel 123.

44. JA to TJ, 9 October 1787, *AJL* 1:202–3.

45. JA to Benjamin Waterhouse, 16 August 1812, in Worthington Chauncey Ford, ed., *Statesman and Friend: Correspondence of John Adams with Benjamin Waterhouse, 1784–1822* (Boston, 1927), 81; JA to Hezekiah Niles, 3 January 1817, *MAP,* Reel 123.

46. JA to Mercy Otis Warren, 8 August 1807, 19 August 1807, *Warren-Adams Letters,* Massachusetts Historical Society, 2 vols. (Boston, 1925), 1:477–78.

47. *Works* 6:248.

48. Ibid., 245, 397. The seminal study of fame as a goal of the founding generation is Trevor Colbourn, ed., *Fame and the Founding Fathers: Essays by Douglass Adair* (Chapel Hill, N.C., 1974), 3–26.

49. *Works* 6:247–49.

Now: Our Gilded Age

Atkinson, Anthony B. *Inequality: What Can Be Done.* Cambridge, Mass., 2016.

Bartels, Larry. *Unequal Democracy: The Political Economy of the New Gilded Age.* Princeton, 2016.

Dionne, E. J. *Why the Right Went Wrong: Conservatism from Goldwater to the Tea Party and Beyond.* New York, 2016.

Feuer, Alan. "Tycoons to the Barricades." *New York Times,* 5 July 2015.

Formisano, Ronald. *Plutocracy in America: How Increasing Inequality Destroys the Middle Class.* Baltimore, 2015.

Foroohar, Rana. *Makers and Takers: How Wall Street Destroyed Main Street.* New York, 2017.

Frank, Thomas. *Listen, Liberal: Or Whatever Happened to the Party of the People?* New York, 2016.

Fraser, Steve. *The Age of Acquiescence: The Life and Death of American Resistance to Organized Wealth and Power.* New York, 2015.

Freeland, Chrystia. *Plutocrats: The Rise of the New Super-Rich and the Fall of Everyone Else.* New York, 2013.

Goldstein, Amy. *Janesville: An American Story.* New York, 2017.

Gordon, Robert J. *The Rise and Fall of American Growth: The U.S. Standard of Living Since the Civil War.* Princeton, 2016.

Hacker, Jacob, and Paul Pierson. *American Amnesia: How the War on Government Led Us to Forget What Made America Prosper.* New York, 2016.

Irwin, Neil. "Economic Expansion for Everyone? Not Anymore." *New York Times,* 27 September 2014.

Johnston, David Kay. *Divided: The Perils of Our Growing Inequality.* New York, 2013.

Klein, Naomi. *This Changes Everything: Capitalism Versus the Climate.* New York, 2014.

Leonhardt, David. "The Great Wage Slowdown of the 21st Century." *New York Times,* 27 October 2014.

Lepore, Jill. "Richer and Poorer." *New Yorker,* 16 March 2015.

Lewis, Michael. *Liar's Poker: Rising Through the Wreckage of Wall Street.* New York, 1989.

Lin, Ken-Hou, and Donald Tomaskovic-Devey. "Financialization and U.S. Income Inequality." *American Journal of Sociology* 118, no. 5 (March 2013): 1284–1329.

Madrick, Jeff. *Seven Bad Ideas: How Mainstream Economists Have Damaged America and the World.* New York, 2014.

Mann, Thomas E., and Norman Ornstein. *It's Even Worse Than It Looks: How the American Constitutional System Collided with the New Politics of Extremism.* New York, 2012.

Mayer, Jane. *Dark Money: The Hidden History of the Billionaires Behind the Rise of the Radical Right.* New York, 2016.

Murray, Charles. *By the People: Rebuilding Liberty Without Permission.* New York, 2015.

Noah, Timothy. *The Great Divergence: America's Growing Inequality Crisis and What We Can Do About It.* New York, 2012.

Packer, George. "The Republican Class War." *New Yorker,* 9 November 2015.

———. *The Unwinding: An Inner History of the New America.* New York, 2014.

Piketty, Thomas. *Capital in the Twenty-First Century.* Cambridge, Mass., 2014.

Porter, Eduardo. "A Proposal to Help Falls Short." *New York Times,* 15 July 2015.

Putnam, Robert. *Our Kids: The American Dream in Crisis.* New York, 2015.

Reich, Robert B. *Aftershock: The Next Economy and America's Future.* New York, 2010.

Royce, Edward. *Poverty and Power: The Problem of Structural Inequality.* New York, 2014.

Stiglitz, Joseph. *The Great Divide: Unequal Societies and What We Can Do About Them.* New York, 2015.

Surowiecki, James. "Why the Rich Are So Much Richer." *New York Review of Books,* 24 September 2015.

White, Richard. *The Republic for Which It Stands: The United States During Reconstruction and the Gilded Age.* New York, 2017.

Wiebe, Robert H. *A Cultural History of American Democracy.* Chicago, 1995.

Wills, Garry. *A Necessary Evil: A History of American Distrust of Government.* New York, 1999.

CHAPTER 3: LAW

Then: James Madison

1. The quotation is from JM to Jared Sparks, 1 June 1831, in Gaillard Hunt, ed., *The Writings of James Madison,* 10 vols. (New York, 1890–1910), 9:460. For obvious reasons, the scholarship on Madison is extensive. The "great" biography on Madison is Irving Brant, *James Madison,*

6 vols. (Indianapolis, 1941–61), though its extensive affection for Madison has not aged well. More detached is Jack N. Rakove, *James Madison and the Creation of the American Republic* (Glenview, Ill., 1990), and Richard Brookhiser, *James Madison* (New York, 2011), which is excellent on Madison as a pragmatic politician. Two other books strike me as most perceptive on Madison's thought process and personality: Marvin Meyers, ed., *The Mind of the Founder: Sources of the Political Thought of James Madison* (Hanover, N.H., and London, 1981), and Drew R. McCoy, *The Last of the Founders: James Madison and the Republican Legacy* (Cambridge, U.K., 1989). Though it appeared too late to influence this chapter, Noah Feldman's *The Three Lives of James Madison: Genius, Partisan, President* (New York, 2017) is a major contribution that aligns with my interpretive convictions.

2. *MP* 9:3–24, for "Notes on Ancient and Modern Confederacies"; ibid., 315–58, for "Vices of the Political System of the United States."

3. This is an argument that I have made at somewhat greater length in *The Quartet: Orchestrating the Second American Revolution, 1783–1789* (New York, 2015).

4. *MP* 8:xix–xxii, *MP* 9:261–66, for editorial notes in the *Madison Papers* summarizing his service in the Virginia legislature and Confederation Congress from 1784 to 1787.

5. This is a very succinct summary based on the following letters, documents, and notes from 1782 to 1786: *MP* 4:56, 73, 254–55, 444–46, 450–51; *MP* 5:56–57, 82–83, 177–78, 227, 331, 443; *MP* 6:40–41, 139–40, 141–49, 225–26; *MP* 6:232–33, 265–66, 297–98, 328–29, 375, 392, 471–73, 487–94; *MP* 7:124, 202–3, 397; *MP* 8:152–53, 201, 333–36, 373–76, 406–9; *MP* 9:25–26, 181–84.

6. *MP* 6:144–45.

7. JM to Richard Henry Lee, 25 December 1784, *MP* 8:201.

8. JM to TJ, 12 August 1786, *MP* 9:96. See also JM to James Monroe, 19 March 1786, *MP* 8:505.

9. Editorial note, *MP* 9:115–19; Address of the Annapolis Convention, 14 September 1786, *HP* 3:687–89.

10. The best recent history of the rebellion is Leonard L. Richards, *Shays's Rebellion: The American Revolution's Final Battle* (Philadelphia, 2002).

11. JM to George Muter, 7 January 1787, *MP* 9:230–31, for Madison's apocalyptic response to Shays's Rebellion.

12. Notes on debates, 21 February 1787, ibid., 291–92; Bill Providing Delegates to the Convention, 6 November 1786, ibid., 163–64.

13. JM to GW, 8 November 1786, ibid., 166–67.

14. The quotation comes from GW to Joseph James, 31 May 1780, *WW* 18:453; for a similar statement to Madison see GW to JM, 5 November 1786, *PWCS* 4:331–32.

15. GW to John Jay, 15 August 1786, ibid., 213.

16. GW to Lafayette, 10 May 1786, ibid., 42.

17. JM to GW, 7 December 1786, 24 December 1786, *MP* 9:199–200, 224–25.

18. Edmund Randolph to GW, 6 December 1786, *PWCS* 4:445; JM to Edmund Randolph, 15 April 1787, *MP* 9:378.

19. Henry Knox to GW, 14 January 1787, *PWCS* 4:518–23; David Humphreys to GW, 20 January 1787, ibid., 526–30; GW to Henry Knox, 8 March 1787, *PWCS* 5:74–75.

20. Henry Knox to GW, 19 March 1787, Henry Knox to GW, 19 March 1787, *PWCS* 5:95–98.

21. GW to JM, 31 March 1787, ibid., 116–17.

22. JM to GW, 16 April 1787, ibid., 144–50.

23. JM to Edmund Randolph, 8 April 1787, *MP* 9:370.

24. Ibid., 371.

25. *MP* 9:357–59.

26. The scholarly literature on this topic is huge, but two assessments of Madison's thinking are seminal: Douglass Adair, "That Politics May be Reduced to a Science: David Hume, James Madison, and the Tenth Federalist," in Trevor Colbourn, ed., *Fame and the Founding Fathers: Essays by Douglass Adair* (New York, 1974), 93–106; and Larry Kramer, "Madison's Audience," *Harvard Law Review* 112 (January 1999), 611–99.

27. *MP* 10:15–17, for the Virginia Plan.

28. The best scholarly synthesis of the debates in the Constitutional Convention is Richard Beeman, *Plain, Honest Men: The Making of the American Constitution* (New York, 2003). Among the countless studies of this crucial moment in American history, four other books stand out: Max Farrand, *The Framing of the Constitution of the United States* (New Haven, Conn., 1913); Catherine Drinker Bowen, *Miracle at Philadelphia* (Boston, 1966); Jack Rakove, *Original Meanings: Politics and Ideas*

in the Making of the Constitution (New York, 1986); and Carol Berkin, *A Brilliant Solution: Inventing the American Constitution* (New York, 2003).

29. This is an overly succinct summary of my attempt to identify the political ingredients that shaped the outcome at the Constitutional Convention, provided more expansively in *The Quartet*, 135–53.

30. JM to TJ, 6 September 1787, *MP* 10:163–66.

31. GW to Lafayette, 18 September 1787, *PWCS* 5:334; Franklin's speech is reproduced in Edmund S. Morgan, ed., *Not Your Usual Founding Father: Selected Readings from Benjamin Franklin* (New Haven, Conn., 2006), 286–87.

32. Remark on Signing the Constitution, 17 September 1787, *HP* 4:253.

33. Madison's assessments of the likely outcome in the state ratifying conventions are littered throughout his correspondence in the fall of 1787. The most comprehensive estimate is in JM to Ambrose Madison, 8 November 1787, *MP* 10:243–44. The authoritative scholarly work on the ratification process is Pauline Maier, *Ratification: The People Debate the Constitution, 1787–1788* (New York, 2010).

34. JM to Edmund Pendelton, 28 October 1787, *MP* 10:223–24.

35. JM to TJ, 24 October 1787, ibid., 205–20, provides the first and fullest version of his recognition that the compromise reached in Philadelphia had produced a document that made argument itself the ongoing answer.

36. The term *consolidation* was a central feature of the argument against Parliament's authority over the American colonies in the prerevolutionary years. The seminal study of its quasi-paranoid implications is Bernard Bailyn, *The Ideological Origins of the American Revolution* (New York, 1967). The same extreme apprehension about consolidated government was a centerpiece of Antifederalist hostility toward the Constitution. See Saul Cornell, *The Other Founders: Antifederalism and the Dissenting Tradition in America, 1788–1822* (Chapel Hill, N.C., 1999).

37. The shift in Madison's thinking, or at least his strategic argument, occurred in late January 1788 and appeared in the Federalist Papers, numbers 44 through 48, *MP* 10:420–54. His earlier preference for a more expansive and clearly defined federal government is in JM to Edmund Randolph, 8 April 1787, *MP* 9:367–71.

38. Henry's orations are reproduced in *DHRC* 9:951–59.

39. Madison's response is in ibid., 995–96.
40. Richard Labunski, *James Madison and the Struggle for the Bill of Rights* (New York, 2006), is the authoritative study. Maier, *Ratification*, 443–68, provides an elegant synthesis. The most convenient collection of documents is Helen E. Viet et al., eds., *Creating the Bill of Rights: A Documentary Record from the First Federal Congress* (Baltimore, 1991).
41. Address of the President to the House of Representatives, 30 April 1789, *MP* 12:121–24. Address of the House of Representatives to the President, 5 May 1789, ibid., 132–34.
42. TJ to JM, 6 February 1788, *RL*, 529–30; TJ to JM, 18 November 1788, ibid., 567; TJ to JM, 15 March 1789, ibid., 584–85; JM to TJ, 17 October 1788, ibid., 564–65.
43. JM to TJ, 17 October 1788, ibid., 564.
44. JM to George Eve, 2 January 1789, *MP* 11:404–5.
45. JM to TJ, 29 March 1789, *RL*, 609.
46. Amendments to the Constitution, 13 August 1789, *MP* 12:196–97.
47. Amendments to the Constitution, 13 August 1789, ibid., 333. JM to Alexander White, 24 August 1789, ibid., 352–53.
48. Amendments to the Constitution, 17 August 1789, ibid., 344.
49. Amendments to the Constitution, 13 August 1789, ibid., 201.
50. John K. Mahon, *History of the Militia and the National Guard* (New York, 1983), 52–53.
51. Mary Sarah Bilder, *Madison's Hand: Revising the Constitutional Convention* (Cambridge, Mass., 2015), follows Madison's editorial efforts to revise the text of his notes for the Constitutional Convention in order to accommodate his several shifts in thinking over the succeeding decades.

Now: Immaculate Misconceptions

Amar, Akhil Reed. *America's Constitution: A Biography.* New York, 2005.

Balkin, Jack. *Living Originalism.* Cambridge, Mass., 2011.

Biskupic, Joan. *American Original: The Life and Constitution of Supreme Court Justice Antonin Scalia.* New York, 2009.

Bork, Robert. *The Tempting of America: The Political Seduction of Law.* New York, 1990.

Breyer, Stephen. *Active Liberty: Interpreting Our Democratic Constitution.* New York, 2005.

Calabrese, Stephen G., ed., *Originalism: A Quarter-Century of Debate.* Washington, D.C., 2007.

Cornell, Saul. "Originalism on Trial: The Use and Abuse of History in the District of Columbia *v* Heller." *Ohio State Law Journal* 69 (2008): 625–52.

Coyle, Marcia. *The Roberts Court: The Struggle for the Constitution*. New York, 2013.

Ellis, Joseph J. "Immaculate Misconception and the Supreme Court." *Washington Post*, 7 May 2010.

Feldman, Noah. *Scorpions: The Battles and Triumphs of FDR's Great Supreme Court Justices*. New York, 2010.

Horowitz, Morton J. *The Transformation of American Law, 1870–1960*. New York, 1992.

Kramer, Larry D. *The People Themselves: Popular Constitutional and Judicial Review*. New York, 2010.

Mayer, Jane. *Dark Money: The Hidden History of the Billionaires Behind the Rise of the Radical Right*. New York, 2016.

Neff, Michael. "Original Sins: Justice Scalia and Constitutional Interpretation." Unpublished essay, Harvard Law School, 2011; by permission of author.

Rosen, Jeffrey. *The Supreme Court*. New York, 2007.

Scalia, Antonin. *A Matter of Interpretation: Federal Courts and the Law*. Princeton, 1997.

Strauss, David A. *The Living Constitution*. New York, 2010.

Sunstein, Cass. *Radicals in Robes: Why Extreme Right-Wing Courts Are Wrong for America*. New York, 2005.

Teles, Stephen. *The Rise of the Conservative Movement: The Battle for Control of the Law*. Princeton, 2008.

Toobin, Jeffrey. *The Nine: Inside the Secret World of the Supreme Court*. New York, 2007.

———. *The Oath: The Obama White House and the Supreme Court*. New York, 2012.

CHAPTER 4: ABROAD

Then: George Washington

1. Marcus Cunliffe, *George Washington: Man and Monument* (New York, 1958), was the first biography to focus on the monument problem. My own effort, *His Excellency* (New York, 2004), tries to move a bit further

down the same trail. See also Barry Schwartz, *George Washington: The Making of an American Symbol* (New York, 1987).

2. Paul Staiti, *Of Arms and Artists: The American Revolution Through Painters' Eyes* (New York, 2016), 265–70, for Gilbert Stuart's portraits of Washington.

3. Daniel K. Richter, *Facing East from Indian Country: A Native History of Early America* (Cambridge, Mass., 2001), for the Native American population in 1783. See also the epic account by Fred Anderson, *Crucible of War: The Seven Years' War and the Fate of Empire in British North America, 1754–1766* (New York, 2000), for more background on the struggle for control of the American interior and for the valuable insight that the Treaty of Paris (1783) transferred control to white Americans of the same region the British had won from the French in the Peace of Paris (1763).

4. On the trials and tribulations of the Continental Army during the Newburgh encampment, see Thomas Fleming, *The Perils of Peace: America's Struggle for Survival After Yorktown* (New York, 2013).

5. Circular Letter to the States, 8 June 1783, *WW* 26:483–88.

6. Ibid., 492–96. See the seminal essay by W. W. Abbot, "George Washington, the West, and the Union," in Don Higginbotham, ed., *George Washington Reconsidered* (Charlottesville, Va., 2001), 198–211.

7. GW to Richard Henderson, 10 June 1788, *PWCS* 6:339–42.

8. GW to David Humphreys, 25 July 1785, *PWCS* 3:69.

9. David Howell to Jonathan Arnold, 10 October 1784, *LDC* 21:281.

10. Plan for the Government of the Western Territory, 3 February–23 April 1784, *JP* 6:580–616.

11. GW to James Duane, 7 September 1783, *LDC* 21:101–4. See also Virginia Delegates to Benjamin Harrison, 1 November 1783, ibid., 128–29, for the chaotic consequences of unregulated migration.

12. Wilcomb E. Washburn, ed., *The American Indian and the United States: A Documentary History*, 4 vols. (New York, 1973), 4:2267–77. The standard works are Francis P. Prucha, *American Indian Policy in the Formative Years* (Cambridge, Mass., 1962), and Reginald Horsman, *Expansion and American Indian Policy, 1783–1812* (East Lansing, Mich., 1967).

13. Cherokee Chiefs to GW, 19 May 1789, *PWPS* 2:325–26.

14. Washburn, *Documentary History*, 2:2140–43. For the Native American perspective on American policy, see Richter, *Facing East from Indian*

Country; also Daniel K. Richter, *Before the Revolution: America's Ancient Pasts* (Cambridge, Mass., 2011), for the longer historical perspective.

15. Philip Schuyler to President of Congress, 29 July 1781, *LDC* 13:601–7.

16. Washburn, *Documentary History* 2:2144–50.

17. Henry Knox to GW, 7 July 1789, *PWPS* 3:138–41. My earlier attempt to tell this story can be found in *American Creation: Triumphs and Tragedies at the Founding of the Republic* (New York, 2007), 127–64.

18. Henry Knox to GW, 7 July 1789, *PWPS* 3:138–41.

19. GW to Lafayette, 18 June 1788, *PWCS* 6:3327–38.

20. Henry Knox to GW, 7 July 1789, *PWPS* 3:138–40.

21. Henry Knox to GW, 6 July 1789, ibid., 123–28.

22. Linda Grant DePauw, ed., *Documentary History of the First Federal Congress of the United States of America,* 15 vols. (Baltimore, 1972–76), 2:31–36; 9:128–32.

23. Quoted in John W. Caughey, *McGillivray of the Creeks* (Norman, Okla., 1931), 90–91.

24. Editorial Note, *PWPS* 4:86–89; David Humphreys to GW, 26 September 1789, ibid., 89; Caughey, *McGillivray,* 251–54.

25. GW to U.S. Senate, 4 August 1790, *PWPS* 6:188–86.

26. *National Advertiser and Gazette of the United States,* 14 August 1790. See also *PWPS* 6:253–54.

27. AA to Mary Smith Cranch, 8 August 1790, *AFC* 9:84–86.

28. GW to Tobias Lear, 3 April 1791, GW to Alexander Hamilton, 4 April 1791, *PWPS* 8:49, 57–58. For the "Chinese wall" reference, see GW to Secretary of State, 1 July 1796, *WW* 35:112.

29. GW to Edmund Pendleton, 22 January 1795, *WW* 34:98–101.

30. *AP* 4:260–78, for the full text of the Plan of Treaties, along with an editorial note on the political context and diplomatic legacy.

31. Lawrence Kaplan, *Entangling Alliances with None: American Foreign Policy in the Age of Jefferson* (Kent, Ohio, 1987), emphasizes the consensus among American political leaders. Stanley Elkins and Eric McKitrick, *The Age of Federalism: The Early American Republic, 1788–1800* (New York, 1993), 375–450, takes the party divisions more seriously as expressions of deep divisions.

32. Ellis, *His Excellency,* 188–89. See also Elkins and McKitrick, *Age of Federalism,* 33–34.

33. Samuel Flagg Bemis, *Jay's Treaty: A Study in Commerce and Diplomacy* (New Haven, Conn., 1962); Jerald A. Combs, *The Jay Treaty: Political*

Background of the Founding Fathers (Berkeley, Calif., 1970); Elkins and McKitrick, *Age of Federalism*, 375–450.

34. *RL* 2:882–83, for Madison's reaction; JA to William Cunningham, 15 October 1808, *Correspondence Between the Honorable John Adams . . . and William Cunningham, Esq.* (Boston, 1823), 34; GW to Edmund Randolph, 31 July 1795, *WW* 34:26–32.

35. TJ to Philip Mazzei, 24 April 1796, *WTJ* 7:72–76.

36. TJ to Edward Rutledge, 30 November 1795, ibid., 39–40.

37. TJ to James Monroe, 21 March 1796, ibid., 80. For my early effort at a synthesis of this supercharged moment, see *American Sphinx: The Character of Thomas Jefferson* (New York, 1997), 151–52.

38. GW to John Jay, 21 April 1796, *WW* 35:321.

39. Matthew Spalding and Patrick J. Garrity, *A Sacred Union of Citizens: George Washington's Farewell Address and the American Character* (Lanham, Md., 1996), 55–58. See also Burton J. Kaufman, *Washington's Farewell Address: The View from the Twentieth Century* (Chicago, 1969).

40. Arthur A. Markowitz, "Washington's Farewell Address and the Historians," *Pennsylvania Magazine of History and Biography* 94 (1970): 173–91.

41. *Aurora*, 17 October 1796, 6 March 1797.

42. *WW* 35:224.

43. John M. Murrin, " 'A Roof Without Walls': The Dilemma of American National Identity," in Richard Beeman, Stephen Botstein, and Edward C. Carter, eds., *Beyond Confederation: Origins of the Constitution and National Identity* (Chapel Hill, N.C., 1987), 333–48.

44. Victor H. Paltsits, ed., *Washington's Farewell Address* (New York, 1935), 252–53.

45. Ibid., 258–59.

46. William Duane, *A Letter to George Washington . . . Containing Strictures of His Address* (Philadelphia, 1796), 22.

47. Paltsits, *Farewell Address*, 256.

48. P. S. Brunt, ed., *Thucydides: The Peloponnesian Wars* (New York, 1963), 179–87; George Kennan, *American Diplomacy*, expanded ed. (Chicago, 2012).

49. Peter Henriques, *The Death of George Washington: He Died As He Lived* (Mount Vernon, 2000), 9–10.

Now: At Peace with War

Allison, Graham. *Destined for War: Can America and China Escape Thucydides' Trap?* New York, 2017.

Ambrose, Stephen E. *Rise to Globalism: American Foreign Policy, 1938–1970.* Baltimore, 1970.

Anderson, Perry. *American Foreign Policy and Its Thinkers.* London, 2016.

Aron, Raymond. *The Imperial Republic: The United States and the World, 1945–1973.* London, 1975.

Bacevich, Andrew. *American Empire: The Realities and Consequences of U.S. Diplomacy.* Cambridge, Mass., 2002.

Bremmer, Ian. *Superpower: Three Choices for America's Role in the World.* New York, 2015.

Clarke, Richard A. *Against All Enemies: Inside America's War on Terror.* New York, 2004.

Danner, Mark. *Spiral: Trapped in the Forever War.* New York, 2016.

Diamond, Jared. *Guns, Germs, and Steel: The Fate of Human Societies.* New York, 2005.

Ferguson, Niall. *Colossus: The Price of America's Empire.* New York, 2004.

———. *Empire: The Rise and Demise of the British World Order and the Lessons for Global Power.* New York, 2002.

Friedman, Thomas. *The World Is Flat: A Brief History of the Twenty-First Century.* New York, 2006.

Fukuyama, Francis. *Political Order and Political Decay: From the Industrial Revolution to the Globalization of Democracy.* New York, 2014.

Gaddis, John Lewis. *We Now Know: Rethinking Cold War History.* Oxford, 1997.

Haass, Richard N. *Intervention: The Use of American Military Force in the Post–Cold War World.* Washington, D.C., 1999.

———. "Paradigm Lost." *Foreign Affairs* 74 (Jan.–Feb. 1995): 43–58.

Herring, George C. *America's Longest War: The United States and Vietnam, 1950–1965.* New York, 1979.

Huntington, Samuel P. *The Clash of Civilizations and the Remaking of World Order.* London, 1999.

Johnson, Chalmers. *Blowback: The Costs and Consequences of American Empire.* London, 2000.

Judt, Tony. *When the Facts Change: Essays, 1995–2013.* New York, 2014.

Kagan, Robert. *Of Paradise and Power: America and Europe in the New World Order.* New York, 2003.

———. *The World America Made.* New York, 2012.

Kaplan, Robert D. *The Coming Anarchy: Shattering the Dreams of the Post Cold War.* New York, 2000.

———. *Earning the Rockies: How Geography Shapes America's Role in the World.* New York, 2017.

Kennan, George. *American Diplomacy,* expanded ed. Chicago, 1984.

Kennedy, Paul. *The Rise and Fall of Great Powers.* New York, 1987.

Kissinger, Henry. *World Order.* New York, 2014.

Landes, David. *The Wealth and Poverty of Nations.* New York, 1999.

Maddow, Rachel. *Drift: Unmooring American Military Power.* New York, 2012.

Mandelbaum, Michael. *Mission Failure: America and the World in the Post–Cold War Era.* New York, 2016.

Posen, Barry. *Restraint: A New Foundation for the U.S. Grand Strategy.* Ithaca, N.Y., 2016.

Risen, James. *Pay Any Price: Greed, Power, and Endless War.* New York, 2014.

Rodrik, Dani. *The Globalization Paradox: Democracy and the Future of the World Economy.* New York, 2011.

Rothkopf, David. *National Insecurity: American Leadership in an Age of Fear.* New York, 2014.

Slaughter, Anne-Marie. "The Real New World Order." *Foreign Affairs* 76 (Sept.–Oct. 1997): 183–97.

Tierney, Dominic. *The Right Way to Lose a War: America's Age of Unwinnable Conflicts.* New York, 2015.

Tucker, Robert W., and David C. Hendrickson. *The Imperial Temptation: The New World Order and America's Purpose.* New York, 1992.

Weston, J. Kael. *The Mirror Test: America at War in Iraq and Afghanistan.* New York, 2016.

Wright, Lawrence. *The Terror Years: From al-Qaeda to the Islamic State.* New York, 2016.

Zakaria, Fareed. *The Post-American World.* New York, 2011.

EPILOGUE

The following books either are mentioned in the epilogue or influenced my thinking.

Adair, Douglass. "Fame and the Founding Fathers." In Trevor Colbourn, ed., *Fame and the Founding Fathers: Essays by Douglass Adair*. New York, 1974.

Arnn, Larry P. *The Founders' Key: The Divine and Natural Connection Between the Declaration and the Constitution and What We Risk by Losing It*. Nashville, 2012.

Bailyn, Bernard. *To Begin the World Anew: The Genius and Ambiguities of the American Founders*. New York, 2003.

Ellis, Joseph J. *American Creation*. New York, 2008.

———. *Founding Brothers: The Revolutionary Generation*. New York, 2000.

Goethals, George R., and Douglas Bradburn, eds. *Politics, Ethics, and Change: The Legacy of James MacGregor Burns*. Northampton, Mass., 2016.

Koehn, Nancy. *Forged in Crisis: The Power of Courageous Leadership in Turbulent Times*. New York, 2017.

Mann, Thomas E., and Norman J. Ornstein. *It's Even Worse Than It Looks: How the American Constitutional System Collided with the New Politics of Extremism*. New York, 2012.

Peterson, Merrill D. *The Jefferson Image in the American Mind*. New York, 1960.

Pincus, Steve. *The Heart of the Declaration: The Founders' Case for an Activist Government*. New Haven, Conn., 2016.

Toynbee, Arnold. *The Study of History*. 2 vols. Oxford, 1954.

Wood, Gordon S. *Revolutionary Characters: What Made the Founders Different*. New York, 2006.

INDEX

abortion rights, 111

Adair, Douglass, 224, 229

Adams, Abigail, 4, 44, 190

Adams, Charles Francis, 72–3

Adams, John, 20, 71–101, 169, 174, 190, 195
  on American exceptionalism, 92, 99–100, 215, 252n34
  on banks and finance capitalism, 90–1, 110
  candor and outspokenness of, 72–4
  constitutional proposals by, 71, 85–9, 101
  death of, 74
  Declaration of Independence and, 18–19, 20
  on entrenched inequality and oligarchy, 88–9, 92–101, 104–5, 114–15
  on equality, 73–84, 110
  Federalist views of, 114
  on founding fathers as icons, 97–100
  friendship and correspondence with Jefferson of, 20, 38, 44, 71, 73–4, 83–4, 114, 223
  on grief and emotional motivations, 78–80, 92–6
  on Jefferson's *Summary View*, 17
  lack of national memorial to, 71–3
  on leadership vs. popular opinion, 76–8, 80–1, 86–8, 230
  marginalia in books of, 93
  Massachusetts Constitution of, 4
  as minister to Britain, 85
  Plan of Treaties of, 192
  political talent and leadership of, 223–39
  presidential titles proposed by, 95–6
  on the quest for fame, 98–100, 229
  response to Taylor of, 84–93
  on the spread of slavery, 38
  study of history by, 5–7, 96–7, 213
  Thoughts on Government of, 86, 131
  Treaty of Paris and, 235–6
  See also income inequality

Adams, John Quincy, 215

Adams, Samuel, 130–1

Afghanistan invasion and occupation, 210, 220

African American Museum of History and Culture, 50

African Americans, 60
  Baldwin's view of history of, 64–6
  First Reconstruction era and, 54–5, 58
  Great Migration of, 52–3
  imprisonment rates of, 60–1
  Jim Crow policies toward, 52–61, 111

African Americans *(continued)*
  Middle Passage of, 17–22, 50–1
  in our minority-majority population,
    66–7
  percent of U.S. population of, 50–1
  police interactions with, 50, 61
  poverty and economic inequality of,
    58–9
  racial stereotyping of, 63, 65
  Second Reconstruction era and, 54–9
  in urban ghettos, 53, 59, 61–3
  See also race/racism; slavery
Alexander, Michelle, 60–1
"all men are created equal," 9, 21,
    55, 57
American aristocracy, 92–101
  See also oligarchy
American Creed, 3, 8, 21, 55–6, 103,
    239
American Daily Advertiser newspaper,
    198
American Dilemma (Myrdal), 55–9,
    65–6
American Enterprise Institute, 157
American exceptionalism
  Adams's views of, 92, 99–100, 215,
    252n34
  Jefferson's views of, 92, 99–100, 104,
    215–16
  role in foreign policy of, 9, 204,
    215–16
  role of the middle classes in, 104–5
  Washington's understanding of,
    203–4
American Revolution, 5, 110, 228–9
  Board of War and Ordnance of, 5
  cooperation among the states after,
    177
  Enlightenment ideals of, 176, 203,
    227
  Madison's reformulation of, 126

  mythologized leaders of, 97–100,
    120, 130–1, 157, 159, 223–4
  Native American support of British
    in, 182, 188
  Shays's Rebellion and, 124–5
  Treaty of Paris conclusion of, 23–4,
    122, 175, 188, 194, 226, 234–7,
    261n3
  U.S.'s anti-imperial legacy from,
    17–21, 110, 218–20
  veterans' benefits from, 175
  Washington's personal commitment
    to, 233–4
  western territory acquired from, 173,
    175–7, 188, 226, 231, 235
  See also founders
Annapolis Convention, 124–5
Antifederalists, 113
Aranda, Count, 235
aristoi, 80–4, 86–8
Aristotle, 80, 139, 225
Arnold, Benedict, 195
Articles of Confederation, 113, 131
  Constitutional Convention and,
    129–30, 237
  foreign policy under, 177–8
  Madison's arguments against,
    120–6
  political cooperation among the
    states under, 177
  Washington's critique of, 127
Atkinson, Anthony, 105–6, 107
"Attack on the American Free
    Enterprise System" (Powell),
    156–7
Aurora newspaper, 194–5, 199, 201

Bache, Benjamin Franklin, 194–5,
    198–9
Bailyn, Bernard, 231–2
Baldwin, James, 49–50, 53, 63–6

banking, 108–9
  government regulation of, 91,
    108–11
  Hamilton's National Bank proposal
    for, 90–1, 122, 149
Berlin Wall, 207
Between the World and Me (Coates), 50
Bill of Rights, 119, 141–9, 154
  Brown v. Board of Education decision
    and, 152–3
  as epilogue to the Constitution,
    145–6
  Madison's drafting of, 121, 141, 144
  ratification of, 146–8
  Second Amendment of, 147–9,
    160–7
  state models for, 144–5, 167
  See also Constitution of the United
    States
black Americans. *See* African
  Americans; race/racism; slavery
Black Lives Matter, 50
Black Metropolis (St. Clair and
  Cayton), 62
Bland, Richard, 16
Bork, Robert, 155–6
Boston Massacre, 92
Boston Public Library, 93
Brant, Irving, 255n1
Brennan, William, 160
Britain, 193
  Brexit decision of, 217–18
  colonial revolutionaries' complaints
    of, 17, 19–21, 32, 78, 110, 219
  imperialist legacy of, 17–21, 110,
    218–20
  Jay Treaty of 1795 with, 194–9, 202,
    218
Brookhiser, Richard, 255n1
Brown v. Board of Education, 56,
  152–3, 158, 160, 161

Buffett, Warren, 100
Burger, Warren, 161
Burns, James MacGregor, 224
Bush, George H. W., 208–9
Bush, George W., 158, 210–12
Bush v. Gore, 158

Caesar Augustus, 223
Calhoun, John C., 32, 149
Callender, James, 44
capitalism, 90–1, 96, 101
Carnegie, Andrew, 100, 105
Cary, Robert, 204
Catiline, 218
Cato Institute, 157
Cayton, Horace, 62
Cherokee Nation, 182–3
Cicero, 218
Circular Letter to the States
  (Washington), 175–7
*Citizens United v. Federal Election
  Commission,* 109, 158, 160
Civil Rights Act of 1964, 56–7
civil rights movements, 54–9, 217
  Brown v. Board of Education and, 56
  desegregation of armed forces in, 56
  of the First Reconstruction, 54–5, 58
  of the Second Reconstruction, 55–9
  See also race/racism
Clarke, Richard, 210
Cleon, 218
Clinton, George, 137, 144
Clinton, Hillary, 224
Coates, Ta-Nehisi, 50, 66
Cold War, 8, 107, 174
  coherent international framework
    of, 217
  ending of, 207–10, 214
  expanded executive power of, 209
  Kennan's containment strategy for,
    213–16

Cold War (continued)
  nuclear missiles of, 210
  realist debates of, 203
  Vietnam War of, 112, 212, 214
  See also post–Cold War foreign
    policy
Coles, Edward, 36
color-blind racism, 59–61
Colossus: The Price of America's Empire
  (Ferguson), 219
commercial aristocracy, 94–6
Commonwealth Club Address of 1933
  (FDR), 110
Compromise of 1850, 151–2
Condorcet, Nicolas de, 93
Confederate States of America, 113
Confederation Congress, 120–4
  absent delegates from, 120, 123
  Annapolis Convention of, 124–5
  calls for Constitutional Convention
    by, 124–6, 129
  failures of, 122–3
  financial obligations to war veterans
    of, 175
  governance of new western territory
    by, 178–91
  imperialist rule of Native Americans
    by, 181–4
  perpetual movement of, 123
  ratification of the Constitution and,
    136–8
  Treaty of Paris and, 23–4, 122, 175,
    188, 194, 226, 234–7, 261n3
Constitutional Convention, 227,
  237–9
  agenda for, 121, 237
  Committee on Style and
    Arrangement of, 237–9
  Confederation Congress calls for,
    124–6, 129
  debates on judicial power in, 153

delegate attendance at, 135
executive power proposals for, 134
Great Compromise of, 135–6
Madison's planning of, 126–31,
  133–4
Madison's record of, 134
Madison's Virginia Plan proposal for,
  131–4, 257n26
Virginia Delegation to, 133
Washington's participation in,
  126–31, 133–7
The Constitution of England (de
  Lolme), 88
Constitution of the United States, 6,
  85, 119–70
  Adams's proposals for, 71, 85–9, 101
  Bill of Rights of, 119, 121, 141–9,
    154
  on divided federal and state
    jurisdictions, 139–41, 225–26, 237,
    248nn36–7
  emancipation amendments to, 54
  empowerment of the federal
    government in, 113
  on judicial power, 153
  as living document, 119, 139–41,
    149, 153–6, 158, 160, 161, 164,
    258n35
  Madison's political evolution and,
    121–6
  originalist approaches to, 119,
    155–70
  preamble "We the people" of, 9,
    140–1, 200, 237, 239
  ratification of, 121, 132, 136–41, 227,
    228
  Second Amendment of, 147–9,
    160–7
  on separation of church and state,
    225
  signers of, 135

on slaves as property, 6

on tripartite national government, 131–4, 153, 225–6, 257n26

Twenty-Second Amendment of, 198

on war-making powers, 209, 211

writers of, 119–20

See also Madison, James; Supreme Court of the United States

Continental Congress, 18–22

See also Declaration of Independence

Cornwallis, Charles, 234

Cosway, Maria, 79

cotton gin, 35

Cotton Kingdom, 35, 227

Creek Nation, 186–91

Croly, Herbert, 75

Crusades, 209

Dark Money (Mayer), 103, 111–12, 156–7

Darwin, Charles, 27

Declaration of Independence

Enlightenment principles of governance in, 21–4, 45–6, 48, 78, 239, 245n15

Jefferson's writing on slavery in, 18–22

prohibition of the term "slavery" from, 6, 20

on self-evident truths and natural rights, 18, 21–2, 55–6, 113, 154

unanimous support for, 135

The Declining Significance of Race (Wilson), 62–3

A Defence of the Constitutions of the United States (Adams), 71, 85–9

De la législation (Mably), 93

de Lolme, John Louis, 88

Democracy in America (Tocqueville), 55, 222

Democratic Party, 57

Democratic-Republican Party. *See* Republican Party of Jefferson and Madison

"Dialogue Between the Head and Heart" (Jefferson), 79

Diggins, John Patrick, 252n34

Discourses on Davila (Adams), 93–6

District of Columbia v. Heller, 158, 160–70

historians' perspectives on, 168–70

originalist opinion on, 160–8

precedent overturned by, 158, 160–1, 166–7

Second Amendment and, 163, 166

Stevens's dissent to, 164–5

divided America, 7–8

Drake, St. Clair, 62

Dred Scott v. Sandford, 6, 151–2

Du Bois, W. E. B., 54–5

Dunmore, John Murray, 20

Earning the Rockies (Kaplan), 221–2

economic inequality. *See* income inequality

Eisenhower, Dwight, 109

Electoral College, 140

Ellison, Ralph, 53

emancipation of slavery, 46–8

constitutional amendments on, 54

expectation of segregation in, 47

proposals for expatriation and, 23–8, 34–6, 39–40, 47–8, 51–2

See also civil rights movements

Emancipation Proclamation, 51–2

English Bill of Rights, 163

Enlightenment principles, 176, 203, 227

Adams's response to, 92–3

on economic equality, 75–7, 101

on natural rights, 21–4, 45–6, 48, 55, 57, 245n15

Enlightenment principles *(continued)*
  on racial differences, 9, 26–7, 39, 50
  of the Scottish Enlightenment, 93–4,
    133, 231
European Union, 217–18
evangelical Christians, 111
exceptionalism. *See* American
  exceptionalism
executive power, 237
  in foreign policy and war-making,
    187, 193–7, 209, 211
  Madison's views on, 132, 134
  two-term precedent set for, 198

"Fame and the Founding Fathers"
  (Adair), 229
Faulkner, William, 64
Federalist Papers (Publius), 113, 239
  pluralist vision of, 133
  on the power of the judiciary, 153
  on state and federal jurisdiction,
    139–41, 149*n*51, 248*nn*36–7
  writers of, 121, 137
Federalist Party, 31–2, 90, 113–14
Federalist Society, 157
Federal Reserve Board, 91, 111
Feldman, Noah, 255*n*1
Ferguson, Niall, 219
finance capitalism, 90–1, 107–13
  See also second Gilded Age
The Fire Next Time (Baldwin), 65
First Reconstruction era, 54–5, 58
foreign policy, 173–222
  Adams's Plan of Treaties on, 192
  American exceptionalism in, 9, 204,
    215–16
  in America's new western territories,
    175–91, 226
  with Britain, 193–8, 202
  of the Cold War, 8, 107, 174, 203,
    207–10, 213–17

commercial vs. diplomatic goals of,
  192, 201–2
executive power in, 187, 193–7, 209,
  211
with France, 83–4, 191–4, 197,
  262*n*31
imperialist rule of Native Americans
  in, 173, 175–7, 181–91, 205
Jay Treaty of 1795 and, 194–9, 202,
  218
Kaplan's views on, 221–2
post–Cold War era of, 8, 173–4,
  207–22
realist doctrine in, 203–5, 221–2
U.S.'s anti-imperial legacy in, 17–21,
  110, 218–20
Washington's Farewell Address on,
  173, 175, 198–202, 215, 218, 222
Washington's isolationism in, 193–4,
  201–5, 214–15, 262*n*31
See also post–Cold War foreign
  policy; Washington, George;
  western territory
forgetting. *See* history
Fossel, Joe, 248*n*52
founders
  classical code of, 229
  diverse views of, 232
  iconic status of, 97–100, 120, 130–1,
    157, 159, 223–4
  on Native Americans, 25, 27, 34, 173,
    175–7, 181, 184–91, 205, 226–7
  ongoing dialogue with, 7–9, 232–9
  originalist evocation of, 159, 167,
    169–70
  political talent and leadership of,
    223–39
  presidential campaigns of, 230
  on slavery, 5–7, 226–8
  voluminous writings of, 8–9, 229
  See also names of individual founders

France
  Franco-American Treaty of 1778
    with, 193, 262*n*31
  French Revolution of, 83–4, 191–2,
    203, 238
  Washington's foreign policy with,
    191–4
Franklin, Aretha, 53
Franklin, Benjamin, 87
  Constitutional Convention and, 129,
    136
  Declaration of Independence and, 3,
    18–19
  as minister to France, 181, 235–6
  political talent and leadership of,
    223–39
Freud, Sigmund, 79, 92–3

Garvey, Marcus, 64
Gates, Bill, 100
Gay, Peter, 3, 7
George III, King of England, 20, 113,
    132
  Adams's characterization of, 84
  Jefferson's critique of, 17, 19–21, 32,
    78, 110
Gilded Age, 92, 96, 99
  philanthropists of, 100
  Progressive Era's response to, 103,
    112
  Twain's depiction of, 105
  See also second Gilded Age
Gini index, 105
Glass-Steagall Act of 1933, 108–9
globalization, 107–15, 169, 217–22
Glorious Revolution, 163
Goldwater, Barry, 109
Gordon-Reed, Annette, 246*n*28
Great Compression, 106–7
Great Debate of 1787–88, 113
Great Divergence, 106

Great Migration, 52–3
Great Recession of 2008, 210
Great Society, 107
Griswold v. Connecticut, 155
Gulf War, 208–9
gun rights, 158, 160–7

Hamilton, Alexander, 31, 75, 110, 121,
    169, 204
  Constitutional Convention and,
    124–5, 136, 238
  Federalist Papers and, 137
  Federalist views of, 114
  National Bank proposal of, 90–1,
    122, 149
  political talent and leadership of,
    223–39
  on the power of the judicial branch,
    153
  Washington's Farewell Address and,
    198
Hanna, Mark, 103, 109
Hatch, Orrin, 162
Heller, Joseph, 160–1
Hemings, Beverly, 43
Hemings, Burwell, 248*n*52
Hemings, Elizabeth (Betty), 41
Hemings, Eston, 29, 43–4
Hemings, Harriet, 43
Hemings, John, 248*n*52
Hemings, Madison, 43–4
Hemings, Sally, 28–30, 36
*The Hemingses of Monticello: An
    American Family,* 246*n*28
Hemings family, 41–4
Henry, Patrick, 224
  as NRA hero, 163
  U.S. Constitution and, 130–1, 140–1,
    144, 147–9, 237–8
Heritage Foundation, 157
Hidden Agenda (Wilson), 63

history, 4–9
  Adams's reliance on, 96–7
  Baldwin's take on, 64–6
  detachment vs. objectivity in, 7
  in dialogue between past and present,
    7–9, 57, 232–9
  founder writings as record of, 8–9
  Jefferson on burden of, 64
  memorializing vs. remembering of,
    47–8, 249n59
  utility in the present of, 4–7
History of the American Revolution
    (Ramsay), 228
Holocaust Museum, 48
Houdon, Jean-Antoine, 238
Howell, David, 178–9
Hume, David, 86, 93, 96, 133, 231
Humphreys, David, 129
Hussein, Saddam, 210–11

ideology, 76–7, 92
imperial overstretch, 213
imprisonment rates, 60–1
income inequality, 8–9, 71–115
  Adams on economic oligarchy and,
    88–9, 92–101, 104–5, 114–15
  Adams on equality as illusion and,
    73–4, 80–4, 110
  Adams on motivations to acquire
    wealth and, 94–6
  American exceptionalism and, 92,
    99–100, 104, 252n34
  banking and finance capitalism in,
    90–1, 107–13
  costs of post–Cold War foreign
    policy and, 220
  debates on the role of the federal
    government and, 113–15
  Enlightenment thought on, 75–7, 101
  erosion of the middle classes in,
    104–5, 112–15

  in European countries, 81–2, 107
  of Gilded Ages past and present, 92,
    96, 99, 103–15
  New Deal and Great Society
    response to, 91, 107–11
  political plutocracy of, 92, 95–6, 99,
    109
  precedence of capitalism over
    democracy in, 105
  "pursuit of happiness," 9, 103–4,
    245n15
  race and urban zones of poverty in,
    53, 58–9, 61–3
  structural forms of, 92, 107–13
  See also Adams, John; second Gilded
    Age
inequality. *See* income inequality
*An Inquiry into the Principles and Policy
    of the Government of the United
    States* (Taylor), 84–5, 88–93
intercontinental ballistic missiles,
    210
Iraq invasion and occupation, 210–11,
    220
Iroquois Confederation, 182
ISIS (Islamic State), 211
Islamic terrorism, 210–11
isolationism, 193–4, 201–5, 214–15,
    217–20, 262n31

Jackson, Andrew, 90
Jackson, Michael, 53
Jacksonian Democrats, 31
James II, King of England, 163
Jay, John, 137, 194–8, 234–7
Jay Treaty of 1795, 194–9, 202, 218
Jefferson, Isaac, 246n27
Jefferson, Jane Randolph, 14–15
Jefferson, Martha Wayles Skelton,
    15, 41
Jefferson, Peter, 14

Jefferson, Thomas, 13–48, 174, 204, 234
  on American exceptionalism, 92, 99–100, 104, 215–16
  antifederalist views of, 113–14
  on a bill of rights, 142–3
  biographers of, 14
  on British imperialism and the slave trade, 17–21, 110
  death of, 74
  Declaration of Independence and, 18–22, 78, 239
  duplicity on race and slavery of, 16, 43–8, 66–7, 248n53
  Enlightened governance project of, 21–4, 39, 45–6, 48, 203, 245n15
  enslaved offspring of, 13, 43–4
  on equality, 74–84
  faith in the will of the people of, 76–8, 80–1, 87, 109–10, 143, 193, 203
  family background of, 14–15
  financial challenges of, 45, 195, 248n54
  freed slaves of, 29, 43–4, 248n52
  friendship and correspondence with Adams of, 20, 38, 44, 71, 73–4, 83–4, 114, 223
  on governance of western territories, 179–81
  Hamilton and, 75
  on incompatibility of the races, 13–14, 29–30, 34–7, 40–1, 49–50, 248n52
  on inferiority of blacks, 25–7, 36, 43, 46–7, 57
  on interpreting the Constitution, 151, 154–5
  Jay Treaty and, 196–7
  Louisiana Purchase of, 33–6, 179, 227
  marriage of, 15, 29, 41
  as minister to France, 28, 181
  Missouri Crisis and, 35–9
  Monticello home of, 15–16, 27
  national political service of, 30–5, 44, 77
  on Native Americans, 25, 27, 34
  Notes on the State of Virginia of, 24–8
  political talent and leadership of, 223–39
  proposal for gradual emancipation and expatriation of slaves, 23–8, 34–6, 39–40, 47–8, 51
  Sally Hemings and, 28–30, 36, 41–4
  on self-evident truths, 3, 9, 18, 21–2, 55–6, 58–9
  on Shays's Rebellion, 125
  slaves owned by, 13, 15, 22, 39, 41–6, 246n28
  "The Solemn Declaration and Protest of the Commonwealth of Virginia" of, 38–9
  states' rights doctrine of, 31–3, 57, 247n34
  A Summary View of the Rights of British America of, 17, 20, 32
  temperament of, 74, 79–80
  on the utility of grief and emotions, 78–80
  See also race/racism; slavery
Jefferson Memorial, 14, 47–8, 73
Jim Crow, 52–61, 111
  See also segregation
John Adams and the Fear of American Oligarchy (Mayville), 252n34
John Adams and the Spirit of Liberty (Thompson), 252n34
John Birch Society, 112
Johnson, Andrew, 52
Johnson, Lyndon B., 57
Jupiter (enslaved servant), 13, 15

jurisprudence. *See* Constitution of the United States; Supreme Court of the United States

Kaplan, Lawrence, 221–2, 262*n*31
Kaplan, Robert D., 207
Kennan, George, 203, 213–16
Kennedy, Paul, 213
Kentucky Resolution of 1798, 31–2
Kentucky statehood, 122
King, Martin Luther, Jr., 49, 56–8
Kissinger, Henry, 203
Knox, Henry, 129–30, 148, 185–91, 204
Koch, Charles and David, 111–13, 162
Kuznets, Simon, 106–7

Lafayette, Marquis de
visit to Monticello by, 39
Washington and, 128, 136, 177, 186, 204
La Rochefoucauld-Liancourt, François Alexandre Frédéric, 30
Laurens, Henry, 234–5
law. *See* Constitution of the United States; Supreme Court of the United States
law and order policies, 59–61
leadership, 223–9
failure on Native Americans of, 226–7
of the founders, 223–9
impact of geography on, 231–2
vs. popular opinion, 76–8, 80–1, 86–8, 230
requirement of great crises for, 228–29
slavery as original sin of, 226–8
unprecedented opportunity for, 229–30
Lee, Billy, 233

Lee, Henry, 233
Lee, Richard Henry, 18–19
liberal tradition, 3, 207–9
contemporary failures of, 211–13, 216–19
Jefferson's faith in, 215–16
Lincoln, Abraham, 115, 125, 219, 223
Cooper Union Address of, 6
Emancipation Proclamation of, 51–2
on interpreting the Constitution, 154
prohibition of expansion of slavery by, 38
rejection of racial equality by, 55–6
Republican Party of, 31
research on slavery by, 5–7
"Living Constitution," 139–41, 149, 153–6, 158, 160, 164, 258*n*35
See also *District of Columbia v. Heller*
Livingston, Robert, 18–19
Locke, John, 21, 77
The Lost Soul of American Politics (Diggins), 252*n*34
Louis, Joe, 53
Louisiana Purchase, 33–9, 179, 227

Mably, Abbé de, 93
Machiavelli, Niccolò, 86, 96
Madison, James, 119–49, 238–9
antifederalist conversion of, 114
Bill of Rights and, 121, 141–9
biographers of, 255*n*1
Constitutional Convention planning by, 126–31, 133–4
Constitutional ratification strategy of, 136–41
on executive power, 132, 134
Federalist Papers and, 121, 137–41
federalist views of, 123–4, 130–1, 135–6

financial challenges of, 45, 195
on the Great Compromise, 135–6
Jay Treaty and, 196–7, 218
on Jefferson's views on slavery, 24–5,
 38–9
political evolution of, 120–6, 169
political talent and leadership of,
 223–39
relationship with Washington of,
 125–6, 137, 142
Republican political party of,
 31–2, 44
on secession, 149, 149*n*51
Second Amendment and, 148, 166
on states' rights, 149
tripartite model for national
 government of, 131–4, 257*n*26
See also Constitution of the United
 States
mandatory minimum sentences, 60
Marshall, John, 114, 153, 169, 224
Martin Luther King, Jr. Memorial, 57
Marx, Karl, 104
Mason, George, 21, 224
Massachusetts Constitution, 4
Mayer, Jane, 103, 111–12, 156–7
Mayville, Luke B., 252*n*34
Mazzei, Philip, 196
McCoy, Drew R., 255*n*1
McGillivray, Alexander, 186–90
Medicare, 111
Meese, Edwin, 157
Melian Dialogue (Thucydides),
 203
Mendel, Gregor, 27
Meyers, Marvin, 255*n*1
middle classes, 104–5, 112–15
Middle Passage, 17–22, 50–1
military service, 212
Militia Act of 1792, 148
minority-majority population, 66–7

Missouri Compromise, 151–2, 227
Missouri Crisis, 36–9
moneyed aristocracy, 94–6
 See also oligarchy
Monroe, James, 31, 34, 45, 197
Montesquieu, 131
Monticello, 15–16, 27
 Hemings family of, 28–30, 36, 41–4,
  246*n*28
 slave population of, 13, 15, 22, 39,
  41–6, 246*n*28
Morris, Gouverneur, 133, 141, 238–9
Morrison, Toni, 53
Mount Rushmore, 47, 71, 115
Mount Vernon, 233–4
"My Dungeon Shook" (Baldwin), 65
Myrdal, Gunnar, 21, 55–9, 65–6

Napoleon, 83–4
National Bank proposal, 90–1, 122,
 149
National Rifle Association (NRA),
 161–6
Nation of Islam, 64
Native Americans, 173–91
 expropriation of land of, 181–91,
  226
 government treaties with, 182–4,
  186–91
 Jackson's removal of, 90
 Jefferson's views of, 25, 27, 34
 Washington's concern for, 173,
  175–7, 181, 184–91, 205, 226–7
NATO (North Atlantic Treaty
 Organization), 217
natural aristocracy, 82–3
neoisolationism, 216–18, 220
New Deal, 107–11, 156
 banking regulations of, 91, 108–10
 FDR's proposal for, 110
 Reagan's repudiation of, 109–11

The New Jim Crow (Alexander), 60–1

New Right, 109, 111–13, 156–7
  funding of, 111–12, 156–7, 162
  Second Amendment activism of,
    162–4

Nixon, Richard, 109, 112, 161,
    211–12

North American Free Trade
  Agreement (NAFTA), 217

Northwest Ordinance of 1787, 6, 184

Notes of a Native Son (Baldwin), 49,
    50, 65–6

"Notes on Ancient and Modern
  Confederations" (Madison), 120–1

Notes on the State of Virginia
  (Jefferson), 24–8

nuclear weapons, 210

Nullification Crisis, 149

Obama, Barack, 50

Ohio peoples, 182, 194

oligarchy, 88–9, 92–101, 104–5, 109,
    114–15

Olin Foundation, 157

Ordinance of 1784, 23–4, 179–80

Ordinance of 1785, 180–1

originalism, 119, 155–70
  conservative uses of, 156–60, 169–70
  definition of, 157
  distorted legal scholarship on, 162–3
  District of Columbia v. Heller and,
    160–70
  evocation of founders in, 159, 167,
    169–70
  influence of public opinion on, 160,
    163–4
  law office history methods of, 168
  political detachment claims of,
    156–7, 160, 167–70
  prism of the present in, 164

Owens, Jesse, 53

Paine, Thomas, 87, 199

Paris Climate Accords, 217

Parker, Theodore, 49

Parton, James, 14

peace dividend, 209, 211

perpetual war. *See* post–Cold War
  foreign policy

Piketty, Thomas, 105–6, 107

Plan of Treaties (Adams), 192

Plato, 83

Plessy v. Ferguson, 152

political architecture. *See* Constitution
  of the United States; Madison,
  James; Supreme Court of the
  United States

political plutocracy, 92, 95–6, 99, 105,
    109
  See also oligarchy

Populism, 90

post–Cold War foreign policy, 8,
    173–4, 207–22
  absence of public sacrifice in, 211–12,
    216
  absence of strategy for, 209–10,
    212–13, 216
  Afghanistan and Iraq wars in,
    210–11, 220
  American exceptionalism in, 216
  anti-imperial legacy in, 218–20
  costs of, 220
  failure of liberal nation-building in,
    207–9, 211–13, 216–19
  Gulf War in, 208–9
  Kaplan's views on, 221–2
  lack of peace dividend in, 209,
    211–12
  militarized foreign policy of, 213,
    216
  Muslim world in, 209–11
  new world order of, 209
  Paris Climate Accords in, 217

perpetual wars and occupations of,
211–13, 216, 219–20

September 11, 2001, attacks and,
210

Trump's isolationist stance in, 200,
217–18

U.S. as global superpower in,
208–11, 217–22

Powell, Lewis, 156–7

the presidency. *See* executive power

Proclamation of Neutrality, 193–4,
201–4, 262n31

Progressive Era, 103, 112

The Promise of American Life
(Croly), 75

pseudo aristocracy, 82–3

Publius. *See* Federalist Papers

Puritanism, 95

"pursuit of happiness," 9, 103–4,
245n15

race/racism, 8–9, 49–67
backlash in response to progress on,
49–50, 57–9, 66–7
Baldwin's depiction of, 63–6
civil rights movements against,
54–9
contemporary forms of, 58–63, 111
Democrats' loss of Southern states
and, 58–9
Enlightenment views of, 9, 26–7,
39, 50
history's acknowledgment of, 47–8,
249n59
Jeffersonian legacy of, 43–8, 66–7,
248n53
Jefferson on incompatibility of blacks
and whites, 13–14, 29–30, 34–7,
40–1, 46–7, 49–50, 248n154
Jefferson on inferiority of blacks,
25–7, 36, 43, 46–7, 57

Jim Crow policies of, 52–61, 111
Lincoln's rejection of racial equality
and, 55–6
minority-majority population and,
66–7
poverty and economic inequality in,
58–9, 62–3
proposals for expatriation of blacks
and, 23–8, 34–5, 39–40, 47–8,
51–2, 249n57
race-neutral responses to, 63
racial mixing of slavery, 41–4
racial stereotyping in, 63, 65
Supreme Court decisions regarding,
151–3
See also Jefferson, Thomas; slavery

racial science, 26–7

Radical Republicans, 52, 54

Rakove, Jack N., 255n1

Ramsay, David, 26, 228

Randolph, Edmund, 128, 130

Randolph, Martha, 44, 45

Randolph, Thomas Mann, 44–5

Reagan, Ronald, 216
conservative agenda of, 109–11
Supreme Court nominees of, 157
war on drugs of, 59–61

realist foreign policy, 203–5, 221–2

Reconstruction era, 54–5, 58

Redeeming American Political Thought
(Shklar), 252n34

religion, 225

Republican Party of Jefferson and
Madison, 31–3, 44, 113–14

Republican Party of Lincoln
contemporary racial policies of, 58
on equal rights for ex-slaves, 52, 54
origins of, 31

The Republic of Letters (ed. Smith),
247n34

republics (definition), 101, 225

Revolutionary War. *See* American
  Revolution
The Rise and Fall of the Great Powers
  (Kennedy), 213
Roberts, John, 157–8
Robinson, Jackie, 53
Rockefeller, John D., 100, 105
Roe v. Wade, 111, 155, 158
Roosevelt, Franklin D., 110, 115, 146,
  169, 223
Roosevelt, Theodore, 115
Ross, Diana, 53
Rousseau, Jean-Jacques, 86, 93
Rubens, Peter Paul, 98
Rush, Benjamin, 26, 74–75, 92
Russell, Richard, 57

Sallust, 96
Scalia, Antonin, 151, 160–8
Schuyler, Philip, 183–4
Scottish Enlightenment, 93–4, 133, 231
Second Amendment of the
  Constitution, 147–9, 160–7
second Gilded Age, 92, 96, 103–15
  Citizens United decision and, 109
  dark money in, 111–13
  debates on the role of the federal
    government in, 113–15
  decreased market regulation in,
    107–11
  eroded middle classes of, 104–5,
    112–15
  financialized economy of, 107–13
  income inequality in, 105–7
  New Right constituency of, 109,
    111–13
  philanthropists of, 100
  precedence of capitalism over
    democracy in, 105
  tax reductions of, 108
  See also income inequality

Second Reconstruction, 54–9
Second Treatise on Government
  (Locke), 21
secularism, 225
segregation, 47
  of the armed forces, 56
  Jim Crow policies of, 52–61, 111
  of schools, 56, 152–3
  See also race/racism
self-evident truths, 3–4, 113
  as American Creed, 3, 8, 21, 55–6,
    103, 239
  civil rights movement and, 56–9
  Declaration of Independence on, 18,
    21–2
September 11, 2001, attacks, 210
Shays's Rebellion, 124–5
Sherman, Roger, 18–19, 145
Shklar, Judith, 252n34
Short, William, 29–30, 40
Siegel, Reva, 164
slavery, 13–48
  as America's original sin, 226–7, 237
  broken families of, 45
  Compromise of 1850 on, 151–2
  economic reparations for, 52, 58
  emancipation of, 46–8, 51–2
  founders' views on, 5–7, 226–8
  gradual emancipation and
    expatriation proposals for, 23–8,
    34–6, 39–40, 47–8, 51–2, 249n57
  as inherited status, 16–17
  Lincoln's prohibition of expansion
    of, 38
  Lincoln's research on, 5–7
  Louisiana Territory and, 33–6
  Missouri Compromise on, 151–2,
    227
  Missouri Crisis and, 35–9
  at Monticello, 13, 15, 22, 39, 41–6,
    246n28

moral corruption of masters in, 25

Northwest Ordinance on, 6

racial mixing in, 41–4

slave trade of, 17–22, 50–1, 227

states' rights doctrine and, 31–3, 247*n*34

ubiquity in the South of, 14–16

See also Jefferson, Thomas; race/racism

Smith, Adam, 86, 93–6, 133, 231

Smith, James Morton, 247*n*34

Smith, Samuel Stanhope, 26–7

Social Darwinism, 112

Social Security, 111

"The Solemn Declaration and Protest of the Commonwealth of Virginia" (Jefferson), 38–9

"Sources of Soviet Conduct" (Kennan), 214

Soviet Union, 48

demise of, 207–10, 214

Kennan's containment strategy for, 213–16

Stalin's brutality in, 214

Spirit of the Laws (Montesquieu), 131

Stalin, Joseph, 214

Stanton, Lucia, 246*n*28

states' rights, 31–3, 57, 149, 247*n*34

Stevens, John Paul, 164–5

Stowe, Harriet Beecher, 47

structural inequality, 92, 107–13

structural racism, 59–61

Stuart, Gilbert, 174, 229

A Study of History (Toynbee), 228–9

Style in History (Gay), 7

A Summary View of the Rights of British America (Jefferson), 17, 20, 32

Supreme Court of the United States, 56, 151–70, 158

Brown v. Board of Education decision of, 56, 152–3, 158, 160, 161

Bush v. Gore decision of, 158

Citizens United v. Federal Election Commission decision of, 109, 158, 160

District of Columbia v. Heller decision of, 158, 160–70

dominance in domestic policy of, 152–3

Dred Scott v. Sandford decision of, 6, 151–2

Griswold v. Connecticut decision of, 155

influence of public opinion on, 160, 163–4

judicial review principle of, 153

"Living Constitution" approach of, 139–41, 149, 153–6, 158, 160, 164

originalist approach of, 119, 155–70

Plessy v. Ferguson decision of, 152

Roe v. Wade decision of, 111, 155, 158

U.S. v. Miller decision of, 161, 166–7

See also Constitution of the United States

Tacitus, 96, 213

Taney, Roger, 6, 152

Taylor, John, 84–5, 88–93

technology and globalization. *See* globalization

The Theory of Moral Sentiments (Smith), 93–5

Theory of the Leisure Class (Veblen), 95

Thompson, C. Bradley, 252*n*34

"Those Who Labor for My Happiness" (Stanton), 246*n*28

Thoughts on Government (Adams), 86, 131

Thucydides, 5, 96, 203, 218

Tocqueville, Alexis de, 55, 104, 207, 222

Toynbee, Arnold, 228–9
Treaty of Fort Harmar of 1789, 183
Treaty of Fort Stanwix of 1784, 182
Treaty of Hopewell of 1785, 182–3
Treaty of New York of 1790, 190–1
Treaty of Paris of 1783, 23–4, 122,
    175, 188, 194, 226, 234–7, 261n3
Truman, Harry, 21
Trumbull, John, 19, 229
Trump, Donald, 217–18, 224
Turner, Frederick Jackson, 178
Twain, Mark, 105
Twenty-Second Amendment of the
    Constitution, 198

Uncle Tom's Cabin (Stowe), 47
United States. *See* Constitution of
    the United States; Declaration of
    Independence; founders; Supreme
    Court of the United States
Up from Slavery (Washington), 58
U.S. v. Miller, 161, 166–7

Vanderbilt, Cornelius, 105
Veblen, Thorstein, 95
"Vices of the Political System of the
    United States" (Madison), 121–2,
    131
Vietnam War, 112, 212, 214
Vietnam War Memorial, 48
Virginia
    Constitutional ratification convention
        of, 121, 140–1, 143, 149
    Declaration of Rights of, 143, 147
    proposal for tripartite national
        government of, 133–4
Virginia Resolutions of 1798–99,
    31–2
Voltaire, 93
voter fraud claims, 59
Voting Rights Act of 1965, 56–7

War of 1812, 201, 210
war on drugs, 59–61
Warren, Earl, 157–8
Washington, Booker T., 58
Washington, George, 44, 71–2,
    173–205, 222, 233–4
    Adams's military advice to, 5
    on America's Native American
        problem, 173, 175–81, 184–91, 205,
        226–7
    Bache's impeachment proposal for,
        195, 198–9
    Constitutional Convention and,
        125–31, 133–7
    on declarations of war, 211
    Farewell Address of, 173, 175,
        198–202, 215, 218
    Federalist views of, 114
    inaugural message of, 142
    isolationist goals of, 193–4, 201–5,
        214–15, 262n31
    last Circular Letter to the States of,
        175–7
    on national unity, 199–200
    policies toward Britain of, 194–8,
        202, 219
    policies toward France of, 191–4,
        262n31
    political talent and leadership of,
        223–9
    popular mythology about, 98, 174–5,
        205
    presidency of, 185–200
    on ratification of the Constitution,
        228
    retirement from military leadership
        by, 127–9
    tour of the Western territories by,
        177
    two-term precedent set by, 198
    See also foreign policy

Washington, Lund, 233–4
Washington, Martha, 174, 204, 233
Washington Monument, 72, 174,
    260n1
Watergate scandal, 112
Wayles, John, 28, 41
The Wealth of Nations (Smith), 95–6,
    133
West, Benjamin, 236
western territory, 173–91, 231
    Native American lands in, 182
    Northwest Ordinance of 1787 on,
        6, 184
    Ordinance of 1784 on, 23–4, 179–80
    Ordinance of 1785 on, 180–1
    republican governance of, 179–80,
        184
    rule of native populations of, 173,
        175–7, 181–91, 205
    settler migration and expansion into,
        180–2, 190–1, 226
    U.S. acquisition of, 173, 175–7, 235,
        261n3
    Washington's tour of, 177
    See also Native Americans
"We the people," 140–1, 200, 237,
    239
Whitehead, Alfred North, 223
Whitman, Walt, 232
Whitney, Eli, 35
Wilson, James, 133
Wilson, William Julius, 62–3
Wilson, Woodrow, 201
Winthrop, John, 216
Wood, Gordon, 229–30, 232
Woodward, C. Vann, 53
World War I, 201
Wright, Richard, 52, 53

THE QUARTET
Orchestrating the Second American Revolution, 1783–1789

Joseph J. Ellis tells the unexpected story of why the thirteen colonies, having just fought off the imposition of a distant centralized governing power, would decide to subordinate themselves anew. Alexander Hamilton, George Washington, John Jay, and James Madison—with the help of Robert Morris and Gouverneur Morris—created the new republic by diagnosing the systemic dysfunctions created by the Articles of Confederation, manipulating the political process to force the calling of the Constitutional Convention, conspiring to set the agenda in Philadelphia, orchestrating the debate in the state ratifying conventions, and drafting the Bill of Rights to assure state compliance with the constitutional settlement. Ellis gives us a dramatic portrait of one of the most crucial and misconstrued periods in American history.

History

FIRST FAMILY
Abigail and John Adams

In this rich and engrossing account, John and Abigail Adams come to life against the backdrop of the republic's tenuous early years. Drawing on more than 1,200 letters exchanged between the couple, Ellis tells a story both personal and panoramic. We learn about the many years Abigail and John spent apart as John's political career sent him to Philadelphia, Paris, and Amsterdam; their relationship with their children; and Abigail's role as John's closest and most valued advisor. Exquisitely researched and beautifully written, *First Family* is both a revealing portrait of a marriage and a unique study of America's early years.

History

REVOLUTIONARY SUMMER
The Birth of American Independence

The summer months of 1776 witnessed the most consequential events in the story of our country's founding. While the thirteen colonies came together and agreed to secede from the British Empire, the British were dispatching the largest armada ever to cross the Atlantic to crush the rebellion in the cradle. The Continental Congress and the Continental Army were forced to make decisions on the run, improvising as history congealed around them. In a brilliant and seamless narrative, Ellis meticulously examines the most influential figures in this propitious moment, including George Washington, John Adams, Thomas Jefferson, Benjamin Franklin, and Britain's Admiral Lord Richard and General William Howe. He weaves together the political and military experiences as two sides of a single story and shows how events on one front influenced outcomes on the other.

History

ALSO AVAILABLE

American Creation
American Sphinx
Founding Brothers
His Excellency

VINTAGE BOOKS
Available wherever books are sold.
www.vintagebooks.com